Routledge Revivals

A History of the Modern Church

First published in 1930, A History of the Modern Church is a scholarly and readable account of the church from the beginning of the Reformation to modern times. It traces the rise of many attitudes towards life, many conceptions of the faith, and many ecclesiastical systems. This book will be of interest to students of religion and history.

A History of the Modern Church
From 1500 to the Present Day

J. W. C. Wand

First published in 1930
Seventh edition (revised) 1952
By Methuen & Co. Ltd.

This edition first published in 2024 by Routledge
4 Park Square, Milton Park, Abingdon, Oxon, OX14 4RN
and by Routledge
605 Third Avenue, New York, NY 10017

Routledge is an imprint of the Taylor & Francis Group, an informa business

© Methuen & Co., 1952

All rights reserved. No part of this book may be reprinted or reproduced or utilised in any form or by any electronic, mechanical, or other means, now known or hereafter invented, including photocopying and recording, or in any information storage or retrieval system, without permission in writing from the publishers.

Publisher's Note
The publisher has gone to great lengths to ensure the quality of this reprint but points out that some imperfections in the original copies may be apparent.

Disclaimer
The publisher has made every effort to trace copyright holders and welcomes correspondence from those they have been unable to contact.

A Library of Congress record exists under ISBN: 0416181201

ISBN: 978-1-032-73506-1 (hbk)
ISBN: 978-1-003-46454-9 (ebk)
ISBN: 978-1-032-73509-2 (pbk)

Book DOI 10.4324/9781003464549

A History of
THE MODERN CHURCH
FROM 1500 TO THE PRESENT DAY

BY

J. W. C. WAND, D.D.
FORMERLY BISHOP OF LONDON

METHUEN & CO. LTD.
11 New Fetter Lane, E.C.4

First published January 30th 1930
Reprinted six times
Seventh Edition, revised, October 1952
Reprinted, with minor corrections, 1955
Reprinted 1957
Reprinted 1961
Reprinted with corrections 1965

First published as a University Paperback 1971

Hardback SBN 416 34080 6
University Paperback SBN 416 18120 1

Printed in Great Britain by
Latimer Trend & Co. Ltd.

This title is available both as a hardbound and as a paperback edition. The paperback edition is sold subject to the condition that it shall not, by way of trade or otherwise, be lent, re-sold, hired out, or otherwise circulated without the publisher's prior consent in any form of binding or cover other than that in which it is published and without a similar condition including this condition being imposed on the subsequent purchaser.

MATRI MEAE
QUAE MATRIS ECCLESIAE AMOREM
INSTILLAVIT

PREFACE

IT was possible for Miss Deanesly in the Preface to her *History of the Medieval Church* to speak of one attitude towards life, one faith, and one Church system. The student must be prepared for a complete change when he turns to the present volume. In the modern period it is necessary to trace the rise of many attitudes towards life, many conceptions of the faith, and many ecclesiastical systems. And these have to be set against so complicated a background of general history that it is impossible to tell their story in a strictly chronological order. An effort has here been made to avoid any resultant confusion by the provision of a table of parallel dates which may help the reader to form a coherent picture of the whole period. Moreover, certain features of contemporary Church life have been deemed so important as to merit a distinctive historical account for themselves, and the growing friendliness between the English and Eastern Churches has demanded a somewhat fuller treatment of Orthodoxy than is usually accorded to it in works of this kind.

My thanks are due to the Rev. J. F. Clayton,

viii HISTORY OF THE MODERN CHURCH

who read the proofs; to my son who helped to prepare the map material for the draughtsman; and to Dr. A. J. G. Hawes, Vice-Principal of Salisbury Theological College, who spared himself no pains in the compilation of the Index. I must also express my deep gratitude to my colleague, Mr. G. N. Clark, who has saved me from a number of errors both of thought and expression.

J. W. C. W.

July 1929

NOTE TO THE SEVENTH EDITION

IN this edition the book has been brought up to date by the insertion of a few paragraphs in the last chapter showing the main events and trends in the ecclesiastical history of the last quarter of a century. There have also been some appropriate additions to the lists and tables in the appendix.

J. W. C. W.

April 1952

NOTE TO 1965 PRINTING

I HAVE merely to repeat what is said in the note to the seventh edition. The chronicle of events and the bibliography have again been brought up to date. I am very happy to find that the book is still regarded as useful.

J. W. C. W

St. Paul's,
1964

CONTENTS

		PAGE
	PREFACE	v
CHAPTER		
I.	THE NEW AGE	1
II.	BEGINNING OF THE REFORMATION	12
III.	THE MOVEMENT BECOMES GENERAL	28
IV.	REFORM BEGINS IN ENGLAND	41
V.	ALTERNATION BETWEEN EXTREMES	53
VI.	THE COUNTER-REFORMATION	63
VII.	THE ELIZABETHAN SETTLEMENT	79
VIII.	THE BORDERS OF EUROPE	91
IX.	THE SEVENTEENTH CENTURY	105
X.	THE SEVENTEENTH CENTURY IN ENGLAND	120
XI.	THE EXPANSION OF CHRISTENDOM	135
XII.	THE EASTERN CHURCH	144
XIII.	NATIONALISM AND TOLERATION	159
XIV.	DEISM AND THE ENLIGHTENMENT	171
XV.	PIETISM AND METHODISM	182
XVI.	VICISSITUDES OF ROMAN CATHOLICISM	192
XVII.	THE OXFORD MOVEMENT	205
XVIII.	EDUCATIONAL AND SOCIAL MOVEMENTS	221
XIX.	THE EASTERN CHURCH IN RECENT TIMES	232
XX.	AMERICAN CHRISTIANITY	245

CHAPTER		PAGE
XXI.	REUNION MOVEMENTS	256
XXII.	MODERN MISSIONS	272
XXIII.	CONCLUSION	285
	SELECT BOOK LIST	298
	PRINCIPAL EVENTS, 1509–1929	304
	POPES AND ARCHBISHOPS OF CANTERBURY	310
	INDEX	313

MAPS

EUROPE AT THE REFORMATION	32
THE EASTERN ORTHODOX CHURCH	239

A HISTORY OF THE MODERN CHURCH

A History of the Modern Church

CHAPTER I

THE NEW AGE

By the beginning of the sixteenth century the intellectual world was fully conscious that it had entered upon a new age. This is shown by the unanimity with which the previous period was now being recognised as the Middle Age. Who first used that expression is not known, but the conception is already that of Flavio Biondo (1388–1463), the humanist secretary of four successive popes, and the name *Medium Aevum* is found six years after his death. Like most theologians, the scholars of this generation delighted to characterise the particular genius of their own day as a mere recovery of a glorious past, and they called by the name of the Middle Age those centuries that had intervened between the decay of the old classical culture and their own revival of it at the end of the fifteenth century. But history never slavishly repeats itself, and they were the inaugurators of a period that was even newer than they realised. During the modern period we trace the history of an outbursting of the human spirit that shattered the old authoritative unity of life and seemed to hold the promise of a great inheritance for individual effort. In the consequent struggles much is gained, but there is also a measure of disillusionment, and at the end of the story we see our own generation striving in a new period of transition to regain some, at least, of

2   HISTORY OF THE MODERN CHURCH

that which was heedlessly lost when the Middle Age was left behind.

The dividing line between the medieval and the modern periods is formed by the Renaissance. The immediate cause of a great impetus to this movement was the capture of Constantinople by the Turks in 1453, which drove a number of scholars to seek refuge in Italy, bringing with them their Greek manuscripts and Hellenic culture. Hitherto the great classics had been known mostly in Latin translations which had been handed down through the agency of Arabic learning. Greek was but little known, although there had been professors of Greek in Florence since the beginning of the fifteenth century; and they had no small influence in preparing the way for the Constantinopolitan scholars who arrived there half a century later.

Several countries dispute with each other the honour of being the true home of the Renaissance. There can be little doubt that the decision should be given in favour of Italy, although the very fact that there can be a dispute shows that the influence of the movement was much more widespread, as well as much deeper, than is generally recognised. In Italy it was warmly welcomed by the highest ecclesiastical authorities, and the best that can be said of such a Pope as Julius II is that he possibly saw, and tried to seize, the opportunity of repeating the exploits of early Christianity and of bringing the full, free-flowing life of classical antiquity under bondage to Christ. Such a combination of what is best in both worlds may be seen in the creations of Bramante's architectural genius at S. Peter's and the Vatican, and in the artistic splendours of Raphael and Michelangelo. But the aim proved too high both for the popes and for their Italian fellow-countrymen. The scholars fell back upon a pedantic imitation of the approved masters of classical literary style, and the people as a whole were content with a recovered sense of natural beauty which allowed free reign to sensual passions and destroyed the old grounds of moral restraint. In this sense the Italian Renaissance may be viewed as a complete revolt against the Age of Faith.

The extent to which the new paganism had abandoned

THE NEW AGE

the old Christian standards can be seen from the writings of Machiavelli, who asserted that you cannot govern the world with paternosters, and had so taken to heart the fate that had overtaken idealism in the person of Savonarola that he made a courageous and ruthless cynicism the most necessary requisite for a successful prince. This essential characteristic was to be found not only in Caesar Borgia, but also in his father, Pope Alexander VI, whose private and public life made the title 'Vicar of Christ' the most appalling mockery that has ever been perpetrated in the name of religion.

In Germany the Renaissance took on much more definitely the character of a religious Revival of Learning. There the way had been prepared by the Brethren of the Common Life, a mystical organisation founded towards the end of the fourteenth century by Gerhard Groot. When printing began in 1455, they published editions both of classical authors and of the Fathers, and encouraged such a love of education as led to the foundation of no fewer than nine universities between the years 1456 and 1506. Here not only Greek but also Hebrew was carefully studied and laid under contribution for the better understanding of the Scriptures. It is not to be supposed that such advance could be made without much opposition. The protagonist against obscurantism was the famous scholar Reuchlin (b. 1455). He was attacked by the Dominicans, who had, at least, this to say for themselves: that Reuchlin had been led astray by his devotion to Hebrew studies into some of the errors of the Cabbalists. Nevertheless it was altogether too much to ask him to consent to the opinion that all Jewish books, except the Old Testament, ought to be burnt. The case set all learned Europe aflame and was carried to Rome. Out of it arose the most famous pasquinade in all literary history. A number of scholars had written to Reuchlin to show their appreciation of his work in defence of sound learning, and a collection of their letters was published under the title *Clarorum Virorum Epistolae*. This was followed by an amazingly successful parody, *Epistolae Obscurorum Virorum*, addressed to Reuchlin's enemies. In this collection the monks are represented as writing congratulatory letters to one of their own heroes, a professor at Cologne, and exhibiting, all unconsciously, both their ignorance of classical Latin and their revolting coarseness of manners. It is said that Erasmus laughed so heartily over these letters as to cure himself of a quinsy.

In England the Renaissance took the same serious turn as in Germany. Here the way had been prepared for it by Henry VI's foundations of Eton College and King's College, Cambridge, which had some imitators; and the effort to reform the Church by an intellectual revival was warmly supported by Warham, the Archbishop of Canterbury and trusted adviser of Henry VII. But its leaders were the great trio known as the Oxford Reformers, Colet, More, and Erasmus.

John Colet (1466–1519) was the son of a Lord Mayor of London. He was educated at Oxford and afterwards in Italy, where he met Erasmus and imbibed that love of Greek learning which made his fame when he came home and began to lecture on the Pauline Epistles. He became Dean of S. Paul's, but his teaching attracted the Lollards and drew suspicion on himself. His Bishop, Fitzjames, cited him for heresy before Warham, but the Archbishop dismissed the charge. Colet's aim was to bring back the Christianity of the apostles and to clear away the 'thorns and briars' with which it was overgrown, owing to the still prevailing influence of medieval scholasticism. He spoke against images and written sermons, but believed that the Church had full power to reform itself if only the old canons were enforced. It was he who founded S. Paul's School for the free teaching of 153 poor children.

Sir Thomas More was the dearest friend of Erasmus, who said of him: 'Nature never framed anything gentler, sweeter, happier, than the temper of Thomas More. His whole house breathes happiness, and no one enters it who is not the better for the visit.' He, too, studied at Oxford and meditated priesthood, but finally selected the law for his profession and became speaker of the House of Commons and afterwards Lord Chancellor. He advocated the study of Greek and thought that learning was the best protection against heresy and obscurantism. He was thus a thorough believer in the possibility of reform *from within*, and fully accepted the papal jurisdiction, not knowing that the

THE NEW AGE

famous decretals were forged, although they had recently been proved false. It is interesting that men of this type could use the New Learning as an instrument of attack against the later Reformers. In his dialogue of 1528, More complains of them, and especially of Tyndale, that they garble the meaning of the New Testament by bad translation and worse annotation.

Erasmus has been called 'the father of the theological scholarship of the Reformed Churches'. He would himself have disliked the title, for he hated the prospect of war and revolution, through which alone these churches came into being, and all his own scholarship was meant to purify and enrich the intellectual life of historic Christianity. 'My work', he said, 'has been to restore a buried literature and recall divines from their hair-splittings to a knowledge of the New Testament.' He wished to reduce the articles of the faith to the fewest and simplest, and showed himself no dogmatist, although he was the most cultured man of his day. For this reason it is sometimes thought that he may yet be found to have been the precursor of a movement deeper than that of the Reformation and the inaugurator of a future age of undogmatic Christianity. But this is to go too far. Certainly the instruments upon which he relied were wit and learning, but the ecclesiastical system was in his blood, and the actual fact is that he was a monk and priest who gave himself to scholarship. He was born at Rotterdam in 1467, and was attracted to England both by its freedom and by the pension which Warham awarded him. Without the moral earnestness of Colet and More he had greater intellectual gifts. He levelled all the resources of a matchless wit against the coarse obscurantism which his early upbringing had taught him to understand so well. His *Praise of Folly* was a satire which 'left monks and clergy in wreck and confusion, the objects of universal laughter'. His greatest work was an edition of the Greek New Testament with a new Latin translation. It was the first-fruits of Biblical criticism, and laid down for all time the proper method—a comparison of manuscripts—for the finding of the true text, and it was published in 1516 with the sanction of Leo X. He died in 1536 in communion with Rome.

Such, then, was the intellectual atmosphere of the new age. But scarcely less important for our study is a knowledge of the political situation. The Christian and pagan elements, which had been combined in medieval culture, but now showed a tendency to fall apart under the fresh influx of classicism at the Renaissance, had been held together by international institutions, which themselves broke up at this period. Those institutions owed their inspiration ultimately to Augustine's 'City of God', which had been Charlemagne's favourite reading, and had taught men to think of one Christian commonwealth linked together in the bond of Divine love under one emperor and one pope. In this unity the spiritual and the secular were closely intertwined. Consequently, any tumult that arose must affect the security both of Church and State, and also the harmony of the relation between the two. On the secular side the unity of command was threatened by the rising spirit of nationalism. Charles V was the last effective Holy Roman Emperor and he inherited a host of troubles. In Germany, where the individual strength of the medieval towns still made for local independence, he could not produce enough cohesion to check the corrosive influence of reform, and in Italy he could only join in that squabble of petty princedoms that turned the headquarters of Catholicism into a cock-pit and made effective control of her forces against the new enemy impossible. Everywhere else in Europe the nations were forming their own independent unities and trying their strength against centralised authority.

In France the Hundred Years War with England had come to an end in 1453. Louis XI, by consummate diplomacy, had taken advantage of the destruction of the power of the feudal nobility in that war to bring the provinces under the control of the crown; and Francis I, a true Machiavellian despot, found himself strong enough to try conclusions with the Emperor on every occasion. In England the Wars of the Roses, ended in 1485, had given the nobility a chance of destroying itself, and the rise of Tudor autocracy, broad-based upon the will of the people, resulted in the creation of the most effective of the new nationalities. Spain, after eleven years' fighting against the Moors, had conquered Granada in 1492, freed her territory from the last relics of Mohammedan rule, and so consolidated her sincerely Catholic monarchy that it could no longer be used as a mere pawn in imperial ambitions. And still earlier the cantons of Switzerland had freed themselves from Austrian domination and were developing a cohesion that was to preserve the commonwealth against all outside attacks.

This independence was won in spite of the fact that Christendom was fighting against the infidel, not only in Spain, but also in Hungary and on the Neapolitan coast. Indeed, it was preoccupation with the Turkish menace that distracted attention from the growing power of early Protestantism. For Islam was not satisfied with the capture of the capital of Eastern orthodoxy. A fresh push was made when Solyman the Magnificent came to his throne in 1520. He first took Belgrade, and then in 1526 destroyed the independence of Hungary at the Battle of Mohacs. The Turk was not repulsed until he had reached Vienna in 1529, nor finally checked until the Battle of Lepanto in 1571.

One other series of events was to have a profound effect in forming new political unities, although its significance was somewhat slow in working itself out. The amazing discoveries made chiefly by the sailors of Spain and Portugal succeeded both in their original object of circumventing the Turk and also (by chance) in opening up a new world. Since India, with its store of spices, was too dangerous of approach by the old route through the Mediterranean, a new way must be sought by the south of Africa. Henry, the sailor prince of Portugal, was the instigator of many adventures. Afraid to trust their small vessels to the open sea, his people explored the west coast of the great continent, marking their slow advance by crosses and converting here and there a negro or two to the Christian faith. The equator was crossed in 1471, but it was not until 1486 that Bartholomew Diaz, following the same course, was blown out to sea, and after weathering the storm gave up the effort in despair, turned north, touched land, and found to his amazement that he had rounded the Cape. But it still required another twelve years before Vasco da Gama completed the voyage and reached India. In the meantime

Columbus had tried to reach the same country by sailing due west. In 1492 he landed in the Bahamas thinking that he had reached his destination, and even when, on a later voyage, he disembarked upon the mainland he was convinced that he had discovered that eastern paradise, the Garden of Eden. America was added to the world by the most magnificent miscalculation in history. It is a curious reflection that it was Alexander VI, the most infamous of popes, who had the right to divide the New World between Spain and Portugal.

On its ecclesiastical side also the old unity was now being destroyed. The seeds of disruption had been long sown, and the danger should have been obvious before ever the fruit was plucked at the Reformation. It is true that no check had been found to papal absolutism. The conciliar movement, in which the bishops had tried to secure the recognition of their own divine right, had failed; but the popes, becoming anxious merely to build up the fortunes of their own families, found themselves ever more and more engrossed in Italian affairs and used the local Churches only as a means for obtaining supplies. This had left the Churches free to assert some measure of independence. France had obtained its Pragmatic Sanction of Bourges in 1438. England had long resisted papal exactions, and the appointment of Wolsey as legate made him practically supreme head of the Church in this country. Germany had tried to follow the example of France, but her internal disorganisation left her open to extortion, and the burden fell all the more heavily upon her since English contributions had grown smaller. Italy, of course, found financial advantages in the situation, but her attitude was the more cynical since Lorenzo Valla had exposed the true nature of the Donation of Constantine, and the character of the popes appeared ever less worthy of their office.

Alexander VI spent all his thoughts upon the project of carving out of the estates of the Church a dominion for his son, the infamous Caesar Borgia, and then in 1503 died, it is said, as the result of poison that he had intended for one of his own cardinals. Julius II (1503–13), having enriched his own kindred, set himself to build up the estates of the Church. This he did *vi et armis*, taking the field in person and leading his own troops across the frozen ditches and through the breach at Mirandola. But when he made war against Louis XII, the French king retaliated by arranging for a council to be summoned at Pisa in 1511. This endeavoured to restrain the madness of the Pontiff and to initiate reform in the Church; but as the Emperor changed sides from the King to the Pope it proved abortive, and Julius replied by summoning a council at the Lateran in 1512, which annulled the proceedings of the Pisan Council and was still sitting when Leo X succeeded to the papal throne. As its composition was entirely Italian, the world was not willing to recognise in it any oecumenical authority, although it claimed the title of Fifth General Lateran Council. Consequently its conclusions fell a little flat, not even the clergy of Spain and Germany showing themselves willing to pay the tax levied upon them for a crusade against the Turk. Its projects for reform were rendered abortive by the opposition that appeared between the bishops and the Curia, but the former gained a slightly increased power over the monasteries and convents, and the printing presses were put under their control. In the weakness of the constitution the authority of the Papacy stood out all the more clearly, and its prestige was for the moment heightened by the success of Julius in adding to the papal States. By the League of Cambrai against Venice (1508) he had gained Rimini, Faenza, and Ravenna, and by the Holy League against France he had annexed Parma and Piacenza. Leo X, who guided the Lateran Council to its conclusion, was a typical Renaissance pope, but even in his patronage of art and letters he was so ineffective as to make him unworthy of the praise that has sometimes been bestowed upon him, for the signs of decay were already evident in his day. His most important task was to meet the French, who under their new king, Francis I, marched to regain possession of Naples, and won a great victory at Marignano. Leo was compelled to give up Parma, but he gained a diplomatic success over the King at Bologna (1516), when the Pragmatic Sanction was abrogated and a Concordat concluded, by which the King received the right of appointment to the bishoprics and other ecclesiastical dignities, but the Pope regained the annates. Thus Leo and Francis divided between them the rights of the Church in France and the old Gallican liberties were quietly set on one side.

Such, then, was the state of things, intellectual, political, and ecclesiastical, during the opening years of the sixteenth century. It was out of this confusion that the Reformation suddenly blazed and caught the old-established authority unawares. It has often been asked whether there were any special premonitions of impending change. Abuses, indeed, there were and to spare, but they had existed for centuries past, and many voices had been raised against them. Why had they not long ago provoked the cataclysm that was now to burst upon the world? It may be answered that hitherto there had appeared upon the stage no figure commanding enough to claim universal attention. And that, indeed, is part of the truth, but it is not the whole. Wonderful as is the power of personality, the individual is himself too puny for so great a task. For the initiation of a movement of such magnitude there is demanded both the hour and the man.

In the present instance the arrival of the hour was signalised, not by any one of the facts we have enumerated, but by the convergence of many. Intellectually the Renaissance had set free the human spirit, and inasmuch as it was a revival of learning the Renaissance may be regarded as the direct parent of the Reformation. But on its moral side the Renaissance can make no such claim. The more serious section of Christendom was immeasurably shocked by the effects of the classical revival in the lives of the Italian ecclesiastics. Consciously or unconsciously it was felt that here was no true synthesis between paganism and the gospel. Consequently the Reformation may be regarded as a revolt against the Renaissance just as truly as the Renaissance itself may be regarded as a revolt against the Age of Faith.

Politically two forces now emerge, that of nationalism and that of individualism. Medieval Christendom had moved forward as an army with banners, and that had often been glorious for the army, but terrible for the individual. Its authority had cramped both his body and his mind. The Renaissance had brought relief only to the wealthy, the powerful, and the learned; but now the individual became conscious of himself as such and claimed a right of place for his own reason, his own judgment, irrespective of rank and station. How could it be otherwise when scholars asserted that they translated a Book out of the dim past to be read and known by 'every ploughman at his plough'? And nationalism was a kind of individualism, seeing itself writ large in the glory of its country and the splendour of its king. Hence everywhere the loosening of old bonds and the sympathy with revolt.

Ecclesiastically, too, the time was fully ripe. The whole vast medieval system had become top-heavy: it was all system, there was no spirit discernible in it. When it should have spoken of God, it talked only so loudly of rights and claims, of war and money, that the voice of the gospel was stifled. Granted that the most difficult task before the Church is always to reconcile the apparently conflicting claims of this world and the next—while remaining itself in space and time to bring its members into touch with the eternal and the infinite—yet here was a Church that used spiritual sanctions for sordid ends, and that did not even seem to believe seriously in its own spiritual foundation. Certainly there were exceptions, and where the Church showed itself officially serious, as in Spain under the influence of Ximenes and even of Torquemada, there no revolt had the least chance of success. There was also a real spiritual faith, as we shall see, in some, at least, of the German monasteries, and there were still faithful parish priests ministering to their people the true Bread of Life, but to all these alike the official Church showed itself hopelessly corrupt. It satisfied no religious need, and religion was then, as always, the essential hunger of humanity.

Thus in every department the Church of the day was at feud with the aspirations of mankind. Mind, body, and soul were alike left unsatisfied. It wanted but an occasion when this gigantic failure should be thrown into glaring light for the great upheaval to begin.

CHAPTER II

BEGINNING OF THE REFORMATION

THE hour and the man met in the life of Martin Luther, the son of a Turingian peasant. The land of his birth exemplified to the full the conditions that paved the way for revolt: the lack of a strong central government, the papal exactions that had made Germany in England's default the milch-cow of the Papacy, the encouragement of the new learning resulting in the rapid growth of new universities, the grave inefficiency and even degradation of the parochial clergy which had driven evangelical religion to shelter under the revived asceticism of some of the mendicant Orders. All these helped to produce in Luther the experience which was to set the whole world ablaze. At first sight he seems signally deficient in the gifts that make the successful reformer. Without ever perceiving it, he was essentially a revolutionary. Interested in the new learning so far as it affected Biblical studies, he was no humanist, and ultimately he broke with the leaders of that movement. A founder of Churches, he could not organise his followers into a truly independent body. A theologian, he was completely incapable of organising a consistent theological system. His titanic strength lay in the supreme fervour of his spirit. He recapitulated more completely than anyone else has ever done the experience of S. Paul, and felt as whole-heartedly as the great apostle the tragic conflict between works and grace. With all the force of his being he had felt the terror of the wrath to come, and had sought escape from it by his own efforts. And then he had realised that his own merits could avail nothing, but that he must accept God's free gift simply, like a little child who could do nothing to deserve it. To him, as to countless others who have in some small degree shared that experience, it made the universe a new creation. This was essential Christianity, the good news, to proclaim which the Saviour came from heaven and gave His life. And this it was that the Church should have proclaimed. But as he looked round upon the Church of his day, Luther found it intent only upon using its great powers as means of sordid gain. It was for this reason that he came to the conclusion that the whole imposing structure of medieval Catholicism must be swept away and a return made to the stark simplicity of the original gospel.

As we look back upon his early years we see now, plainly enough, how everything combined to produce this cataclysmic figure. Carlyle draws a moving parallel between the birth of Luther in the midst of the Winter Fair at Eisleben in 1483 and that of Mary's greater Son in the crowded village of Bethlehem so long before. His father was at this time a pitman, who afterwards became a master-miner. Consequently in his early life Luther knew the hard but efficient training of poverty, helping to pay for his own elementary schooling by singing in the church choir and even in the streets. But by the time that he was ready to go to the biggest of German universities, that of Erfurt, his father had prospered sufficiently to make such expedients no longer necessary. Here he read the Latin classics and studied the nominalist philosophy preparatory to entering upon that training in Law for which his father designed him. But suddenly, in 1505, he abandoned this career and entered a monastery. The stories that attribute this decision to the death of a friend in a storm or elsewhere have not been substantiated, and it is probable that in any case the change was due to the continued oppression of a doubt whether he could save his soul if he remained in the world.

The Order to which Luther thus joined himself was that of the Augustinian Eremites. Originally hermits, they had been gathered together to live according to the Rule of S. Augustine by Pope Alexander IV. The convent at Erfurt belonged to a reformed congregation, the members of which had a great reputation as spiritual directors, preachers, and teachers of philosophy and theology. Among these companions Luther's inward struggle worked itself out. Dogged by the sense of his utter sinfulness in contrast with the overwhelming righteousness of God he strove to find relief along the path of a stern asceticism. But no solution of his difficulties appeared until he became acquainted with Staupitz, the Vicar-General of his Order, who taught him that in His Son God had already held out His hand to the fallen sinner, and that those were freely forgiven who were found in Christ. To attain this fellowship with Christ all that was necessary was to have faith in Him, to put in Him a trust that brought about a sense of personal friendship. Thus one did not attain to justification with God as the crown and consummation of one's own meritorious endeavour, but one received it as the largess of God which could alone turn all subsequent efforts into true riches.

Shortly after attaining inward peace, Luther was ordained to the priesthood (1507), and felt no more difficulty than did Staupitz himself in administering the Catholic system from this point of view. In the following year he was called by the Elector Frederick of Saxony to assist in the work of building up the new and struggling University of Wittenberg. His duties here were interrupted by a visit to Rome on the business of his Order. He went with the highest hopes and came back shocked to the soul by the corruption of the Church in the great city. He realised now, with a vividness that could never have been derived from any source but personal experience, what could be made of Christianity by such Vicars of Christ as Alexander VI and Julius II, and the disillusionment must have affected him greatly during the period after his return to Wittenberg, which was normative for his theology. After taking his doctor's degree, he succeeded Staupitz as Professor of Theology. He was glad to be quit of Aristotle and the scholastics, and discovered a natural affinity with the mystics—Augustine, Tauler, and the author of the *Theologia Germanica* being his favourites. But beyond these he found an absorbing interest in the text of Scripture, making the Old Testament the prophet of Christ and S. Paul the interpreter of the gospel. He received rapid promotion in his Order, and soon had a thorough knowledge of the monastic system. He visited no fewer than forty monasteries on a tour of inspection, and he had himself, as Vicar, the oversight of eleven such conventual houses.

It was in the midst of these multifarious interests that Luther found himself challenged by the crying evil of indulgences. Leo X was in need of money in order to complete the building of S. Peter's at Rome, and sought to raise it by proclaiming an indulgence to all who should contribute. Albert of Brandenburg was also interested in furthering the campaign, because part of the money raised in his Archbishopric of Mainz was to count towards the vast charge that had been levied upon him when he first entered into possession of his office. The indulgence was preached by the Dominican, John Tetzel, who had already performed the same office for the Elector when he wished to pay for his bridge at Torgau. Whether Luther knew how strong were the interests that might be arrayed against him is questionable; what is certain is that he saw in the sale of indulgences a grave practical abuse. No doubt the best Roman theologians can defend it on the ground that the gift of money was an act of charity, and that in consideration for such an act the Church could remit certain temporal penalties for sin (including those of Purgatory), which the Church having herself inflicted could herself forgo. But others went farther than that and said that an indulgence could remit not only the penalty but the very guilt of sin, and Luther himself had penitents who had bought this latest indulgence and had demanded that he should recognise its complete efficacy. He saw that these sinful souls were relying upon the lowest kind of satisfaction for their sins; to encourage them to do so was to make a mockery of religion and to destroy that sincerity which was the very foundation of true penitence. Consequently he proceeded to attack, not the doctrine of indulgences, but the sale of them as a means of raising money. On this subject he prepared ninety-five theses, which he proposed as matter for debate, and nailed them up on the door of the castle church at Wittenberg, the usual place for university notices, on All Saints' Day, 1517. It was a purely academic proceeding, but it was the starting-point of the Reformation.

Luther does not seem to have expected the commotion he aroused. He thought that authority would be on his side. On the same day that he posted his theses he sent a copy of them with a covering letter to the Archbishop, and indeed in the theses themselves he had assumed that his own view was that of the Pope. But the horror there expressed of the system of payments, and the determined limitation of the efficacy of an indulgence to the penalty for sin, roused a storm of protest. Several replies were at once forthcoming, notably one from Eck, the Professor of Theology at Ingoldstadt, and another from Prierias, the Master of the Papal Palace, who equated all Church custom with the papal authority and denounced any questioning of it as heresy. The Archbishop and the Dominicans denounced Luther at Rome, but Leo thought the affair merely a monkish quarrel and requested the General of the Augustinian Eremites to call his people to order. Luther appeared before the Chapter at Heidelberg, but proved unbending, and was summoned to Rome. Thereupon the Elector, unwilling to sacrifice a favourite professor, successfully intervened and arranged for the case to be heard before the Legate, Cardinal Cajetan, on German soil at Augsburg in October 1518. After an unavailing effort to reconcile their views, the Cardinal ordered Luther to retract, but this he refused to do, appealing from the Pope ill informed to the Pope better informed, and afterwards, from his refuge in Wittenberg, changing this into an appeal to a General Council. But how little chance there was of an agreement was shown by the Pope's publication in that same month of a Bull defining indulgences in the very terms to which Luther had already made objection.

Attempts at mediation were not, however, immediately abandoned. The impending Imperial election made it advisable for the Pope to keep on good terms with the Elector, and he sent a Saxon nobleman, Charles von Miltitz, to confer upon Frederick the honour of the Golden Rose and to arrange, if possible, the matter of Luther. So well did the monk and the nuncio agree that after a convivial evening they kissed one another; Tetzel was disgraced, and Luther wrote a letter of submission to the Pope. But Miltitz had gone too far. He had promised that his own side as well as Luther's should be forbidden to preach upon the disputed points, and he had not persuaded Luther to retract any of the statements he had made, only to acknowledge that he had perhaps spoken the truth out of season. The

BEGINNING OF THE REFORMATION

controversy between Eck and one of Luther's Wittenberg friends, named Carlstadt, already begun, made it impossible for Luther to keep silence, and it was revealed how wide yawned the gulf between the new and the old opinions.

The differences between them were thrashed out in the Leipzig Disputation of 1519. With Carlstadt, Eck discussed the subjects of grace and free-will, but with Luther discussion centred in the question of papal authority. Luther had by this time made himself acquainted with the history of the forged decretals, and he was beginning to doubt the whole basis of current ecclesiastical jurisdiction. Eck skilfully pushed him into an admission that he believed it possible even for a General Council to err, and that, in opposition to the Council of Constance, he believed some of the statements of Huss and Wycliffe to be most Christian and evangelical. Thus, in effect, Luther was forced to emancipate himself from Pope and Councils, and, the old authority being broken, the Reformation became an established fact. But Eck rightly saw in such a plain admission of heresy a tactical triumph for himself, and the way was open for him to demand a Bull of Excommunication, which the Pope at length published on June 15, 1520.

Before the Bull arrived Luther wrote and published three of his most important treatises. The first of these, the *Address to the Christian Nobility*, challenged the old system by emphasising the responsibility of the laity in Church affairs. The three walls of the papal defence, he says, have been the superiority of the spiritual to the temporal power, the prohibition to anyone but the Pope of the right to interpret the Scriptures, and the refusal to anyone but the Pope of the power to summon a council. But these are all undermined at once if it is remembered that in case of necessity every man can baptise and absolve. Essentially, then, every believer is a priest, and between spiritual and temporal persons the only real difference is one of office and function, not of estate. Consequently to reduce the Church to one man is a devilish and damnable heresy. Where the Pope refuses to act it is allowable for the temporal authorities to step in, for they are fellow-Christians, fellow-priests. Thus Luther made his great political effort. In the second treatise, the *Babylonish Captivity*, he made his doctrinal effort. This was a trenchant criticism of the current sacramental system, which he believes to be simply an endeavour to bring the faithful into bondage to the priest, whereas the true function of the sacraments is to witness to the divine promise which we receive freely by faith. Transubstantiation is denied on the ground that Christ is able to include His body within the actual substance, as well as within the accidents of the bread. The Mass is not to be looked upon as a good work by which we can make ourselves all-powerful with God. Our works are nothing and faith is all. It was against this treatise that Henry VIII wrote his exposition of sacramental doctrine, which won for him the title *Defensor fidei*. In his third effort of this year Luther put forth an eirenicon to the Pope, *Concerning Christian Liberty*, in which he set out as against contemporary misconceptions his view of the true nature of personal religion, telling the Pope that this is the kind of thing he would much rather be working at if it were not for the many controversies by which he was beset. It is indeed amazing that some of these fine passages could have been struck off in the heat of controversy. 'A Christian man is the most free lord of all, and subject to none; a Christian man is the most dutiful servant of all, and subject to everyone.' 'One thing, and one thing alone, is necessary for life, justification, and Christian liberty.' Scripture is divided into two parts—precepts and promises; the precepts were ordained to show man his own impotence for good, so that when he has found no source for justification in himself he may be ready to receive it as the fulfilment of God's promises. And this must become a matter of personal experience. 'It is not sufficient to preach the works, life, and death of Christ in an historic manner, as facts which it suffices to know as an example how to frame our life. . . . Preaching ought to have the object of promoting faith in Him, so that He may not only be Christ, but a Christ for you and for me, and that what is said of Him may work in us.' Faith, then, must come first, and works only as its consequence: 'Good works do not make a good man, but a good man does good works.' And his attitude towards ceremonies is well expressed in the following passage: 'In the Christian life, ceremonies are to be no otherwise

BEGINNING OF THE REFORMATION

looked upon than builders and workmen look upon those preparations for building or working which are not made with any view of being permanent or anything in themselves, but only because without them there could be no building and no work. When the structure is completed they are laid aside. Here you see that we do not contemn these preparations, but set the highest value on them.'

These are the three great Reformation treatises of Luther, and in them 'the whole genius of the Reformer appears in its most complete and energetic form'. But Eck had already published the Bull of Excommunication. The Elector refused to carry it into effect and demanded that Luther's case should be tried before impartial and learned judges. Nevertheless the Reformer's works were publicly burned in Louvain and Cologne. After making another appeal to a General Council, Luther definitely threw off his allegiance to the Papacy, and finally he retaliated in the most dramatic manner by burning both the Bull and a copy of the decretals at Wittenberg on December 10, 1520, before the assembled University.

Events now occurred that were to lift this struggle to the stage of world affairs. In 1519 Leo's political schemes had been defeated, and at the election that followed upon the death of Maximilian I, the young Habsburg prince, Charles, already heir of Spain, the Netherlands, Austria and part of Italy, and the newly discovered portion of America, was selected to succeed him as Holy Roman Emperor. A sincere Catholic, it looked for the moment as if he might bring about a return to the old unified conception of political and spiritual life that had dominated the Middle Ages. But his interests were mainly dynastic, and he pushed the fortunes of his family in a struggle with Francis I, King of France, for the possession of Italy, which gradually spread over Europe and made centralised government impossible. The real drama of Charles V's reign was indeed caused by the interaction of two conflicts, the one with Francis and the other with the followers of the new religious movement. There was always the chance that the two forces might join against him, as we shall see that they did in 1552. It is important to remember this political situation, for it was Charles's preoccupation with it that alone gave the Reformation breathing-space to grow. An instance of the way in which the various influences acted was seen in 1521. The Pope in January of that year issued a stronger Bull against Luther and called upon the new Emperor to see it carried out. Charles, who had been advised to use the threat of Luther to draw off the Pope from his friendship with Francis, and was also under obligations to Frederick the Elector for help given him in the election, contented himself with summoning the Reformer to appear under safe-conduct at the Diet which he was to hold at Worms. Here, on April 18th, Luther made his famous refusal to recant. The next day the Emperor stated his own view of the situation: 'A single monk, led astray by private judgment, has set himself against the faith held by all Christians for a thousand years and more, and impudently concludes that all Christians up till now have erred.' Charles expressed his own determination to follow the example of his forefathers in putting down heresy at whatever cost. In May he secured his alliance with the Pope, and extracted from the Diet the Edict of Worms, which put Luther under the ban of the Empire. But everyone knew that Luther had by this time departed on his homeward journey. As he approached Eisenach, friendly hands seized him and carried him away to the Elector's castle of the Wartburg, and the Emperor presently departed from Germany for an absence of ten years during which the Reformation was comparatively free to work itself out.

There can be no doubt that the German nation as a whole was behind Luther in the stand he had made. Even the princes who helped to pass the Edict presented their own demand for a disciplinary reform of the Church. They also saw that Luther's proposals would deliver secular government from ecclesiastical control. The monks, too, favoured his views. His own Augustinian Brethren followed him, and so did many of the Franciscans. But the Dominicans and the parochial clergy were against him. His most important allies were the trading classes. It was indeed in this movement that the bourgeois emerged into an even greater prominence in public life than they had already enjoyed in the medieval cities. They felt the attractiveness of Lutheranism because it emphasised the value of ordinary natural human life, while the Church had made monasticism the ideal of Christianity. Hence the popularity of Luther's writings. His were the most profitable books for the Press to publish, and the Venetian ambassador tells in a dispatch how 'his books are sold publicly in Worms, although the Pope and the Emperor, who is on the spot, have prohibited them'.

Luther had plenty of leisure for writing in his ten months' retirement at the Wartburg. It was now that he set himself to the task of translating the New Testament. His was not the first German translation, but the others were from the Vulgate, while his was from Erasmus's second edition of the Greek text. It had a great place in the history of German literature, for it fixed Luther's own dialect as the norm, and had as much influence on the national tongue as our own Authorised Version did on the development of the English language. His first edition of the New Testament appeared in 1522, the Old Testament was not complete till 1534, and in that he had the assistance of other scholars, notably of Philip Melanchthon.

Melanchthon (German Schwartzerd—'Blackland') was a grandnephew and protégé of Reuchlin. He had become Professor of Greek at Wittenberg in 1518, and had been confirmed in his leaning towards Luther's teaching by the arguments to which he had listened at the Leipzig Disputation. He was more of a scholar than Luther and always more ready to make intellectual concessions, but he was never so great a leader. The contrast between them is best expressed in Luther's own words: 'I am rough, boisterous, stormy, and altogether warlike. I am born to fight against innumerable monsters and devils. I must remove stumps and stones, cut away thistles and thorns, and clear the wild forests; but Master Philip comes along softly and gently, sowing and watering with joy.' His great contribution to the literature of the Reformation was his *Loci Communes* (*Commonplaces*), of which Luther said that it was the best book next to Holy Scripture, 'a book invincible, imperishable, even of canonical value'. Originally it was nothing but a collection of notes for systematic expansion in oral lectures on the Epistle to the Romans; but between its first publication in December 1521 and its seventeenth in

1523 it was successively enlarged until it made its author the great systematiser of Lutheran theology and almost the mediator between that expression of reformed opinions and Catholicism.

Melanchthon kept his leader in touch with what was going on in Wittenberg. It was not all pleasant hearing. Things were moving rapidly and there was a consequent state of confusion. Carlstadt had encouraged some of the secular clergy to marry, and had also, in spite of the Elector's request for restraint, instituted a liturgical reform by making alterations in the Mass. Zwilling, an Augustinian, had attacked private Masses and monastic vows. But more disturbing than this had been the arrival of the Zwickau Prophets. These were two preachers named Storch and Strubner, the representatives of a kind of Montanistic-Hussite sect lately founded in Zwickau by Thomas Munzer, the precursor of the Anabaptists. They provided a strong reinforcement for Carlstadt's radical party. Even Melanchthon was impressed by them, they claimed such wonderful things for themselves—'that they had been sent to teach by the manifest voice of God, that they held familiar conversations with God, that they saw the future, that, in short, they were prophetic and apostolic men'. This confidence in the immediate possession of the Spirit placed them above Scripture; it also enabled them to dispense with infant baptism; and, further, it convinced them that the millennium was shortly to appear. While the Golden Age tarried they endeavoured to prepare the Church for it by a baptism of blood, but the plot had been discovered and they had been ejected from Zwickau. Luther was not so easily taken in as Melanchthon; he demanded some clear proof of their divine vocation, and when it was not forthcoming decided to leave the Wartburg, return to Wittenberg, and make an attempt to restore order, the credit of the Reformation, and his own prestige. He succeeded admirably. In a course of eight sermons he appealed to the good sense of the community, established the twin principles of liberty and regularity, and laid it down as a canon that in matters of discipline anything is lawful that is not contrary to Scripture. The prophets left to seek a more congenial atmosphere.

It was well that Luther acted so promptly, for in this

same year (1522) began the Diet of Nürnberg, which was definitely to make of the Reformation a national question. Leo X had died and was succeeded by Charles's old tutor, Adrian VI, a Netherlander and the last of the non-Italian popes. He was a serious man, full of the grave obligations of his office and clearly seeing the necessity of a disciplinary reform. But he was frugal, and the Italians preferred the scandalous, but open-handed, prodigality of his predecessors. Consequently when he died, broken-hearted, after less than two years of fruitless struggle, the wits wrote over his physician's door the legend: 'To the liberator of his country.' It was he who sent his nuncio to the Diet of Nürnberg, promising reform, but asking as a preliminary for the repression of heresy. The reply of the Diet was that to enforce the Edict of Worms was impossible, but that Luther should keep silence if the Pope would promise a free council on German soil within the year; and in the meantime attention was again called to the *Centum Gravamina*, or the *Hundred Grievances* of the Germans against the Church. This was, in effect, to make the Reformation a national movement, and to put it under the protection of the princes. There is little doubt that if a council had been held, either general or national, it would have resulted in a Germany united and reformed. The situation was saved for the Papacy by the death of Adrian. He was succeeded by the much shrewder Medicean, Clement VII, who dispatched Cardinal Campeggio as his legate to the Diet. The legate arrived in March, and to 'avoid scorn' entered the hostile city 'like a mere horseman' and not like a prince of the Church. Nevertheless he was able to break up the solid body of opposition, gathering together the better disposed princes of the south and welding them together into a papal party by the League of Ratisbon, 1524. Thus the possibility of a united Germany was postponed for three centuries.

After this, several events conspired to check the spread of reform. The most important of these was the Peasants' War, which broke out in 1524 and lasted for two years. Luther has often been charged with the responsibility for this disastrous revolt, but in truth its origin was entirely agrarian. The tradition that places the beginning of the war in the action of the Countess von Lupfen, who compelled her tenants to spend a holiday in gathering snail shells upon which she might wind her wool, is sufficiently indicative of the sense of oppression that set the peasants against their lords. No doubt that sense had been deepened by the teaching of men like Carlstadt, who had actually wished to close the schools on the ground that learning was not required to understand the Scriptures, and even Luther's own emphasis on the universal priesthood of all believers helped to fan the flame. Luther at first attempted to mediate between the opponents, but when that proved impossible he chose to link his cause with the power of the rulers rather than discredit it by association with armed rebellion, which in any case he abhorred. But he went to such extremes of language as to make him the scandal of social reformers in later days, bidding the nobles to treat the peasants as brute beasts and to stab, slay, and strangle without restraint. The struggle did not die down till 100,000 peasants had been slaughtered, and after that the lower classes of Germany were the most wretched in Europe till the middle of the eighteenth century, living in a misery that was productive of materialistic atheism and was largely responsible for the almost complete sterility of German thought during that period.

At the height of this conflict, Luther gave a shock to his friends and a cause of rejoicing to his enemies by marrying an 'escaped' nun. The act caused the more consternation as it was entirely unexpected, not even Melanchthon being admitted to the secret, although he loyally defended his leader when it was done. Erasmus, who had said of another such marriage that he supposed the bridegroom did it because he wished to afflict the flesh, said of this that it turned what people had called the Lutheran tragedy into a comedy. But Erasmus and Luther had now drifted apart. The later developments of Lutheranism, as seen both in the Peasants' War and in the doctrinal emphasis upon predestination, were repellent to the exact and fastidious scholar. In 1524 he published his *De Libero Arbitrio* in which he claimed the freedom of the will as the ground of human responsibility. The following year Luther replied in the *De Servo Arbitrio*, affirming in the strongest terms the Augustinian doctrines of predestination and reprobation. This led to the widening of the breach between the humanists and the reformers.

Political events also seemed to be telling against reform. Charles, in pursuit of his quarrel with Francis, inflicted upon him a severe defeat and actually took him prisoner at Pavia in 1525. This led to the Treaty of Madrid between the two in the following year, and it looked as if the Emperor would at last have his hands free to deal with the religious question. But reform was once again saved by the Turks. On August 28, 1526, Solyman the Magnificent defeated and slew Louis II, King of Hungary, at the great Battle of Mohacs. News of this Turkish advance closely affected the course of the discussion of religious questions at the Diet of Speier, which had been sitting since June. There the parties were clearly defined. Philip of Hesse had formed a strong opposition to the League of Ratisbon in his own League of Torgau. Both sides stood their ground, and Ferdinand, who was presiding for his brother Charles, soon saw that while the one insisted upon the Edict of Worms the other would have none of it. Under the circumstances it was clearly impossible to get them to agree upon any common programme of reform, and this was the last time that particular expedient was ever tried. Also, the Pope had forfeited the Emperor's good will by allying himself in the League of Cognac with Francis against Charles. And to crown all, Ferdinand badly wanted help from both parties against the Turk. Thus it came about that the Edict of Worms was neither enforced nor repealed, and it was decided that the religious question should be settled on the principle of inter-territorial toleration. Each prince should be free to fix the religion within his own boundaries, and each should respect the right of the others. It is the principle designated by the famous phrase: *'Cujus regio, ejus religio.'*

There now ensued a short period of comparative quiet in which Luther set himself to build up again on new lines the religious sanctions that had been broken down by the upheaval necessarily consequent upon his teaching. In this effort at reconstruction he was greatly helped by the new Elector of Saxony, John the Steadfast. Frederick had died during the Peasants' War in 1525, and he had always been a moderating influence. John, his brother, was a much more ardent supporter of the Reformation, and it was by his order that a series of *Instructions*, drawn up by Melanchthon with a preface by Luther, were administered throughout the Electoral territory in 1528-29. As the bishops would not undertake this duty it was given to six different commissions, but the provisions were not very stereotyped. Thus arrangements about the ministry were to be made simply as occasion served with the secular Government, the state being regarded as responsible for the supply of pastors, who were to be set up where necessary in the parishes with a superintendent over each group. The Mass had already been translated into the vernacular and made into a sacrament simply, without any sacrificial significance. The daily Mass was abandoned as a cause of superstition, but a Mass with lights and vestments and a sermon on the Gospel was retained as the Sunday morning service, and at the afternoon service there was a sermon on the Old Testament. Here we see the undue prominence of the Old Testament which was to prove the bane of much of the later preaching. Popular education was not neglected, and to further it Luther composed his *Greater Catechism* (1528), and in the following year the *Short Catechism*, which is one of the most famous of the Reformation documents. Practically the whole of Lower Germany adopted similar measures, but they seem to have availed little in checking the deterioration in morals, of which Luther has the bitterest things to say.

It was certainty time for the reformers to set their house in order, for Charles was now carrying all before him. In 1527 his troops sacked Rome and made Clement a prisoner. Two years afterwards he concluded the Peace of Barcelona with Clement and the Peace of Cambrai with Francis. As the negotiations for these treaties were under way, Ferdinand felt the moment opportune to reverse the decision of the Diet of Speier. A new Diet was held in the same place in 1529, with the Catholics in the majority. The *cujus regio* principle was annulled, and the new institutions promulgated in the evangelical states were, in effect, disallowed. The followers of reformed opinions were powerless; all they could do was to protest. This protest, joined in by the Elector of Saxony, the Landgrave of Hesse, and fourteen imperial cities of Upper Germany, was embodied in an open appeal to the Emperor and a future council. It is from this that Protestantism has received its name.

CHAPTER III

THE MOVEMENT BECOMES GENERAL

THE story of the beginning of the Reformation in Germany is almost exclusively the story of Luther's own life, but at about the same moment a parallel movement was started in German Switzerland by one who would admit no indebtedness to Luther. Zwingli (1484–1531) was the son of well-to-do peasant parents, but his education was under the care of his uncle, the Rural Dean of Wesen, by whom he was put to school, and then sent to the University of Vienna. Here he came under the influence of the humanist, Wyttenbach, and was imbued with that love of the new learning that was to fill him with so ardent an admiration for Erasmus and to govern his whole career. It is from this point of view that Zwingli's later work can best be understood. He had none of Luther's moral strength —his own life was far from being without reproach—but he had a keen intellectual sincerity that laid bare to him all the abuses of the contemporary ecclesiastical system. Also he had a shrewd eye for practical abuses, and of these he had an early taste, for when in 1506 he was ordained to the priesthood and received the charge of Glarus, he found that he had to pay no less than a hundred gulden before he could enter upon his cure.

He was at Glarus for ten years, and distinguished himself as an opponent of the custom by which the Swiss were wont to hire themselves out to foreign princes for military service. The only service Zwingli allowed was that of the Pope. But in that service he was invaluable, thrice accompanying the troops as chaplain and earning for himself a papal pension. This explains the difference in the treatment meted out by the Papacy to him and to Luther; even the high-souled Adrian could not afford to be harsh with so

THE MOVEMENT BECOMES GENERAL 29

valuable an ally. From Glarus, owing to political differences, he moved to the humanist stronghold of Einsiedeln, where he was not afraid to say that the present authority of the Papacy could not be justified from Scripture, and where he joined in the scoffing outcry that prevented the success of a campaign on behalf of an indulgence. Nevertheless in 1518 he received an honourable appointment as Acolyte Chaplain to the Pope, and as such was able to secure election as People's Priest of the Great Minster of Zürich.

Here he had scope for his talents as a preacher, which he had taken the greatest pains to cultivate, and was thus enabled to carry out the great effort of his career, which, more circumscribed and concentrated than that of Luther, had as its practical result the emancipation of the city from the control of its bishop. In 1520 he resigned his pension, but in the next year he became Canon, and his seat in the chapter brought him the privileges of a citizen, which enabled him in his future agitations to bid for and secure the support of the Town Council. The Zwinglian Reform began in 1522 with the question of Lenten observance. In that year some of Zwingli's followers ate meat during the fast and were supported by their leader in a sermon 'On the Choice and Freedom of Food'. This brought a remonstrance from the Bishop, but the Council temporised, and while ordering that for the present the old custom should be observed, prayed the Bishop to take further advice; and so, by showing that they did not regard his present ruling as final, they entered upon that course by which they finally freed themselves from his authority. The same year Zwingli presented a petition on behalf of himself and some friends asking the Bishop's permission to marry, frankly giving their own dubious past as the reason. But no reply was received, and Zwingli himself had entered upon a connexion with a wealthy widow which he legalised by marrying her in 1524.

In 1523 the Council accepted the Zwinglian standard of 'Scripture only' as the basis of doctrine and discipline, and on this ground Zwingli published *Sixty-seven Articles*, which after a public disputation were enforced by a decree of the Council as the norm for all preachers in its territories. After a second Disputation the Council issued a 'Mandate for the Abolition of Images and the Mass', and declared their intention of sending preachers of their own appointment to convert the country districts. Monasteries in the meantime had been suppressed, and some at least of their endowments were devoted to education and the poor, a Latin School being established out of money derived from the Great Minster. A course of studies leading up to the ministry was devised, and Church courts for discipline and marriage cases were set up. When on Maundy Thursday, 1525, a Love-feast had replaced the Mass, the Zwinglian reform, after a development of only three years, was practically complete.

Meanwhile the movement had spread to Bern and Basel, but, as in Germany, difficulties were stirred up by people who wished to go to extremes. The leaders of this radical party were Manz, Grebel, and Hubmaier, supported at a distance by our old friend Munzer and in Zürich itself by Carlstadt. They wished to apply strictly Zwingli's own standard of Scripture and Scripture only. They had been to the fore in image-breaking, but now they extended their criticism to infant baptism. They began to re-baptise adults at first by sprinkling, but soon by immersion, and this was the beginning of Anabaptism. Zwingli, unable on his own premises to meet their argument, denounced them as blockheads before the Council. Twenty-one of them from both sexes were confined in the Witches' Tower to see whether their obstinacy could be broken, and when that expedient failed a grimmer form of humour condemned several of them to death by drowning. Hubmaier escaped and recanted on the rack. More serious difficulties were encountered from the Catholic party, the Forest Cantons allying together against the City Cantons which sided with Zürich. The aggressive attitude of Zürich ultimately led to the First War of Cappel (1529), which was ended after little more than a fortnight's hostilities by an arrangement for mutual toleration.

Zwingli began to look farther afield and to meditate great schemes. Zürich had already joined itself to Constance, and to several other towns where the new opinions were supreme, in a Christian Civic League. Austria and the Catholic States had replied with a 'Christian Union'. This

THE MOVEMENT BECOMES GENERAL 81

new alignment of forces broke through the limits of the Swiss Confederation, but, under the influence of Philip of Hesse, Zwingli dreamt of a great Protestant Union. These projects were defeated by the irreconcilable differences between the reformers. Zwingli has been called 'the revolutionary theologian of the Reformation'. On two points especially he went beyond Luther. The latter was willing to accept all that could be proved not contrary to Scripture, but the former would not allow anything that could not be directly proved from Scripture. Also, Zwingli went far to reject the whole doctrine of the sacraments. To him physical things could not be the vehicles of spiritual grace. Especially he reduced the Eucharist to a bare sign. In the phrase, 'This is my body', the word 'is' must be equivalent to 'represents', as if a woman were to point to her wedding-ring and say, 'This is my husband'. There might be some social significance in the sacrament, but otherwise it was a mere memorial. This was very far from the opinion of Luther, who, as we have seen, actually went so far as to accept the theory of consubstantiation.

In order to compose these differences and so present a united front to the enemy, Philip of Hesse summoned a conference of the reformers at his own castle of Marburg in 1529. It broke down over the question of the Eucharist, Luther chalking on the table at which he sat the words, '*Hoc est corpus Meum*', and refusing to recede from a literal interpretation of them. Luther drew up fifteen articles as a basis of union, and Zwingli was prepared to agree to all except the one dealing with this subject. Luther thereupon revised them in a still more uncompromising spirit; and as the famous 'Articles of Schwabach' they became the basis of Lutheran doctrine and the bond of union for an exclusively Lutheran league of North German states. Philip had the more reason to regret the failure of his attempt at mediation, as at this very time the Turks under Solyman were defeated in an effort to take Vienna, and Charles was once again free to take steps against the Protestants. The breakdown at Marburg was therefore the beginning of a period of religious reaction in Germany.

Charles now (1530) called a Diet at Augsburg, to be attended by himself in person, and in spite of pressure

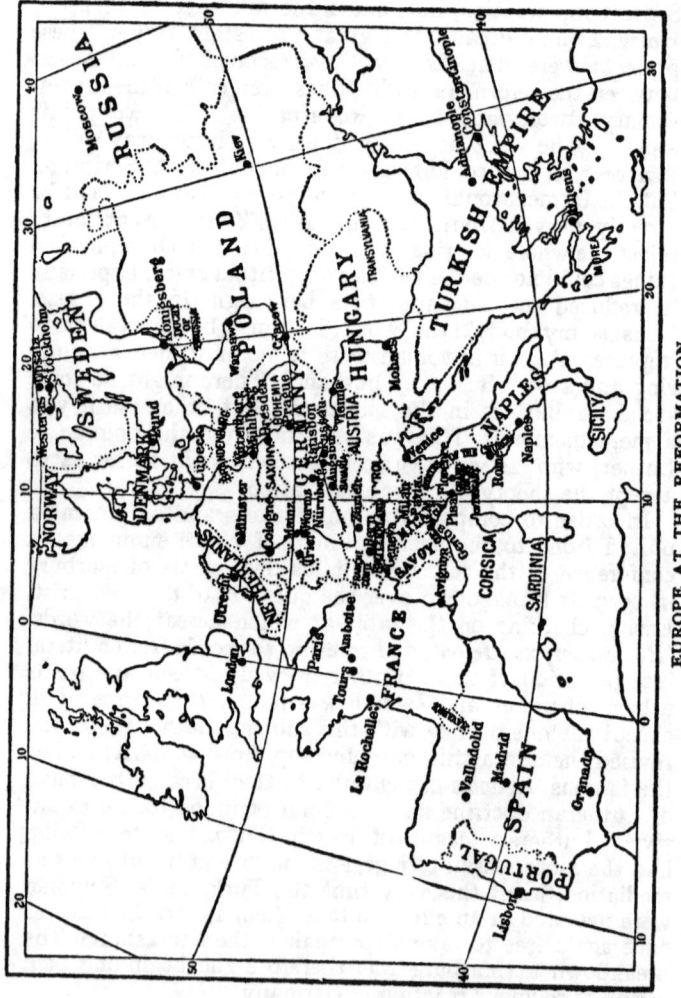

EUROPE AT THE REFORMATION

THE MOVEMENT BECOMES GENERAL 33

from the Pope, who urged him to deal drastically with the situation, promised a fair hearing to every man's opinion. The Lutheran case was presented by Melanchthon in an *Apology* based upon the Articles of Schwabach, which was afterwards known as the *Confession of Augsburg.* It was conciliatory in tone. Melanchthon feared the imminence of war, and he tried to effect a compromise by showing how far Lutheran doctrine differed from Zwinglian, and how closely it approached the old Catholic system. This led to some concessions from the Catholic side, notably from Eck, who agreed that the sacrifice of the Mass was not to be regarded as a bloody offering, but as representative and in a mystery. But Luther himself repudiated all compromise, and the Emperor had no alternative but to demand conformity from all until such time as a council could be called. The Protestants had now nothing to look forward to but war and coercion, and their position was made even worse by the election of Ferdinand as King of the Romans in 1531. They made haste to band themselves together as closely as they could, but this was made difficult by the intransigence of Zwingli. However, four Zwinglian cities of Upper Germany, Strassburg, Constance, Lindau, and Memmingen, put forward a mediating creed, mainly the work of Bucer, called the Tetrapolitana, and the work of conciliation between the two schools of reformers was made easier by the fact that Zwingli himself was killed in the Second War of Cappel, which broke out between the Forest and the City Cantons of Switzerland in 1531. This led to a considerable reaction in Zwingli's own country, where even Glarus once again became Catholic, but it helped to make effective the Schmalkaldic League in which a few months earlier the German Protestants of both north and south had united to face their foes.

These two years, 1530–31, were a period of the greatest peril to the Protestant cause, for there is no doubt that the Emperor could have crushed it if he had acted with energy. But he was prevented, largely by a fresh advance of the Turks, and at the Peace of Nürnberg (1532) he promised, on consideration of help against the infidel, a truce to the heretics until a Council or fresh Diet should meet. When the Turks retreated, Charles left Germany on a nine years'

84 HISTORY OF THE MODERN CHURCH

absence to pursue his schemes elsewhere, and the Reformation was free to spread a little farther. Even the seemingly untoward event of a fresh outburst of Anabaptist madness helped this extension. For when these fanatics set up a kingdom of their own at Münster, in 1533, with John Bockholt, a Leyden tailor, as their king, the Lutherans fought side by side with the Catholics to suppress it, which they succeeded in doing in 1535, and so acquired merit with the Governments for their good sense. Also in that year the Papacy received the news that Henry VIII had abolished the Pontiff's authority in England. But a parallel event to that which was the occasion of reform in England had a very different effect in Germany. Philip of Hesse, who had discovered a strong distaste for his wife and found continence impossible, wished to marry again. The reformers preferred bigamy to divorce, and a marriage took place in the presence of Melanchthon and Bucer in 1540. Luther proposed to cover it up with 'a good strong lie', but Melanchthon nearly died of shame when the truth came out. It was in all respects disastrous, for the obloquy in which it was held drove Philip into the arms of the Emperor and effectively stopped the progress of reform.

A last effort to reconcile Catholic and Evangelical views was made in 1541 at Ratisbon. Paul III was now Pope, and his conciliatory agent, Cardinal Contarini, met Melanchthon with other theologians in the Colloquy of Ratisbon. They came near to succeeding in their task, and actually agreed upon the question of Justification, but neither Luther nor the Roman consistory would accept the compromise, and the theologians on the spot finally disagreed about the constitution of the Church. Nothing now was left but to await the General Council, which the Emperor at last wrung out of the Pope in 1545. The following year Luther died.

The teachings of Luther and Zwingli represent respectively the conservative and liberal elements in the new religious thought. A middle position, which was destined to have a greater future than either, sprang from France and was developed in French Switzerland. The Church in France had long been less dependent upon the Papacy than was the Church in other countries. The Pragmatic Sanction of 1438 had been the joint result of the conciliar theory and a strong monarchy, and the effect of the Concordat of Bologna (1516) had been to place the temporal interests of the Church under the King. Nevertheless, in theology, French churchmen had been content to follow the old lines; the Sorbonne was strongly traditionalist and provided opponents to the humanism of Erasmus. Consequently, where the Renaissance learning did take root, it produced more naturally than elsewhere opinions analogous to those of the Reformation. This was notably true of Lefèvre d'Etaples, who, as early as 1512, had published a commentary on S. Paul's Epistles, in which he had denied the merit of human works apart from the grace of God, and, while admitting the Real Presence, had doubted the doctrine of transubstantiation. Together with his old pupil, Bishop Briçonnet, Farel, and other friends, he settled down in the former's cathedral town of Meaux and established there a centre for the new thought, preaching faith instead of authority as the foundation of religion, denouncing clerical celibacy and Latin prayers, and publishing a French translation of the Bible. His views rapidly spread, and elicited the sympathy of the King's sister, Margaret, afterwards Queen of Navarre. Governmental attitude towards them was dictated by the exigencies of Francis's quarrel with Charles V; and the characteristic French policy was already established, by which they can encourage abroad religious opinions that they do their best to discourage at home. Negotiations were fitfully carried on for an alliance with such reformers as followed the teaching of Bucer or Melanchthon without preventing occasional persecutions of their own Huguenots.

The most important convert of this French school was John Calvin. He was born at Noyon in Picardy 1509, his father being notary to the chapter and secretary to the Bishop. Calvin was thus brought up in aristocratic surroundings, the only gentleman, it has been said, among the reformers. He was a youth to whose seriousness the legend that he was known to his companions as 'the Accusative' Case' is sufficient witness. To provide for his education he was made a prebendary at the age of twelve, though, like

Melanchthon, he was never ordained. At Paris he studied under Cordier, the teacher of the future Jesuit Ignatius Loyola. In obedience to his father he studied law, but his chief interest was in the humanities, his first published work being on Seneca. On his father's death he could follow his own bent, but a sudden conversion in 1532 turned his thoughts to higher things and he became the leader among a little circle of students who favoured reformed views. He was on friendly terms with the new rector of the university, Nicholas Cop, and probably wrote for him the inaugural address, which, when delivered, helped to raise such a storm that they both had to flee. He resigned his benefices at Noyon, and, while living at Basel, in 1535 he finished the first edition of his *Institutes*, a work which placed him in the front rank of theologians. On his journeyings he happened to come to Geneva. Farel, who was struggling hard to preach reform there, hailed him as a heaven-sent recruit, and insisted that he should remain. Thus began a work that was to become of world-wide importance.

Geneva offered the most fruitful soil for the development of Calvin's genius. It was French in sympathy, and had recently acquired an independent status of self-government after ousting the authority of both Duke and Bishop. It gave Calvin the opportunity both to dominate France and to try out to the full his own ideas of ecclesiastical polity. It was in 1536 that he arrived, and was appointed by the Council to be lecturer at the Cathedral. For two years he worked side by side with Farel. Their aim was to make of the city an ecclesiastical state, in which every citizen should be bound, under pain of excommunication, to adopt the statement of belief that they themselves had drawn up. The attempt was premature; the citizens were not yet ready to place themselves under the heel of a new tyranny. Also they were under obligations to Bern, which had helped them in their late struggles for liberty. Consequently, when Bern asked them to adopt a more liberal theology, they made it a test for the ministers, and when Calvin and Farel refused to conform they were both banished from the city in April 1538. On the invitation of Bucer, Calvin settled at Strassburg, where he ministered to the French refugees, lectured in theology, and revised his *Institutes*.

THE MOVEMENT BECOMES GENERAL 87

When Cardinal Sadoleto took advantage of the late dissensions to invite the Genevese to return to the fold of the Church, it fell to Calvin to write a famous and successful reply. The opposition to him in the city was dying down, and the Council showed its appreciation of his defence by ordering it to be printed. Finally, when his enemy, the Captain-General, had been executed, Calvin was officially requested to return. He was most unwilling to do so, but at last, fearing the fate of a Jonah, he gave way and arrived in the city in 1541, and there he worked till his death in 1564.

The system, as now administered, was set forth in the *Ordonnances Ecclésiastiques*. In theology, it was mainly derivative, although more completely organised than any reformed system hitherto set forth. On the Eucharist a position midway between that of Luther and Zwingli was maintained: Christ was truly received, but the reception was due to faith and was not directly associated with the elements. But the real original power of the system lay in its discipline. Authority was vested in the religious body itself represented by the consistory, which was composed of the pastors and elected laymen, and was well fitted to that democratic government which it has always been the boast of Calvinism that it has fostered. But it was indeed a terrible tyranny. It gave an undue extension to the idea of crime, and punished delinquents with an appalling severity. Death was the penalty meted out for adultery, and drowning sometimes followed unchastity. A child was beheaded for having struck its parents. The wife of the Captain-General was imprisoned for scolding and for dancing. A free-thinker who had affixed a placard to Calvin's pulpit was beheaded. But the worst blot on Calvin's name is his treatment of Servetus This unfortunate Spanish scholar sought truth both in the field of medicine and that of theology. In the former he achieved distinction, for he seems to have been the first discoverer of the circulation of the blood. In the latter he was less happy, for he published two books that threw ridicule upon the doctrine of the Trinity. Fleeing from the wrath aroused by these publications, he took shelter with a former pupil who was now Archbishop of Vienne. There he might have remained in peace had he not **engaged in a violent controversy with Calvin, and later** published anonymously another book of strongly heretical views. Calvin, who had seven years before told Farel that if Servetus ever came to Geneva he would see that he never left it alive, actually caused him to be delated to the Inquisition, by whom he was first imprisoned and then, on his escape, burnt in effigy. By an act of madness Servetus then presented himself at Geneva, and there he was burnt in reality (1553).

From all this it can be seen that Calvin's system is that of a lawyer. God's unalterable and unquestionable will is the basis of all. By that will some are from all eternity predestined to everlasting life and others to everlasting death. The law of God must guide men to their destined end, and that law was administered by a Presbyterian system with the aid of a kind of Protestant inquisition above which stood the dominating influence of Calvin himself. The system, with its careful inquiry into the details of private life, pressed more hardly upon the individual than any medieval system, because it had no corollary in a merciful sacrament of penance. Yet it has produced some of the finest types of character, and its merits recommended it so widely as to make of Calvin the only international reformer.

While these events were happening in Geneva, things were going from bad to worse in Germany. The Council of Trent had been called, but it was clear from the first that it could not bring peace. The logic of events had forced Charles to see the identity of the interests of the Empire with those of the Church and to recognise that he must face a life-and-death struggle between their combined forces on the one side and those of Protestant territorialism on the other. The calling of the Council of Trent was the signal for taking up arms. The combatants were unequally matched. On the one side Charles had concerted his measures with the Pope and had been left by the death of Francis I and Henry VIII 'without a rival in Europe'. On the other side the Schmalkaldic League was not even united, and of its leaders Philip of Hesse was discredited, and John Frederick, the new Elector of Saxony, had a rival claimant for his position in his treacherous cousin Maurice. The last named invaded the Saxon territories; the Emperor took

THE MOVEMENT BECOMES GENERAL 89

John Frederick prisoner at the Battle of Mühlberg, 1547, and Philip gave himself up. Protestantism was thus completely crushed, and it looked as if the whole of North Europe might again become Catholic. But in this crisis Charles was feeling particular irritation at the action of the Pope, who, in fear of the sudden growth of the Emperor's power, had withdrawn his troops and called the Council from Trent to his own second capital of Bologna. Consequently Charles tried the path of compromise. He first drew up with representative divines, and then passed through the Diet, the *Interim of Augsburg*, conceding the cup to the laity and marriage to the clergy, but retaining the seven sacraments and transubstantiation. This he sought to force upon the cities, where necessary, at the point of the sword. It, of course, was distasteful both to the stauncher reformers and to Pope Paul III, who only acceded to it on his deathbed. But most of the princes accepted it, and even Melanchthon, who carried the majority of the theologians of his party with him, was willing to receive it in so far as it concerned things indifferent (*adiaphora*), a proposal which produced a great Adiaphoristic Controversy among the Lutherans. Charles's scheme met with a large measure of success, but he alienated Protestant sympathy by the rigour with which he enforced it, and he lost the support of the new Pope, Julius III, by the domineering way in which he forced him to return the Council to Trent, and then sought to manage it. Maurice took the opportunity to change sides once again and rebel against this absolutism. He effected that alliance between the French king (now Henry II) and the German Protestants which was to prove Charles's undoing. While Henry took the field in Lorraine he himself captured Augsburg. Charles was compelled to flee, and by the Convention of Passau (1552) accepted a truce and promised to call another Diet in which the religious differences should be composed. Poetic justice overtook Maurice, who did not live to enjoy his ill-gotten power, but was slain the next year in a private war at Sievershausen.

The end of all this was that a real settlement was effected in 1555 by the Peace of Augsburg, which was to prove the foundation of religious liberty in Germany. By the terms of this Peace religious disputes were henceforth to be settled by the Imperial Chamber; each secular sovereign was to adopt which creed he liked, and was to allow others the same freedom; and confiscated Church lands were to be kept by their present owners, but there were to be no further confiscations. Thus the old unity was finally accepted as broken. Up to this date the possibility of reconciliation was always kept in view, but now there were three rival creeds: Catholic, Lutheran, and Reformed (Calvinist). Yet by the Peace only the first two of these were recognised: Lutheranism obtained legal recognition, Calvinism did not. Secular princes were allowed a choice between two religions, but by the 'Ecclesiastical Reservation' any spiritual prince who forsook the old faith forfeited his lands and status. This victory for the *cujus regio* principle was a step on the road to religious liberty, but 'to define the faith is to limit the faithful'. Religion was actually narrower than it was in the Middle Ages. Within the states there was no toleration.

CHAPTER IV

REFORM BEGINS IN ENGLAND

IT is one of the difficulties in dealing with the Reformation that it can never be discussed in general terms. It means different things in different places, and it may mean different things in the same place at different times. England affords a particular illustration of this. Here the predisposing causes were the same as on the Continent: there was the same hatred of ecclesiastical abuses, the same uprising of nationalist and individualist spirit, the same revival of learning with its rediscovery of the text of Scripture. But the occasion of the beginning of reform in England was quite peculiar to the circumstances of the English king, and both the course that the movement followed, emphasising quite different features in different reigns, and its final issue were unlike anything that was seen on the Continent.

When Henry VIII came to the throne in 1509 he seemed the very embodiment of the new age. Young, masterful, disdainful of authority, every inch a king in athletics, learning, music, diplomacy, religion, he was popular with all classes, but especially with the 'new' men. To Erasmus he said: 'Give me the pleasure of assisting and protecting you as far as my power extends.' Before the death of his elder brother, Arthur, it seems that he was destined for a career in the Church and looked forward to being Archbishop of Canterbury. It was this, no doubt, that gave him his special interest in theology, and he was theologian enough, as we have seen, to reject the Lutheran scheme. No more than his friends, the Oxford Reformers, did he wish to change the old doctrinal order. To the great cataclysmic change that he made he was moved by a worthy motive of anxiety for his dynasty and the subsequent peace of the kingdom, but more by the less worthy motives of lust, greed, and pride. Thus he became the willing leader of the men who saw in the Papacy itself the cause of the current abuses, but in spite of himself he gave a great impetus to a consequent theological revolt against the medieval doctrine.

The occasion of the English Reformation is to be found in Henry's desire to have his marriage with Katherine of Aragon declared null and void. She was the widow of his brother Arthur, but that first marriage had never been consummated, and he himself had married her under a dispensation from Julius II in which the Pope had provided most carefully against any possible dispute about the validity of the marriage. But all Katherine's seven children, with the exception of the weak and sickly Princess Mary, died at birth or shortly after, and Henry saw in this fatality a result of the curse pronounced in Leviticus xx. 21. His fear of the Divine wrath combined with the fact that he was now head over ears in love with Anne Boleyn to make him determined at all costs to set himself free. The agent he employed to this end was his Minister, Wolsey, Cardinal-Archbishop of York and papal legate. This astute ecclesiastic by his foreign policy had made England powerful while Francis I and Charles V were quarrelling. When the question of the 'divorce' came up he first tried to put the King off, and then, not seeing the real motive of the King's determination, tried to make political capital out of it by securing him a French wife. When at last he was enlightened, he tried to get a commission from Clement VII for himself and Cardinal Campeggio to try the case in England. There seemed to be no difficulty about it; such things had often been done by the Papacy before and were being done at that moment. But the request came in 1527, when the sack of Rome had placed the Pope a prisoner in the hands of the Emperor, who was actually nephew to Katherine. For the time nothing could be done, but during a temporary respite from Charles's tyranny in 1528 the Pope allowed the commission, which was actually bringing its proceedings to a close in the following year when pressure once again fell upon the unhappy Pontiff, and he recalled the case to Rome. Filled with wrath at this thwarting of his hopes the King compelled Wolsey to relinquish the Great Seal, and by a premunire dismissed him from all his offices except that of Archbishop of York. Later the fallen Minister was summoned to answer an absurd charge of treason, but he was fortunate enough to die on the way (1530).

Henry was compelled to look round for fresh means of accomplishing his purpose. In the house where his friends stayed after the breakdown of the commission there happened to be a gentle and sensitive student with a leaning to the new theology, a Fellow of Jesus College, Cambridge, named Thomas Cranmer. He suggested the not uncommon expedient of consulting the universities. This pleased the King so much when it was reported to him by Stephen Gardiner, the Bishop of Winchester, that he first had Cranmer made chaplain to Anne's father, the Earl of Wiltshire, and then sent him to the Continent to put his suggestion to the proof. Here Cranmer won good opinions both from Pope and Emperor, but imbibed at least enough of Lutheranism to marry a niece of the scholar Osiander. Shortly after this he received the surprising order of the King to return and take up the office of Archbishop of Canterbury in place of the aged Warham who had died in 1531. He was constrained to obey, but realising the difficulty of his position kept his marriage secret.

The object of the appointment was to secure a sympathetic Archbishop who should try the King's case in his own court. Naturally this could not be done without a good deal of pruning of papal authority, but for this Henry had already taken the necessary steps. He had begun in 1531 by telling the clergy that since they had recognised the legatine authority of Wolsey (which he held by the King's own grace!) they had incurred a premunire. From the consequences of this the Convocation of Canterbury had to buy itself off by a payment of a fine of £100,000 and that of York by a fine of £18,000, and both alike were compelled to recognise the King as the Supreme Head of the Church in England. Warham himself suggested the addition of the words, 'As far as the law of Christ allows', and the only consent given by Convocation to the measure was when one cried out, 'We are all silent'. The next year,

1532, the year from which the English Reformation is usually dated, the Convocations promised by the 'Submission of the Clergy' not to meet henceforth without the King's writ, not to enact any new canon without his assent, and to submit to a revision of the canon law by a committee of sixteen spiritual and sixteen lay persons appointed by the King. This committee, in point of fact, was never appointed in this reign. On the same day that the clergy made their submission, Sir Thomas More resigned his office as Chancellor and retired to his private house. But the work went on. In the same year was passed the Annates Act, by which the archbishops and bishops were to refuse to pay first-fruits to the Pope, who was to accept a composition of five per cent. instead of the first year's income. This Act was only to be operative at the King's pleasure, and Henry used it in order to force the Pope to recognise Cranmer's appointment by sending him the customary pall. The next year came the Act in Restraint of Appeals. Already by the Act of Premunire of 1353 appeals to Rome had been made impossible without the King's consent, but now the King was never to grant his consent.

This at last made it possible for Cranmer to proceed. Having just been made Archbishop he tried the King's case in his own court at Dunstable and pronounced the marriage with Katherine to be invalid. Then five days after he pronounced the King to be lawfully married to Anne. She was already with child, and by an act of poetic justice the babe turned out to be a girl, the Princess Elizabeth. The same year the Pope retaliated by declaring the marriage with Anne void and that with Katherine valid. A breach was thus clearly made, but so far the Pope's spiritual power had not been brought in question, nor had there been any evidence of an intention to alter religion. The gap was widened the next year (1534) by a series of four Acts. The first embodied the 'Submission of the Clergy'; the second was a new Annates Act, decreeing that henceforth none be paid to Rome, and including legislation on the future method of appointing bishops. No Bulls for such appointments were to be required from the Pope, nor any fees paid for them, nor was any pall to be sought for the Archbishop. This was simply to revert to the position of 1416, when,

REFORM BEGINS IN ENGLAND

during the dispute of three rival candidates for the Holy See, Henry V and his Parliament had directed Chichele to act in such matters on his own authority as Metropolitan. The third Act dealt with Dispensations, ruling that henceforth all licences were to be sought from the Archbishop and forbidding payments for licences to the Pope. The last was the 'Supreme Head Act', which confirmed the title already conceded by the Convocations and added a visitatorial power to the ecclesiastical headship of the Crown. The same year both Convocations declared that 'the Bishop of Rome hath not by Scripture any greater authority in England than any other foreign bishop'. As a result of these measures Paul III prepared a Bull of Excommunication, but Henry forestalled him by passing an Act in 1536 'for extirpating the authority of the Bishop of Rome', by which it was provided that every clerk and layman holding office should take an oath renouncing the Bishop of Rome and his authority under penalty of high treason.

It has sometimes been said that by his action Henry VIII had founded a new Church. That is absurd; neither he nor his theologians believed that in shaking off the administrative claims of the Pope they were cutting themselves off from the communion of the historic Church. Unlike the Continental reformers they took care in fixing the outward constitution of the Church to continue it as it had always been, except for the one fact that they would have no foreign interference. That a breach had occurred between the King of England and the Pope, a breach that involved the people of England, was obvious; but such things had occurred before, and that it was not regarded by Rome as a new departure was shown clearly enough in 1554 when, for a season, she closed the breach that had been made.

Henry had thus made himself absolute master in his own territory by removing the one outside power that had interfered all through the Middle Ages. For the rest of his reign neither Law nor Parliament nor the Church dared lift a hand against him. This was in accord with the genius of Tudor government, which recognised that it could be tyrannical so long as it was popular and successful. But while the country benefited the individual suffered. Henry now used his position to accumulate wealth and to direct the religion of his people along the old paths.

His instrument for a few years was Thomas Cromwell. This typical representative of Renaissance statecraft was the son of a Putney blacksmith, and already an able lawyer, when in 1514 he attracted the notice of Wolsey, who used him in the suppression of a few small monastic establishments in order to provide the money for his educational schemes at Oxford and Ipswich. Cromwell deserted the fallen Wolsey for the King's service, and put into practice political ideas learnt from Machiavelli's *Prince*, consulting not the honour but the inclination of his master. Under his malign influence Henry's tyranny in its worst form was embodied in the Act of Succession and the Verbal Treasons Act, both of 1534. The object of the first was to ensure the repudiation of the marriage with Katherine and to secure the succession to the children of Anne. It was accompanied by an oath, which, as administered to More and to Fisher, the Bishop of Rochester, required them also to repudiate the authority of the Pope. This they refused to do and were consequently imprisoned. The second involved in treason any who should use words calculated to deprive the Crown of its dignity. After this, to the horror of all Christendom, Fisher and More were executed. The former had irritated the King by the acceptance of a cardinalate from the Pope, and Henry avenged the insult by ensuring that when the hat arrived there was 'no head to wear it'. Other executions were those of Elizabeth Barton, the nun of Kent, and six monks and friars, chiefly from the London Charterhouse. It is noteworthy that most of the other religious, except the Friars Observant of Greenwich and Richmond, who were suppressed, seem to have accepted the situation.

But this did not save them, for the King and his Minister proceeded to the dissolution of the monasteries. There was precedent for this. Henry V, in his quarrel with the French, had suppressed the alien priories in 1414, and Wolsey had followed the example. There is no doubt that monasticism was a failing institution. Religious zeal was running in

REFORM BEGINS IN ENGLAND 47

other channels; charity was bestowing itself elsewhere; there were too many monasteries; a considerable number were more than half empty; their lands were too extensive; and they were unpopular landlords. The fact that they had become largely a parasitic institution had had a bad effect on the spirituality of the monks, but the cases in which there were grave abuses were few and far between. But that did not matter; abuses were sought only as an excuse. The visitors who were appointed entered no more than a third of the houses and got through their work in six months. The real reason for the suppression was that money was needed, and that papal monasteries were a menace to the Royal Supremacy. Possibly a few idealists thought that the lands formerly gained by the monasteries from the parish churches of which they had become rectors, would now be returned, but others had a better-founded hope that some, at least, of those lands would find their way into private possession.

Cromwell carried through the work in virtue of his position as Vicar-General, which made him superior in authority to the Archbishops and enabled him to preside in Convocation. In 1536 the dissolution of all monasteries was ordered which had an income of less than £200. They amounted to 320 all told. Their monks were transferred to the larger houses and the heads were pensioned off, although in point of fact only those received their pensions who had influence in high places. The north, which was two centuries behind the south in development, and where monks and people retained their old friendly relations, felt the attack most keenly. An insurrection broke out in Lincolnshire, which led to the execution of fifty leaders, but stirred up the Pilgrimage of Grace in Yorkshire and fired almost the whole of the northern counties. Under the lawyer, Robert Aske, and bearing their banner of the Five Wounds of Christ, the rebels set out upon their crusade and seized the City of York. The Duke of Norfolk, who stayed their progress at Doncaster, was compelled to treat with them. They were perfectly loyal to the King, thinking only that he was misled by evil Ministers, and when they heard that he had safeguarded the faith by the issue of articles of religion and that he promised both a free parliament to meet in the north and proper maintainance for the monks from the confiscated lands, they dispersed rejoicing to their homes. Henry then took the opportunity of a few isolated outbreaks to visit his wrath upon the insurgents. Six abbots and a number of the nobility were executed, and the countryside was covered with the gibbets of commoner folk.

The money gained by the suppression of the smaller monasteries not proving sufficient for the Royal purposes, recourse was had to the larger monasteries, although in the report issued by the visitors their morality had been particularly emphasised. By the year 1539 practically all the remaining houses, to the number of 168, had made voluntary or compulsory surrender of their property, and in that year, in order to complete the work, an Act was passed vesting all monastic property in the King. Twelve refractory houses were reduced by attainder, and the abbots of Glastonbury, Colchester, and Reading were hanged for treason. The harm done by this wholesale spoliation was incalculable. The glorious architectural splendours of the countryside were plundered, even after they had been rifled for their treasures, of their very stones and timber, lead and iron. Their relics, a few broken walls and columns, still remain here and there, like bones picked clean by vultures, to witness to the strength and beauty of the living form that once stood amidst scenes of romantic loveliness. Priceless treasures in manuscripts were destroyed. The status of the clergy was degraded by the lay impropriators, who appointed old or ignorant vicars at the lowest possible stipends. By the distribution of the lands a new nobility, including many of the present 'county families', was created and maintained its position by refusing any return to the old regime. A ring-fence formed by their domains was erected round London and controlled the main roads from the north and west. Education gained little but the partial completion of Christ Church, Oxford, and Trinity College, Cambridge, and the foundation of some Regius Professorships. But the Church received one benefit in the carving out of the six new bishoprics of Oxford, Chester, Peterborough, Gloucester, Bristol, and Westminster.

REFORM BEGINS IN ENGLAND

Further spoliation of the Church occurred when Cromwell's injunctions of 1538 forbade images and declared superstitious shrines to be forfeit to the King. If things like the Rood of Boxley were well out of the way, Henry saw to it that the shrine of S. Thomas of Canterbury, against whom as the champion of ecclesiastical liberties he felt a special vindictiveness, yielded him two complete waggon-loads of gold and jewels. Cromwell succeeded, as he had promised, in making his monarch the richest prince in Europe. But he overreached himself when, in order to effect an alliance with the Continental Protestants in a great Protestant League, he tried to induce the King to marry Anne of Clèves. The lady was plain and dull, and Henry could find no better name for her than that of 'the Flanders Mare'. Cromwell was attainted on a charge of treason and beheaded in 1540.

The changes so far enumerated were mostly on the surface: they were a reform of ecclesiasticism rather than of religion. It would be a mistake to think that no deeper impression was made. If the English Reformation produced no great theological figure like Luther or Calvin or even Zwingli, it nevertheless sought to meet the religious needs of the common man. It established, among other things, the private and public use of the Bible in English. So far the only complete English Bible was that of Wycliffe, which still survives in about 170 copies, but popular knowledge of the Bible stories was still derived from such collections as 'the Golden Legend' taken from the Vulgate. The recent publication of Greek and Hebrew texts by Reuchlin and Erasmus had made a greater accuracy possible. Tyndale brought out a translation of the New Testament and part of the Old in 1526. But it was tendencious, replacing 'priest' by 'elder' and 'Church' by 'congregation'. Henry in his orthodoxy would have none of it. Copies were printed at Cologne and Worms and smuggled to England in merchants' bales. The first edition was bought up by opponents and burnt. But the money furnished means for further editions, until Tyndale was discovered in Belgium and died at the stake. The next effort was Coverdale's, not based, like Tyndale's, on the original languages, but on the Vulgate and the reformers' versions. This was not good, and was superseded (1537) by Matthew's or Rogers's Bible, which was, in fact, a reprint of Tyndale with one or two corrections and (where he ended) of Coverdale. But at last there came the Great or Cranmer's Bible, which was a careful revision of Matthew's. This was ordered to be set up in churches in 1538, and its quality may still be judged from the beautiful version of the Psalms in the Book of Common Prayer.

Other attempts to guide religion are to be seen in a series of Articles and Injunctions. In 1536 the Ten Articles were published. These had been drawn up by the King and approved by Convocation. They distinguish between things necessary and things laudable, and it is noteworthy that the former include the Bible, the three Creeds, the four General Councils, and the sacraments of Baptism, Penance, and the Altar. The same year Cromwell, as Vicar-General, issued Injunctions that the clergy should explain these Articles to their flocks and see that everyone knew in English the Apostles' Creed, the Lord's Prayer, and the Ten Commandments. Also the clergy were to denounce the Bishop of Rome in church, and were to set up Matthew's translation beside the Latin Bible in every parish church, so that the people might read them if they would. In 1538 he issued further Injunctions replacing Matthew's Bible by Cranmer's, denouncing images and discouraging any trust in the efficacy of candles. The King became more markedly orthodox towards the end of his reign, and the change was registered in his Six Articles of 1539, which the reformers called the 'bloody whip with six strings'. They insisted on transubstantiation, communion in one kind only, clerical celibacy, vows of chastity, private Masses and private confession. They only passed through Parliament by the persuasion of the King's personal presence. Cranmer fought against them, although neither he nor any other bishop doubted transubstantiation as yet; but he put away his wife and submitted. The penalty for refusing to accept them was death by burning, and it is said that in the year after their publication no fewer than five hundred persons were tried in London alone. Among these was Anne Askew, whose own account of her examination under torture, printed abroad and published throughout England, did as much as her courage at the stake to spread desire for doctrinal change. The articles marked the King's policy till the end of his reign and made further advance in reform impossible for eight years.

An attempt to penetrate still closer into the heart of religion was made in a series of devotional books. In 1537 was issued the Bishops' Book or *Institution of a Christian Man*. It was drawn up at the King's request by a committee of bishops and embodied an exposition of the creed and sacraments on the lines of the Ten Articles. It was superseded in 1543 by the *Necessary Doctrine and Erudition for any Christian Man*, generally called the King's Book, because it was founded on his criticisms of the Bishops' Book, and was compiled from the standpoint of the Six Articles. In 1544 Cranmer issued his English Litany. It was very like the present Litany, but it included three prayers to the saints (the Blessed Virgin, the angels, and the whole company of heaven), and contained a petition against 'the Bishop of Rome and all his detestable enormities'. Finally, in 1545, the King issued his own Authorised Primer as a guide to private devotions. It followed the lines of the medieval primers, but omitted the usual Hours of the Virgin, and (significant hiatus) all allusion to the seven deadly sins.

In any attempt to form a judgment of Henry's reform we are compelled to notice what seems at first sight the haphazard nature of the whole thing. It began as a political movement, seemed likely to become doctrinal, and then fell into sharp and stern reaction. As its occasion the character of the King was all-important, but the real causes were deep-rooted in the nation's experience. It has been said that the future does not come from before to meet us, but streams up from behind over our heads, and never is it more necessary to remember this in the study of any apparent cataclysm than in the ecclesiastical history of England in the sixteenth century. That the changes were accompanied by much indefensible evil is undeniable, but they, at least, freed England from the oppressive dominance of a foreign power and made it possible for Christian men ultimately to penetrate below all the superstructure of medievalism to the primitive origins of their faith. And while they checked the speed of revolution, they enabled Englishmen to produce a result which, if characteristically illogical, was all the more consonant with life itself. And in any case they were quite unlike anything which in these days people have come to know as Protestantism.

CHAPTER V

ALTERNATION BETWEEN EXTREMES

PERHAPS the reason why the English nation has not seen its way to accept either of the two types into which Western Christianity was divided at the Reformation in an extreme form is that during the next two reigns it had an opportunity of seeing them both in the sharpest contrast and of knowing them for what they were. When Edward VI came to the throne as a boy of nine, it was certain that reform would be pressed farther than it had yet gone. There had not been wanting signs towards the close of the last reign that a change from the position of the Six Articles was impending, and the old king had left his son to the care of men who were not likely to be content with things as they were. There arose at once in the country a babel of many voices demanding instant doctrinal changes. But the Protector Somerset left these matters very much to Cranmer, and the instinct of both was to proceed slowly. Cranmer, indeed, was the gentlest, his enemies might say the most timid, of men. 'Do my Lord of Canterbury an ill turn', it was once avowed, 'and you make him your friend for life.' He was on this as on other grounds more nearly comparable to Melanchthon than to any other of the Continental reformers. On one point he was quite clear, and that was the necessity for maintaining the Royal Supremacy. To this principle he showed his adherence on the death of Henry by making all the bishops take out a fresh licence. Somerset, too, was a pious and moderate man with some regard for the poor and a dislike of religious persecution, although after his clever victory at Pinkie against the Scots he preferred military violence to more conciliatory methods, and so lost the hand of Mary Stuart, to which he aspired. But on the whole he was a conservative influence in reform. Consequently the first efforts of the reign were to prevent a stampede, and its first Act was one passed against reviling the sacrament of the altar.

Somerset's influence lasted from 1547 to 1549, and the lines upon which he hoped to proceed were at once shown by the repeal of the notorious Treasons Act, the Six Articles, and other measures that involved persecution. The resultant freedom involved an almost hopeless confusion, and an attempt to straighten things out was made in the *First Book of Homilies*, prepared by Cranmer and published by Royal authority to be read in church every Sunday. Injunctions were also issued forbidding images and all candles except two, ordering the destruction of all pictures of false miracles, and commanding that the Epistle and Gospel at High Mass be read in English. These were enforced by a visitation that superseded the jurisdiction of the diocesans and was conducted on the authority of the Council alone. Next year (1548) an *Order of Communion* appeared. In this the priest's Mass was not altered, but a form of Communion for the laity in English, compiled mainly from the *Consultatio* of Hermann, the reforming Bishop of Cologne, was appended. Then in 1549 the chief liturgical glory of the English Reformation appeared in the First Prayer Book of Edward VI. Its main principles were its great simplicity, its use of the English tongue, its wide and continuous reading of Scripture, its supersession of the many diocesan uses by one use for the whole kingdom, and its drawing of the whole congregation into every act of worship. It is disputed whether the book was brought before Convocation; probably it was only presented in an informal way, but it met with general acceptance, and such a Catholic-minded bishop as Gardiner was apparently satisfied with it. Its rubrics were vague and general, and this meant, no doubt, that there would be a good deal of diversity in the manner in which its services were conducted, but certainly in many, if not in most, churches they would be accompanied by the ancient ceremonies. It was enforced by an Act of Uniformity which enjoined its use upon all the clergy. Thus it was hoped to put an end to confusion by insisting upon a unity of liturgical formula rather than upon a unity of ceremonial or even of doctrine. The phraseology of the new book was carefully framed to admit a wide latitude of view, and an official preacher at S. Paul's Cross proclaimed that belief was to be freer than it had been before. In its resonant language, its exalted piety, its reverence for the continuity of Christian history, and its toleration the book shows Cranmer at his best. Its title alone was enough to show that the Archbishop was fully alive to the practicability of a type of worship that should be both Catholic and in accord with national needs. 'The Booke of the Common Prayer and Administracion of the Sacraments, and other Rites and Ceremonies of the Churche after the Use of the Churche of England.' When it had been published the Reformation in England had reached its high-water mark. Only in Devon and Cornwall did it stir men into open rebellion, and in the latter county the English tongue was almost as foreign as Latin. The insurgents complained that the new services were 'like a Christmas game', perhaps because they were most familiar with English in connexion with the Christmas mummers.

Unfortunately, however, Cranmer himself was not satisfied with it, and almost at once began preparations for a second and more Protestant edition. This coincided with a deepening of foreign influences on his theology. Calvin, indeed, was willing to put up with the English liturgy as a collection of *tolerabiles ineptiæ*, but his influence had hardly yet replaced that of Luther who had now ceased to count for much in England. The chief influences were those of the foreigners who had actually taken refuge in this country. Of these the most important was Martin Bucer. He had already tried his hand at liturgical reform by assisting Bishop Hermann in the compilation of his *Consultatio*. He had also, as we have seen, worked in Strassburg, occupying a mediating position between Luther and Calvin, from which he earned some distrust and the title of 'the limping Strassburger'. He had come to England on Cranmer's invitation and been made Regius Professor of Divinity at Cambridge. Although he knew no English, he compiled a *Censura* of the First Prayer Book, consisting of twenty-eight criticisms, the chief of which attacked the use of the sign of the cross in the Eucharist and at Baptism, the anointing of the sick, and the commendation of the soul at burial. The questions in the new Ordinal that was issued in 1550 came from his *De Legitima Ordinatione*. Another important influence was that of Peter Martyr, an Italian of Florence and an ex-Augustinian canon who had taken on Zwinglian views. In 1549 he became Regius Professor of Divinity at Oxford, and joined in the criticisms of the First Prayer Book, which helped to produce the Second. He had the temerity to introduce women as residents into Christ Church, whereupon the townsfolk broke his windows and compelled him to fortify his garden. The unmeasured acerbity of his disputations so provoked the people that the county rose in revolt under the parish priests and demanded the restoration of the old services and the extermination of heretics.

But the worst feature of this time was the putting into force of the Chantries Act of 1545, which Henry had never enforced. This was based on the belief that Masses offered for the dead were superstitious, and it transferred all endowments for the purpose to the King's purse, which in effect meant into the pockets of his Ministers. As the chantry priests were the elementary school-teachers of the time, and as every guild and hospital prayed for the soul of its founder, it can easily be understood what evil was wrought under the shelter of this Act. The universities and Eton and Winchester were not touched, but the grammar schools suffered, those that are now called 'Edward VI' schools being those that were reconstituted and allowed to continue on diminished endowments. As the guilds were the insurance societies and sick and burial clubs of the poor, the hardship inflicted by their suppression is beyond estimation. But perhaps even worse was the impetus given to the instinct for spoliation already so strong in the breasts of the powerful, encouraging them to go to all lengths in disregard of any rights of property. Even the Protector himself dissolved the new bishopric of Westminster and destroyed six bishops' palaces in London in order to build his own Somerset House. His first intention had been to plant it on the site of Westminster Abbey, but the canons bought themselves off by the surrender of twenty of their manors. However, Somerset had not much more of his course to run. The party against him in the

Council was waxing stronger, and at last he fell before his rival Warwick, afterwards Duke of Northumberland, in 1549, and after three years' respite was beheaded.

Northumberland had climbed into power on the shoulders of the Catholics, who hoped to bring about a reaction in religion; but he was a complete scoundrel, who, although he really shared their convictions, for the sake of his own greed and ambition threw over his friends and pushed reform as far as it would go. If only the English churches could be reduced to the stark bareness of the Calvinistic meeting-places, the greater would be the spoils gathered by himself. Hence his encouragement of further liturgical changes. In 1550 the new Ordinal was issued. It was based on the old Sarum Pontifical, but it omitted the four minor Orders and many of the customary ceremonies. The same year the stone altars were ordered to be replaced by movable tables. In 1552, the year of Somerset's execution and the year in which German Lutheranism won its freedom in the Treaty of Passau, the Second Prayer Book was issued. It broke up the canon, forbade vestments, and omitted certain ceremonies in baptising and the prayers for the dead. It was never submitted to Convocation, and at the very last moment, when some of the copies were already printed, the Black Rubric was inserted, which, while retaining the practice of kneeling to receive Communion, denied that it implied a belief in the Real Presence. This represents the farthest point that the English Church ever reached in the Protestant direction, and it is noteworthy that every subsequent revision of the Prayer Book has been back towards the book of 1549. The changes were enforced by the Second Act of Uniformity, which, unlike the first, affected the laity as well as the clergy, compelling them to attend the services as thus prescribed. Recusants who omitted to do so were punishable by ecclesiastical penalties, and separatists, who attended other services than those set forth, were to be imprisoned after trial by jury. But it is probable that these measures had hardly taken effect throughout the country when the reign came to an end. In 1553 were published the Forty-two Articles. These had been drawn up by Cranmer on the lines of the *Augsburg Confession*, and were intended to be a test for the clergy against medievalism on the one hand and Anabaptism on the other. They were published by Royal authority, but were fathered by a lie on Convocation.

In keeping with all this it was ordered that the old service books should be destroyed, and there was a renewed campaign against all images that were not strictly historical monuments. This had the singular effect in Worcester Cathedral of leaving King John unharmed while the saints were removed. The only actual persecution that occurred during the reign took place under Northumberland; but there were some changes of personnel. Gardiner, Bonner, Day, Heath, and Tunstall were all deprived of their sees and imprisoned, and their dioceses were carefully plundered before reforming bishops were put in. Of the new men the most remarkable was Hooper. He was a Somerset man, and had been a Cistercian monk before he went to Zürich and became Zwinglian. On his return he was made chaplain to Somerset, and showed himself the 'father of Nonconformity' by objecting to vestments. On this ground he refused the bishopric of Gloucester, but after being imprisoned in the Fleet he allowed himself to be constrained to obedience, and was consecrated in 1551. He was a great preacher and proved himself a capable bishop. He was made to realise the bitter results of the late upheaval when he made his visitation, and discovered that out of his 311 clergy ten could not say the Lord's Prayer, twenty-seven did not know who was its Author, thirty could not tell where it was to be found, and 168 could not repeat the Ten Commandments.

When the delicate and precocious boy who had sat upon the throne during this upheaval died (1553), the English nation as a whole was heartily sick of Protestantism and all its works. Bonfires were lighted to greet his successor, the Princess Mary, and she was welcomed with wild manifestations of joy by the people, who thought that the Golden Age of Henry VIII would return. Her rival, the Lady Jane Grey, friend of Edward VI and his nominee for the crown, had no chance against her. Most of the Continental reformers, including the redoubtable Peter Martyr, fled back to the Continent, and some of their English friends followed them. There remained three distinct religious parties: the Roman Catholics, the mediating party, and the Protestants.

To the first belonged the Queen herself. A daughter of the unhappy Katherine of Aragon, herself made illegitimate by the Parliament of 1533, she was not likely to follow her father's faith. And her own conscientious conviction led her in the strictest fashion along the old paths. She had always been devout, and even during her long retirement had refused to give up her Mass, which Cranmer and the Council had been persuaded to concede. Her greatest friend and companion was Reginald Pole. He was a mild scholar with no knowledge of men or affairs. He had been educated at Oxford, Padua, and Paris, and had been at one time a friend of Henry VIII, but he would not support the divorce and stayed out of England for fear of the consequences. The papal party of earlier days had hoped that he would marry Mary, but somewhat to his dismay he was made cardinal in 1536. He was abroad when his family fell from favour and his mother, the Countess of Salisbury, was executed in 1541. On Edward VI's accession he had written to the Council urging them to redress the wrongs of the Church, but their reply had been to exclude him from the general pardon extended to the sufferers under the late tyranny. When Mary succeeded he was made papal legate, but both Pope and Emperor, fearing the combination of his extreme devotion and lack of practical statesmanship, did all they could to keep him out of England as long as possible while things were settling down.

Of the mediating party the most prominent figure was Stephen Gardiner, Bishop of Winchester, of whom we have already seen something. During the late reign he had taken the line that it was not lawful to make changes so long as the King was a minor, and consequently he had spent most of his time in prison. On Mary's accession he was liberated and made Lord Chancellor. His companion was Edmund Bonner, Bishop of London. He had been deprived under Edward, but was restored under Mary, and was to achieve an evil, but not altogether deserved, notoriety in the execution of the heresy laws. He had always been staunch on the subject of transubstantiation, but, like many another during this period, pliant on the subject of the

Royal Supremacy. The difficulty of this party was that they had helped Henry VIII to end the Papal Supremacy, while under Mary they were expected to restore it. For six months they struggled, but finally gave way; and so the field was divided between frank Roman Catholics and Protestants.

Of this last party Cranmer, since the disintegration of his theology, must certainly be reckoned the leader. It would have been in keeping with his character if he had fled with his foreign friends, but he was restrained by a conscientious adherence to his doctrine of the Royal Supremacy, which could not be held to change with the views of the sovereign, and much of his future vacillation must be ascribed to the difficulties occasioned by this doctrine. Hooper we have already described. Most widely influential of the reformers was Hugh Latimer, the Cambridge scholar. He had been tried for heresy as long ago as the time of Wolsey, but was then acquitted. He had helped Henry over the divorce and had received preferment, becoming Bishop of Worcester in 1535. He had resigned on the publication of the Six Articles and lay in prison expecting death, when he was saved by the accession of Edward. He would not resume his bishopric, but had a great vogue as a preacher, holding congregations spellbound for three and four hours at a stretch. Under Mary, he was given an opportunity for flight, but refused, with the direst consequences. Another Cambridge scholar was Nicholas Ridley, lately Master of Pembroke Hall, and successively Bishop of Rochester, and of London on the deprivation of Bonner in 1549. He was the master spirit among the reformers. 'Latimer leaneth to Cranmer, Cranmer leaneth to Ridley, and Ridley to the singularity of his own wit.'

The course of events was swift and dramatic. Edward VI's bishops were at once deposed, Cranmer, Ridley, and Latimer finding themselves in prison, and the deprived prelates, such as Gardiner, Bonner, and Tunstall were restored. The Queen did not abandon the title of Supreme Head, and under that authority restored by an Act of Repeal (1553) the services to the condition in which they had stood at the end of the reign of Henry VIII. Then came a pause while Europe debated the question of her marriage. An heir to the throne was eminently desirable, and Mary agreed that she must marry. The nation was anxious for an English husband, but the only possible candidate was Courtenay, and Mary was not disposed to marry a debauchee. She was already accustomed to lean upon the advice of her cousin, the Emperor Charles V, and in this dilemma he offered his own son Philip to whom he intended to resign Spain and the Netherlands. After due inquiries Mary gladly accepted, and in her married love gained almost the only happiness of her tragic life. Nevertheless even that was 'made in blood'. The marriage was most unpopular in the country, and the revolt against it, headed by Wyatt, was only stayed by the Queen's personal bravery, which secured the sympathy of London. As a result of the revolt the Lady Jane Grey was executed as well as Northumberland, and the Princess Elizabeth was sent for a time to the Tower. The same year (1554) the marriage was celebrated on July 25th.

Injunctions were now issued to deprive all married clergy of their livings. The anti-papal legislation of Henry VIII was repealed and the old heresy laws were re-enacted. In November, Pole arrived, and when he had promised, in the name of the Pope, that the confiscated Church lands should be left in the possession of their present owners, Parliament decided to submit to Rome. Pole solemnly pronounced the absolution on November 30, 1554. The rest of the reign is the story of the growing morbidity of the Queen. Disappointed time and again in her expectation of an heir, realising at last that she was the victim of a mortal disease, smitten with loneliness when her husband left her to attend to necessary affairs on the Continent, grieving over the loss of Calais in 1558, she seems to have become convinced that God's anger against her and her land could only be wiped out by Protestant sacrifice. Little as England suffered in comparison with such countries as Holland, there were three hundred burnings in three years. Things moved too fast for the Pope himself. Not all the fault was Mary's. Some of the heretics were needlessly violent, and the Protestants in safety at Basel agreed that some of the holocaust, at least, was due to the seditious pamphlets of

John Knox. But the persecution was really medieval in that it made the charge not treason, but heresy, and it was an anachronism in an age when men were already beginning to distinguish between external uniformity and private opinion.

Roger of S. Paul's was the first victim, Hooper perished in 1555, Latimer and Ridley in the following year. Cranmer's case was the hardest of all. If he still accepted the Royal Supremacy, ought he not to follow his sovereign in submitting to the Pope? He vacillated; the thought of the sufferings of his two friends, whom from his prison window at Oxford he saw pass to the flames, increased his perturbation. Six times he recanted, and then when in S. Mary's he was expected to make a recantation that would edify all the faithful and so strengthen the Roman cause, he first left out the Hail Mary at the end of the Lord's Prayer and followed up this sign of Protestant sympathies with a recantation of all his former recantations and a bold proclamation of the views that he had originally taught. The great endurance at the stake of one who had so greatly feared did more than anything else to make men detest a fanaticism that could put a gentle scholar and Christian gentleman to so dire an ordeal. Nor was there any sympathy with his successor, Pole, a man of similar temperament, but different views, who had to be ordained priest before he could enter upon his office, and actually said his first Mass on the day that Cranmer died.

Two years more sufficed to complete the alienation of the people. When she died in 1558 Mary was more cordially hated than any English sovereign had been since John. It was fortunate for Pole that he died on the same day as his Queen. Had he been able to advise her better, and taught her to avoid the Spanish marriage, the Pope, and the persecution, Mary might easily have restored the system of Henry VIII. As it was, Roman Catholicism had been as badly represented as Protestantism under Northumberland. The way was open for a new settlement that would satisfy the religious needs of Englishmen better than either.

CHAPTER VI

THE COUNTER-REFORMATION

THE Catholic reaction in England during Mary's reign coincided with a stiffening of Catholicism abroad after its recovery from the first shock of the Reformation. The Church had been slow in realising the importance of that movement and slower still in concerting adequate steps to meet it. One reason was that it had long known its need of reform, but had turned a deaf ear to the cry until it seemed possible to ignore it for ever. The Fifth Council of the Lateran (1512–17) had drawn up a programme of practical measures, but the vested interests of the Papacy and the Curia had prevented anything being done. Nevertheless in Italy itself a whole new generation of earnest men was springing up, which, as it replaced the older men in office, succeeded in making the Church an infinitely more efficient organisation than it had been in the days of the Renaissance.

The school in which the ardour of these men was kindled was the Oratory of the Divine Love, a society both clerical and lay, which had been founded in Rome in the time of Leo X, and, after the sack of that city in 1527, had met again in Venice. The members were about fifty in number and included the future cardinals, Contarini, Sadoleto, Caraffa, and Giberto. They met for mutual edification by prayer and preaching and spiritual exercises, and the things they had in common were a real love for the Church and a desire to recapture that intensity of personal conviction which seemed to have been so fatally lost. But there were grave differences between them, and for long it was uncertain which section would prevail and set the character of the Catholic reform. There were those like Contarini who had much sympathy with humanism and agreed with the Teutonic reformers about the importance of Justification, and were consequently ready to explore every avenue of conciliation. There were many who reacted violently against the half-pagan spirit of the Renaissance, and worked for a practical and ascetic reform. There were others, like Caraffa, who began to set their hopes on a strengthening of the Papacy and a stern attitude against heresy. The lines between them were not at first clearly drawn, but it is one of the strange mischances of history that it was ultimately the last class which won, and so widened the gulf between the Old and the New Learning, which has never since been satisfactorily bridged.

One sign of the revival was the emergence of new types of conventual life. The Order of the Theatines, founded in 1524 and named after Caraffa's see of Theate, endeavoured to improve the standard of life among the secular clergy by binding a number of them together under the same three vows as were taken by monks. The Barnabites, established about 1530, were even more successful in the same effort. Strenuous attempts were also made to revive spiritual life among the laity. The adherence of the Italian peasantry was maintained largely by the Capuchins (so-called from the cowl they wore), who were founded in 1526 as a reformed branch of the Franciscans. The Ursulines were an Order of nuns founded in 1535 to care for the fallen; they afterwards undertook the education of girls and later did a great work in Canada.

Attempts at dogmatic reform were almost negligible, and came from beyond the Italian borders. Juan de Valdes was a Castilian who settled at Naples and was more mystic than theologian. He was not of the kind who willingly overturn established order, and was content to develop among his followers an inward piety which built itself upon the doctrine of justification by faith alone, and was nurtured by frequent confession and communion. His best-known disciples were Peter Martyr, who worked for a time at Lucca and advanced a good deal in his views before coming to England; and Bernardino Ochino, of Siena, who after being Vicar-General of the Capuchins fell into such error as made even the Unitarians fight shy of him. The kind of reform that was more likely to be effected was shown in 1537, when a committee appointed by Paul III, and consisting mostly of members of the Oratory of the Divine Love, put out its famous report *Consilium de Emendenda Ecclesia*. The great evil aimed at is the system of money payments. It is this that has corrupted the Curia and penetrated into the dioceses and parishes. Laws ought not to be dispensed with for money payments. Where there is grave cause for a dispensation, the Church should freely give as she has freely received. Other evils are non-residence, in which the cardinals are as bad as the bishops, and scandals in monastic houses. The Roman See should be the first to redress such evils. This report was too candid to be published, and although the Pope issued a Bull of Reformation and called a General Council at Mantua, the one was never acted upon and the other never met. Nevertheless Contarini tirelessly pressed the aged Pope, and as a result there came the Colloquy of Ratisbon in 1541, in which the reformers, under Melanchthon, were all but reconciled. However, the intransigence both of Luther and of the Pope was too ingrained for such a consummation, and when practical steps were at last taken they were dictated by the austerity of Caraffa and the fanaticism of Spain.

Both the Jesuits and the Inquisition were borrowed from Spain, which was now enjoying its Golden Age. The new discoveries had filled its coffers with wealth and its religion with an adventurous spirit. But the fact that its orthodoxy had been sharpened by the struggle with the Moors and the Jews prevented that spirit from acting against the interests of the historic Church. Even its great mystics of this period were more intensely Catholic than any others. Its Church had reformed itself on practical and ascetic lines under Cardinal Ximenes, before Luther arose, but learning had not been neglected, as witness Ximenes' own *Complutensian Polyglot*, which began to appear in 1520 and made his university of Alcala famous throughout Europe.

Ignatius Loyola (1491–1556) was born of the noblest blood in the land, and was full of knightly ambitions when a wound received at Pampeluna in 1521 produced a conversion that made him resolve to turn knight of Christ. As such he did more than any individual to stay the progress of the Reformation and conserve the Roman Church against the corroding influences of the time. Not that his original purpose was such. In 1522, the very year in which, at the Diet of Nürnberg, the German nation put itself at the head of Luther's movement, Ignatius was at Manresa and went through experiences upon which he modelled his *Spiritual Exercises*, a series of meditations that have as their object the moulding of the personality into a perfect instrument for fulfilling the will of God. He himself thought that his own vocation was to a missionary life, and he set off on a journey to Palestine; but he was evicted from Jerusalem and on his return went to take his degree at Paris. Here others fell under his influence, notably Francis Xavier and his future successor Lainez. They became filled with his ambition to found a society, and in 1534, in the crypt of S. Denis at Montmartre, Ignatius and six friends pledged themselves to poverty and chastity and to go to Jerusalem, or, if that proved impossible, to place themselves at the absolute disposal of the Holy Father. It was the latter eventuality that happened, but the Pope had to be repeatedly besieged before at last he gave his sanction to the Society of Jesus in 1540. Loyola himself was its head from that time till his death, and in those sixteen years he saw the society spread into every country of Europe and into every colony of Spain and Portugal. By that date the members numbered about a thousand, and what manner of men they were can best be judged from the fact that by the *Exercises* they had been schooled actually to desire discomfort rather than ease, and had been drilled into such obedience that they could accept the thirteenth 'Rule for Thinking with the Church': 'To arrive at the truth in all things, we ought always to be ready to believe that what seems to us white is black, if the hierarchical Church so defines it.' Their distinctive feature lay, not merely in this exact obedience to their superior, which involved body, mind, and soul, but in that it was rendered by people who were not shut up within the narrow confines of monastic establishments, but, being free from the obligations of singing the long choir offices and of dressing as monks, could mingle with the world as freely as the secular clergy. At first the Church reaped

THE COUNTER-REFORMATION 67

the full advantage of this system; it was not until later that the evils inherent in it turned many to criticism. Perhaps the best side of it is seen in the devoted life of S. Francis Xavier, who was sent in 1541 to preach in the Portuguese dominions in the Indies, and succeeded in converting to respectability the notoriously profligate town of Goa, afterwards turning his attention to the pearl-fishers on the coast of Comorin. After four years of these labours he went farther east and preached in the Malay Archipelago. In 1549 he became the first to introduce Christianity into Japan, and then, after a visit to Goa, tried to penetrate into China, but died of fever on the way. Thus he fulfilled the first intention of Ignatius to found a missionary society, and became the pioneer in that enterprise that made of the Jesuits one of the greatest agents in Christian propaganda that the world has ever seen.

In Rome the followers of Ignatius were largely responsible for encouraging Paul III to start the Inquisition, although the first impulse in that direction came from Caraffa. The medieval Inquisition had never been under the complete control of the Papacy, and it was actually dying out when it had been reorganised as a much more efficient machine in Spain, to which country it was introduced in 1477. There it had been a purely national affair, but in 1542 Paul III set up in Rome a Holy Office that was both papal and universal. Over this centralised organisation six cardinals presided, their number being afterwards increased to twelve. They not only decided cases themselves, but heard appeals from the branch offices elsewhere. High and low, rich and poor, were all alike brought within its scope, and in 1556 the highest ecclesiastic in Spain, Carranza, Archbishop of Toledo, was condemned by it. Its establishment signalised the abandonment of the policy of conciliation and introduced force instead of persuasion as the means of settling doctrinal disputes. A natural corollary was the refusal to allow books to be printed without the permission of the Inquisition. This prohibition was first issued by Caraffa in 1543, and led to the compilation of the Index, or list of forbidden books, the earliest examples of which appeared in Louvain and Paris and a more complete form in Rome in 1559.

It was natural that in these circumstances the Protestants should have little hope of anything to be gained from the Council of Trent, which lasted from 1545 till 1563. Nevertheless the Council is of the greatest possible importance, for this was the last occasion on which Catholicism was defined. It has been said that if we wish to understand the spiritual zeal of the counter-Reformation we must study the *Spiritual Exercises*, while if we wish to understand its doctrinal attitude we must study the Council of Trent. But its importance goes even farther than that, for without some knowledge of it we cannot understand the Roman Catholicism of to-day. In its effect it produced a solid body of doctrine that could be opposed to the teaching of the reformers, and by emphasising the Papacy at the expense of the bishops it encouraged the tendency by which churches lost their national character and became ever more Roman. Yet it did not exclude all diversity of view, but left it possible for bishops to assert that they derived their authority from Christ and not from the Pope, and also to deny papal infallibility.

To us who know the result it must seem strange that the popes did everything they could to avoid this Council. The reason was that they remembered only too well the Councils of Constance and Basel, and were afraid that they might themselves be made inferior and even responsible to a Council. As long as they could, they struggled to get it held where it would be under their own control, but the Emperor retaliated by threatening them with a Council on German territory. At last Trent was agreed upon as being an imperial city, and 'as subject to its bishop being neither papal nor German'. The life of the Council falls naturally into three sections, the first lasting from 1545 to 1550. At the outset papal preponderance was secured by the arrangement that the representatives present should vote as one body, and not in nations as they had done at Constance. The dispatch of a few Italians could thus be relied upon generally to turn the scale. An important preliminary question was whether reform or dogma should be taken first. The Emperor was anxious to get to work on the abuses that cried aloud for remedy, the Pope was equally anxious that the utmost firmness should be displayed on doctrinal matters. In the end it was agreed that both should be taken together, and that made it easy for the Pope to have his way. Protestantism was thereupon ruled out as early as the fourth session, when tradition was set up as a standard of doctrine on a footing of equality with Scripture, and the Vulgate was designated as the standard text against vernacular versions, and the official interpretations of the Church were accepted to the exclusion of private interpretations. In the sixth session was issued the decree on Justification. This was to deal with the subject that was fundamental to Lutheranism. Luther, who was perfectly right in thinking that the original meaning of the word was 'to reckon as just' rather than 'to make just', was quite mistaken in making justification identical with salvation, and still more mistaken in holding that righteousness is imputed to us as the result of a faith which is a bare *fides informis* rather than *fides formata per caritatem*. The Tridentine view was more balanced and scriptural. It condemned the extreme theory of imputed righteousness, as well as the view that man's depravity, resulting from the Fall, was total. It regarded faith as the beginning of salvation, needing to be informed with love before it could render a man acceptable with God; and while it acknowledged that the beginning of justification is due to God's prevenient grace, it guarded the freedom of the will by asserting that for the completion of the process man's co-operation was needed. This closed the door to Protestant interpretations of doctrine, but left room for much subsequent disputing between Dominicans and Jesuits. The latter had already begun to make their influence felt in the Council, and it was their view, more than that of anyone else, which, under the powerful pleading of Lainez, finally prevailed. The other important doctrinal question discussed at the time was that of the sacraments. These the Council decreed to be seven in number, thus making authoritative the customary reckoning, but it added the surprising statement that they were all instituted by Christ Himself. It further affirmed the *ex opere operato* view of the way in which the sacraments were rendered effectual. Along with these doctrinal matters some practical reforms were also suggested. An effort was made to put a

70 HISTORY OF THE MODERN CHURCH

stop to the evil of pluralities, and the visitation of chapters and churches was confirmed in the hands of the bishops. There was also some attempt to compel bishops to reside in their sees, but it was impossible to enforce this indiscriminately, for the Curia itself consisted largely of titular bishops, and to have insisted upon such a rule would have destroyed the whole centralised power of the Papacy.

During the later sessions Catholicism had proved itself as successful in war as in debate. The victory of Mühlberg was imminent, and it was clear that the Protestant power would be broken as the issue of the Schmalkaldic War. But this was the Emperor's Catholicism, not the Pope's. The latter, by an act of unexpected weakness, at the very moment when he had everything in his favour and might have restored the peace of Europe and won the Teutons back to his Church, let his jealous fear of his rival's power prevail and called the Council from Trent to Bologna. The reason alleged was fear of the plague, but the real cause was known to all, and the Emperor did what he could by the *Interim of Augsburg* to conciliate his defeated foes, forcing the Pope to accept the terms he had made. From 1547 till 1549 the Council nominally sat at Bologna, but in the latter year it was suspended. Not until Paul III had died and been succeeded by Julius III was it possible for the Council to be recalled to Trent.

The second period extends from 1550 to 1552. It was made noteworthy by the arrival of certain Protestant ambassadors from Württemberg, Saxony, and some of the imperial cities, such as Strassburg. This had been one of Charles's arrangements in the Interim, and Julius had agreed to their admission. They came on a safe-conduct and were courteously received, but they did not agree among themselves and they made absurd demands, such as that the Pope should have no authority in the Council and that the bishops should be set free from their oaths to him. Another point that had been agreed upon in the Interim as a temporary measure was also brought before the Council—namely, the question of allowing the chalice to the laity. But this proved so difficult of solution that the Emperor himself proposed its adjournment. It was found easier to protect the doctrine of the Eucharist by passing eleven canons to condemn false teaching. Other sacraments dealt with were Penance and Extreme Unction. Very little was done in the way of practical reform, except to regulate the question of appeals and make episcopal jurisdiction more effective by freeing it from undue interference on the part of the papal court. Larger measures of reform, such as the proposal to restore synodical government, the Council would not accept. Various troubles were oppressing the delegates. Henry II of France had refused to acknowledge the Council at all, and even threatened to withdraw annates from the Pope. The Protestants, disgusted by the slow progress of reform, withdrew. War had broken out again; there was nothing for it but to suspend the sittings.

The political events that intervened before the Council could again be summoned ten years later were of the first importance. In 1552 the French, under Henry II, had at last allied with the Protestant princes; Maurice had turned traitor the second time, and Charles had fled. In 1555 had come the recognition of lost unity in Germany, and the acceptance of the *cujus regio* principle at the Peace of Augsburg. This was the death-blow to Charles's hopes, and in that year he abdicated. Spain and the Netherlands were left to his son Philip, the Empire to his brother Ferdinand, and Charles enjoyed three years' retirement before his death. In the year of his abdication, Cardinal Caraffa succeeded to the Papacy as Pope Paul IV. Of Caraffa's earnest but gloomy disposition we have already had some evidence. His four years' tenure of office served to bring out unexpected faults. He aspired to become the liberator of Italy from Spanish oppression, and hurried into a war which did not end until an army under Alva threatened Rome itself. He enriched his family, and particularly his nephews, with the endowments of the Church in such a way as to bring himself into endless feuds with rival families. It was only when he at last realised how unworthy were the creatures with whom he had surrounded himself that he suddenly surrendered his worldly ambition and gave himself to the work of reform. In this effort he began with his own family, transferring to other officers the places monopolised by his kinsmen, and setting the first example for many centuries of a Pope who ruled without nepotism This spirit he carried into the service of the Church, reducing the opportunity for rapacious clerks to extort money from the faithful and strengthening the hands of the Inquisitors. A medal was struck in his honour showing Christ driving the money-changers from the Temple. But these measures did not serve to make people forget the war that he had made nor the evil done by his nephews, and when news of his death was heard in 1559 the populace broke down a statue that once in happier days had been erected to him, and dragged the head with its triple crown through the streets. He was succeeded by Pius IV, who immediately revenged himself for former insults received from the Caraffa family, and then tried to carry on the reform recently initiated. He had no objection to calling the Council again: 'We might amuse the world for years with difficulties.' The fact that there was now nothing to fear from the Emperor made things all the easier. He invited not only the bishops of his own Church, but also representatives from the Eastern Churches, from the Lutherans and from England. These invitations were refused by all who did not already recognise the papal authority, and when the Council assembled again in 1562 its constitution was as before.

It was natural that under these conditions the Council, instead of endeavouring to conciliate the Protestants, should set itself to codify its own doctrine. This was finally done in the Profession of the Tridentine Faith or Creed of Pope Pius, which was issued for recitation in public by all bishops and holders of benefices. It includes the Nicene Creed, a summary of theological definitions on the points that had been in dispute, and an acceptance of all the decrees of General Councils, including that of Trent. On the practical side the Council dealt with the questions of the Inquisition and the Index, while it left the problem of the use of the chalice by the laity to be settled by the Pope himself. Both Ferdinand and the French king, who had now come to accept the Council, presented 'Libels of Reformation', offering schemes of reform that would have made the Church more favourable to national ideals and much less centralised in its government. But so skilfully

THE COUNTER-REFORMATION 73

were the debates managed that a large programme of reform was carried which actually left the Curia and the College of Cardinals almost untouched and made the bishops more definitely the delegates of the Pope than they had been before. Largely through the influence of the Jesuits the Church closed up around the Papacy with its central offices. The Council left the Roman Church a narrower, but much more efficient organisation than it had ever been since the Great Schism.

The best side of this revitalised Romanism comes out, not in its systematisation, whether of doctrine or organisation, but in the lives of some of its greatest exponents. If Pius IV had no reputation for nepotism, it was not because he did not lean upon his nephew, Charles Borromeo, but because that nephew was too unselfish to clamour for place and honour—although, indeed, for a man of twenty-two to be Cardinal-Archbishop of Milan might be considered honour enough; but he was virtually Pope and managed everything for his aged uncle, so that he might have had anything he pleased. He attracted the Roman citizens by the magnificence and splendour of his tastes, to which the unfailing courtesy and humility of his demeanour offered an engaging contrast. Yet when the Council of Trent castigated the luxury of the cardinals, he was the first to submit to its wishes and doff his splendid apparel for something simpler. After the death of his uncle he proceeded to put an end to the chaos that had long prevailed in his diocese of Milan, continually preaching, turning his palace into a seminary for bishops, building schools and hospitals, restoring discipline in monasteries, and, during a time of plague, tending the sick with his own hands. He had already shown that he was a good Roman by editing the Catechism put out by the Council of Trent, and by helping in its revision of the missal and breviary. Now he showed that he was a good Milanese by refusing to replace the customary liturgy of his cathedral by the Roman use. Thus the Ambrosian liturgy remains to-day one of the three ancient non-Roman Latin rites in use. Yet so much was Borromeo a part of his environment that he had no qualms about the forcible suppression of heresy. He consolidated Catholicism in that part of Switzerland which still retained it by introducing the Jesuits and Capuchins with the usual machinery for dealing with heretical views. Two years after his death, in 1584, the work was carried on by the Borromean League, which bound the Roman Catholic cantons to oppose the Protestants with arms.

Contemporary with him was S. Philip Neri, the founder of the Oratorians, a name taken from the hall or oratory in Rome, where their sermons and lectures were delivered, and the source also of the term Oratorio, from the music which formed an important feature of those gatherings. The first Congregation of the Oratory arose out of these meetings which were held every evening and combined prayer and instruction with lighter pursuits. It was composed of both clergy and laity, and its intention was to further the cause of the counter-Reformation by quickening spiritual zeal. Its members were joined together by common aims, but not by vows. It had already done some years' unofficial work before its constitution was authorised by the Pope in 1576. It spread into every city of Italy, but it did not extend its work to England until it was introduced by J. H. Newman, himself one of its members.

In Spain the counter-Reformation produced a more mystical type of piety. S. Teresa, indeed, is one of the greatest of mystics. Born in 1515, two years before Luther's theses were posted, she became at the age of nineteen a nun and at forty-seven prioress of a new Order of *discalced* (i.e. sandalled, not shod) Carmelites. She established sixteen other branches for women and fourteen for friars of the same Order. In 1562 she published her autobiography, which is a monument of psychological self-analysis. Here she lets us see the record of her visions, which in point of fact became fewer as she grew more busied with practical affairs. It is also possible to see in this narrative the manner in which the Jesuits extended the direction of the spiritual life until it embraced every thought and feeling. After the period of visions ended, she developed the practice of a type of prayer in which the will is quiescent while the memory and the understanding may still be active, and this may be taken as the spring of that Quietist school which was to give so much trouble to theologians later on.

THE COUNTER-REFORMATION 75

But we must not think of Teresa as the half-demented and diseased degenerate that some writers have made her. She was, on the contrary, full of plain common sense with a fund of humour, and her practical ability must be judged from her success in founding so many religious houses.

S. Teresa's first director had been the Franciscan Peter of Alcantara, who revived some of the austerities of the old eastern monachism, never sleeping more than an hour and a half out of twenty-four, and usually eating only one day in three. Her pupil was the famous John of the Cross, who assisted her in the reform of the Carmelites, and incurred much persecution for so doing. In his sufferings he had occasion to experience those derelictions to which, in his *Ascent of Mount Carmel*, he gave the name of the 'dark night of the soul', and they have thus produced the classical description of the difficulties that beset the soul in its effort after perfection. But John's tendency was to check active effort and to encourage passive yielding without intentional thought, will, or desire. He, too, therefore helped in that drift towards Quietism which was characteristic of the country and the period.

It seems a far cry from all this to the severely logical and practical spirit of France, which was as evident a national characteristic in the sixteenth century as it is to-day. But we cannot properly understand the reactions of the counter-Reformation unless we remember that it was during this time that France, after appearing to hesitate for a period between the two types of religion, definitely decided to remain Catholic. We have seen that the general policy of Francis I was to provide difficulties for the Emperor by encouraging the reformers. Nevertheless matters were not so comfortable for them in France itself as to make such an one as Calvin inclined to stay there. Later, when the King's quarrel with the Emperor was quiescent, Francis's attitude changed, and in 1545 he proclaimed his orthodoxy by giving orders for the extermination of the Waldenses. This led to a terrible persecution in which twenty-two villages were burned and three thousand people killed, while of the survivors many were sent to the galleys and most of the rest found refuge in Switzerland. The next year persecution broke out at Meaux, where a sudden raid on the reformed congregation led to the death at the stake of fourteen of its members. In spite of the fact that Henry II's policy was even more definitely opposed to them than his father's, the Protestants carried on a secret propaganda that gave them a footing in every part of France except Brittany. In 1555 they began to organise themselves on the Presbyterian lines already laid down by their own Calvin. Thus the Huguenot system was based on the three 'orders' of minister, elders meeting in consistory, and deacons. The Calvinist type was further followed in 1559 by the production of a Confession and a *Book of Discipline*, and the maintenance of its character was still more assured by the fact that its pastors were drawn from Geneva, which was looked upon as the headquarters of French Protestantism.

In the meantime, however, Henry had decided to introduce an Inquisition after the Spanish model into his territories, and the persecuting spirit would no doubt have gone on increasing had not the King been mortally wounded in a tournament in 1559. In the confusion that followed his death, Coligny, the wisest statesman of his time, made himself champion of the Protestant cause, which gradually became identified with distinctive political views. A Colloquy was held in 1561 at Poissy, between representatives of the Church, among whom was the Jesuit Lainez, and representatives of the Huguenots, among whom were Beza and Peter Martyr. Catherine de Medici, who had initiated the Colloquy, was disappointed with the result, because the two parties failed to come to any agreement. But it actually served the purposes of the Huguenots, who had enjoyed the privilege of having their case ably stated among the most influential people, and expected great accretions to their numbers. In this they were not disappointed, for they were soon able to claim as many as 15,000 adherents in Paris alone. It was rumoured also that some of the bishops were crossing over to their side, and there were even hopes of the new King, Charles IX, himself. In these circumstances the Catholics made great efforts, and as a result of a further conference at S. Germains they procured the Edict of January (1562), which compelled the Huguenots to restore all the churches and buildings

THE COUNTER-REFORMATION

they had appropriated to their own worship, and forbade them to meet together for their services anywhere but in the open air outside city walls. As if that were not enough to satisfy fanaticism, a fresh massacre broke out at Vassy, and the Huguenots were at last goaded into self-defence. Between 1562 and 1598 France endured the agonies of no fewer than eight civil wars, during which the Reformed won for themselves a peculiar and privileged position, but nevertheless failed completely in the effort to change the national religion.

By the Peace of Amboise, which closed the first of these short wars of religion in 1563, the Huguenots were granted a number of 'refuges', cities in which they were allowed to practise their own worship. This principle, once adopted, continued to be applied in subsequent treaties, and enabled the Huguenots to develop their own polity independently of the national government, until they became a kind of *imperium in imperio* with their capital at La Rochelle. Consequently they grew into a political body of great importance in the state, and under their leaders, Condé and Coligny, political and religious motives often mingled. Coligny's influence over the young King, Charles IX, aroused the jealousy of Catherine, and together with the Guises she decided upon a policy of extermination. When all parties were gathered together in Paris to celebrate the marriage of Henry of Navarre with the King's sister, Margaret of Valois, a terrible massacre broke out on S. Bartholomew's Day 1572. Over 8,000 Huguenots perished in Paris, including Coligny himself, and several times that number in the rest of France. Nevertheless the remnants of the party held together and successfully withstood the siege of La Rochelle the next year. The massacre shocked public sentiment everywhere, except in Rome and Spain, and helped to effect an alliance between the Huguenots and a third party, the 'Politiques', who worked for unity on the basis of a common Christianity without a definite credal confession. Their natural leader was Henry of Navarre, who, after saving his life in the massacre by avowing himself Catholic, was now Protestant once more. They succeeded in obtaining the Peace of Monsieur (1576) by which the Huguenots were allowed to worship everywhere in France except within two leagues of Paris. This led to the formation of a League under Henry, Duke of Guise, which sought to defeat Protestantism with the help of Spain. There was much controversy as to which side the new King Henry III would take. His sympathies were with Navarre, but as 'the eldest son of the Church' he found it difficult to change his religion. The disputes led to the War of the Three Henries. Henry of Guise was murdered at Blois in 1588, and Henry III died as the result of a wound inflicted by a Jacobin friar the next year. It had been declared that Henry of Navarre could not succeed because of his religion, but his own attitude is sufficiently summed up in the saying attributed to him that 'Paris is well worth a Mass', and he was received into the Church in 1593. When he had become King as Henry IV, he did not forget his old friends, but in 1598 issued the Edict of Nantes, by which the Huguenots, on condition of renouncing all foreign alliances, were allowed liberty of conscience, the right of worship in all places where they had practised it during the last two years, and admission to all places of education and to all offices.

Thus ended the wars of religion in France. It was a victory for the Church, but fortune might easily have favoured the other side. Political reasons in large measure dictated the issue. A nation which had but recently won freedom and unity found that unity best guaranteed by the old ecclesiastical organisation. But the result was not decided solely by official considerations. It was a genuine choice of the people themselves. Confronted by two quite clear and definite presentations of Christianity, they were repelled by the bareness of Calvinistic worship and preferred the warmth and richness of the old way. The solution offered by the Politiques, men 'who preferred the repose of the kingdom to the salvation of their souls', was too fundamentally irreligious. And Protestantism, once it had been reduced to the position of a sect, had no attraction for a nation essentially gregarious. That is why Roman Catholicism remains to-day the only type of Christianity of which the vast majority of Frenchmen have any comprehension.

CHAPTER VII

THE ELIZABETHAN SETTLEMENT

IT would be difficult to find a stronger contrast than that presented by the French and English methods of settling their religious difficulties. In France the issues had been set clearly before the whole nation and decided by the prolonged arbitrament of war. In England one issue, the break with Rome, had been presented to the nation as an accomplished fact. Having been given this taste of national independence, the people had then had their opportunity to sample two extreme presentations of Christianity and had been disgusted with both. To most it seemed that there must be some way of reconciling what was best in both types without losing what was essential in either. It was left to Elizabeth to guide this attempt at a new synthesis. If, as a wit has remarked, she made of it 'a regular woman's business—a parcel of bits tied up with string and held together with sealing-wax', the same criticism might be made of the whole British constitution and might be met by pointing out that the apparently inchoate pieces have a way of subtly transforming themselves into an organism that is extremely adaptable to changing circumstances.

Elizabeth was well aware of the dangers that beset her path. She had to avoid such civil and religious wars as disgraced the Continent, and she had to free her weakened country from the interference of such foreign States as Spain and France, to say nothing of the difficulties provided by Scotland, and the threat to her personal title represented by the intrigues of Mary Stuart. The state of her own religious views is undiscoverable. She was at least as much the child of the Renaissance as of the Reformation. She had some reverence for antiquity and beauty in worship, as shown by the services in her own chapel. She had a clear abhorrence of the fanaticism of Protestant extremists, and she had all her father's determination to be free of papal dominance. But she was above all a patriot, and was fully determined to seek her country's peace and glory by constitutional methods. There were few at first on whose assistance she could rely. Henry VIII's party had by this time vanished. There were still many Romanists who wished to retain the Marian position, and they were seconded by the Pope, who, it was said, was even willing to sanction the English Prayer Book in order to keep English obedience. And on the other hand there were Protestants returning from their refuge on the Continent to demand still greater and more drastic changes than had been accomplished under Edward VI.

Her first step was to issue a proclamation forbidding any changes in the Latin services until Parliament had met. Thus she checked any tendency to stampede. In 1559 Parliament passed the Act of Supremacy, reviving the statutes of Henry VIII on Annates and Appeals, by which the country had been freed from papal jurisdiction. But the Queen showed her independence of character by refusing the title of Supreme Head, which was thereupon changed for that of Supreme Governor. The earlier title implied a power of initiation which Elizabeth did not wish to claim, while the latter implied only authority to administer fixed law. She herself in the Injunctions of that year explained her authority as that over 'all manner of persons born within these her Realms, Dominions, and Countries, of what estate, either Ecclesiastical or Temporal soever they be, so as no other forraign power shall or ought to have any superiority over them'. Later, in the Articles published in 1563, she inserted with her own hand the statement that 'the Church hath authority in controversies of faith'. In order further to safeguard the exercise of the visitatorial authority of the Crown it was vested in a court of justice, known afterwards as the High Commission Court. Thus did Elizabeth seek to meet the objections that the Marian divines might feel to an acknowledgment of the Royal Supremacy.

The next step was to arrange for the services. The Queen

THE ELIZABETHAN SETTLEMENT 81

herself would, no doubt, have wished to go back to the Prayer Book of 1549, but that was impossible owing to the strong views of the Protestant refugees who were returning to their homes from abroad. She therefore caused the book of 1552 to be revised and its more objectionable features withdrawn. The Black Rubric was deleted, the old formula for use in administering Holy Communion was added to the newer form, and a rubric was inserted ordering the use of 'the same ornaments of the church and the ministers thereof as were in use by the authority of Parliament in the second year of Edward VI'. This book was attached to an Act of Uniformity that bade the attendance of the laity at its services under the penalty of a shilling fine for abstention. It was passed by Parliament without consulting Convocation. All the bishops in the Lords voted against it. Consequently the result was a laymen's settlement carried through by the State in defiance of the clergy. 'The State took the Church in hand and reformed it against its will.' But the laity are, after all, an integral part of the Church, and their work, at least, received such confirmation as is given by a general acquiescence. In the next five years no more than two hundred clergy were deprived for their refusal to accept the changes. That number included the Marian bishops, which, indeed, was inevitable as they had attained office in virtue of their pronounced opposition to any reform. The settlement was enforced by a series of Injunctions which forbade any to 'set forth or extol the dignity of any Images, Relics, or Miracles', or to keep superstitious pictures or monuments even in private houses. The customary Rogation-tide processions were to be held, but no others, and the Litany, said kneeling, was to replace the procession before the Eucharist. In 1571, in order to instruct the people in the faith, the Thirty-nine Articles were published as well as the *Second Book of Homilies*. A great difficulty was experienced in carrying on instruction because of the diminished number of the clergy, and to meet this need the title of Lector, as a sort of minor order, was restored, and in some cases foreigners were set to serve parishes.

There is no doubt that these arrangements were acceptable, not only to the people, but to many of the clergy, who during the late changes had done what they could to preserve religion in their cures. Of this quiet body, who must be looked upon as the founders of distinctive Anglicanism, the brightest example was Matthew Parker (1504–75). He had been chaplain to Anne Boleyn and Master of Corpus Christi, Cambridge. During Mary's reign he had lived in retirement as a deprived married priest. From this obscurity he had been dragged against his will, and was consecrated Archbishop of Canterbury in Lambeth Chapel according to the new ordinal on December 17, 1559, nine months after Elizabeth's accession. This consecration has become famous owing to the desire of controversialists to prove a break in the continuity of Anglican Orders. In 1604 a story was set on foot that the only consecration he received was in a farcical ceremony in the Nag's Head Tavern, but the consecration at Lambeth is attested by contemporary evidence. It is true that the Marian bishops refused to take part in it, but of those who did participate, Barlow of Bath and Wells and Hodgkin of Bedford, had themselves been consecrated according to the Sarum rite, and Coverdale of Exeter and Scory of Chichester according to the ordinal of 1550. In any case it is not likely that the scholarly author of the *De Antiquitate Britannicae Ecclesiae*, an account of the Archbishops of Canterbury from Augustine down to himself, would have been careless about a matter which so vitally concerned his own succession. The tone of his mind can also be judged from the fact that it is to him that we owe the revised calendar of 1561 with its restoration of the Black-Letter days, and that he took up the proposal to revise the Canon Law which had been dropped in Edward VI's reign. In 1571 he revised the *Reformatio Legum Ecclesiasticarum*, which had been first drawn up under Cranmer and was now published by John Foxe, the martyrologist, but it never got further than the Commons. The idea of a new code was therefore abandoned, but new canons were added by Convocation to the old law. The Queen herself revised these, but she refused to give them the Royal Assent. However, ecclesiastical authorisation proved sufficient to secure their observance, and this was, perhaps, what the Queen desired. In spite of the fact that Parker was thus made personally responsible for producing order out of chaos, he never lost

THE ELIZABETHAN SETTLEMENT

his gentleness of disposition, but protected both the Marian bishops and the extreme Protestants from the consequences of their independence. It is to his combination of mildness, strength, and knowledge, no less than to the peculiar character of the Queen, that we owe the preservation of the Catholic spirit of the English Church.

It was not to be expected that the more extreme Protestants could see the settlement take this form without a good deal of disappointment. A fundamental difference in point of view was making itself manifest. While the Continental reformers held that primitive Christianity had come to an end with the Apostolic Age, the English reformers regarded the whole life of the Church down to the fifth or sixth century as good primitive authority. Consequently, while the former reduced the Christian life to the barest essentials of faith and worship, the latter felt much regard for the institutions that had approved themselves in Christian experience. In England the spread of Calvinistic theology and the resultant dislike of ecclesiastical vestments proved to be the origin of Puritanism, which for many years fought hard with the Anglicans for the right to dictate the form of the national religion. At first there were no separatists; some Puritans conformed and others did not, but all remained within the Church. The very absence of separatism explains the fierceness of the struggle. The difficulty came to the front with the publication of Parker's *Advertisements* in 1566. In these he attempted to enforce a minimum observance upon all—the use of the surplice in the parish church and of the cope in the cathedral, and the practice of kneeling at Communion. The leader of the opposition was Thomas Cartwright, who had formerly been Lady Margaret Professor of Divinity at Cambridge, and was certainly one of the most cultured men of his day. Under his auspices were published in 1571 the first and second *Admonitions* in support of the Presbyterian system developed by Calvin. Cartwright's admiration for this system was boundless. 'For the Church modelled after the fashion of Geneva he claimed an authority which surpassed the wildest dreams of the masters of the Vatican.' He was replied to by John Whitgift, the Vice-Chancellor of Cambridge, who had already deprived him of his professorship, and he was sent into exile at Geneva. Later he was concerned with another Cambridge man, Walter Travers, Fellow of Trinity College, in the publication of a *Book of Discipline*, the object of which seems to have been to set up a Presbyterian *classis* in every diocese, thus establishing Presbyterianism by making the episcopal system ineffective. This Travers had been a disciple of Theodore Beza, one of Calvin's successors in Geneva, and later became a chaplain of the Temple. Hooker was at the time Master of the Temple, and the two carried on a prolonged controversy in its pulpit, the lecturer answering in the afternoon the sermon delivered by the Master in the morning. At this time also arose the difficulty about the 'prophesyings' as the Puritan preaching exercises were called. They, of course, were hot-beds of disaffection, and Parker tried in vain to stop them in 1574. When Grindal succeeded as Archbishop he, too, was called upon to suppress them. But he was himself more than half in sympathy with them, and replied that he was willing to regulate them, but not to suppress them. For this he was sequestrated until his death in 1583, and the Queen dealt with the matter by instructing the individual bishops to suppress the prophesyings in their several dioceses. The fact that in most places the same thing went on under another name shows how difficult was Puritanism to deal with under its many forms.

If Elizabeth and her friends had much ado to avoid the Scylla of Puritanism, they were equally threatened by the Charybdis of Romanism. The Jesuits who had done so much for the counter-Reformation elsewhere were not likely to abstain from efforts in England. In 1568 Dr. Allen founded a seminary at Douai, the purpose of which was to train priests as missionaries to England. After ten years the institution was moved to Rheims, and in 1579 a similar seminary was founded at Rome. At first the flocks of missionaries produced by these colleges effected little, but in 1580, when the Jesuits Campion and Parsons landed, there was a great rallying of the Papalist forces. By this time the serious character of the work had been fully recognised by both sides. In 1570 Pope Pius V had taken the deplorably unwise step of publishing a Bull that presumed to depose Elizabeth. The effect of this was to make

THE ELIZABETHAN SETTLEMENT 85

all Roman Catholics potential traitors. Hitherto the bulk of them had obeyed the law and attended their parish churches, but now they had to choose between the Queen and the Pope, and the result had been to make many of them actual traitors, joining in every treasonable plot that was hatched. The State was forced to defend itself, and the inevitable consequence was the passing of a series of Acts against the recusants which gradually deprived them, not only of religious liberty, but also of many of the rights of a citizen. The massacre of S. Bartholomew in 1572 associated Roman Catholicism with the vilest methods of attaining political and religious ends, and the Government had henceforth little mercy on any papal agents who fell into its hands. It has been estimated that under this head two hundred executions took place during the reign. Because of his complicity in the Ridolphi plot, which definitely aimed at the assassination of the Queen, the Duke of Norfolk had already been executed at the beginning of the year 1572. Campion and Parsons were therefore ordered by their superiors to abstain from all interference with affairs of State, but the Government refused to believe in the pacific nature of their mission, and when Campion was caught he was brought to the gallows with several of his companions, while Parsons escaped to begin definitely treasonable undertakings with Mary Stuart. Babington, having made full confession of his part in a similar Jesuit plot, was executed in 1586, and Mary Queen of Scots herself paid the extreme penalty the year after. The year 1588 saw the grand finale of all these Roman efforts when the Armada sailed for England carrying all the hopes of Philip of Spain. The vast fleet was first defeated by the gallantry, gunnery, and seamanship of the English sailors, and the work of its destruction was completed by a providential gale. Thus Roman Catholicism was finally defeated in England. Its long association with treason did more than anything else to give a decidedly Protestant tone to much of English religious thought for the next three centuries, but it had the effect on its own adherents, even while it contrived their ostracism, of developing among them a solidarity and a zeal which in the day of their freedom are at last meeting with some reward.

86 HISTORY OF THE MODERN CHURCH

After Parker's death and Grindal's short but tragic occupation of office the work of guiding the Church through these troubles on either hand was committed to John Whitgift. It was he who had deprived Cartwright of his professorship and championed the Church against the Presbyterian *Admonitions*. Nevertheless he was, and remained, predominantly Calvinistic in his theology. This was shown in the Lambeth Articles that were drawn up under his presidency in 1595. These Articles definitely stated the Calvinistic doctrines of predestination and reprobation, but they raised such a storm, both on the part of the Queen and of the Cambridge theologians to whom they had been sent, that they were practically withdrawn. They were issued on the sole authority of the Archbishop, and neither then nor at any subsequent time has the Church of England shown herself willing to go so far in that direction. Whitgift himself drew a clear distinction between Calvin's theology and his discipline, and the first ten years of his rule were largely taken up with the effort to preserve the Church from falling under the 'reformed' system. We have seen how earnestly the Puritans strove to establish this system. The instrument that Whitgift used against them was the High Commission Court. The Court grew out of the arrangements made by Thomas Cromwell as Vicar-General in 1535 for the trial of heretics. Edward VI had put this authority into commission, and Mary had developed it into a body of bishops, statesmen, and lawyers. Thus until the year 1583 it acted as a kind of Inquisition, completely under the control of the Privy Council, the laymen being thought more trustworthy at this kind of business than the clergy. But in that year it began to exercise new functions. One of the gravest difficulties of the times arose out of the fact that the ordinary ecclesiastical officials had no proper coercive power. They could admonish and excommunicate, but something more was needed to bring recalcitrants to book and so restore order out of chaos. This power was found by recognising the High Commission as a definite court of law. It was thus developed as an administrative instrument for enforcing the new organisation of the Church. It consequently gave to the Archbishop a power that his most authoritative orders would otherwise have lacked,

THE ELIZABETHAN SETTLEMENT 87

and it was by this means that order and decency were evolved. The virulence of the opposition that he had to face can be judged from the venomous character of the Martin Marprelate Tracts which began their appearance in 1588. The first of them was an anonymous pamphlet entitled *An Epistle to the Terrible Priests of the Convocation House*, and their object could be seen from the avowed wish to 'put a young Martin in every parish, every one of them able to mar a prelate'. So the Puritan anger against the bishops expressed itself because they would not push forward to extreme reform. But the tracts went too far, and by uncovering the strength of the early Puritan movement helped to break it up. Their precise author has never been discovered, but there is little doubt that Cartwright's influence was behind them. Of the two publishers, Udall was executed and Penry died in prison. The defeat of the movement was signalised in an Act of 1593 for the banishment of those who refused to attend the services of the Church. After this many of the Puritans fell into line and the rest departed to Holland.

During the remaining ten years of his rule Whitgift, enjoying the strong support of the Queen, was at peace, and in that peace was able to carry on another part of his work, the building up of a school of Anglican theology. The two best examples of the school during Elizabeth's reign were Jewel and Hooker. John Jewel (1522-71) had been a Fellow of Corpus, Oxford, and had listened to the teaching of Peter Martyr. He was Public Orator in time to offer the University's congratulations to Queen Mary on her accession, but lost his fellowship through refusing to attend Mass. He saved his life by subscribing a papal test, but fled the country and found refuge in Frankfort, where he took part on the conservative side in the quarrels worked up among the religious exiles by John Knox. Later he became Professor of Hebrew at Zürich, but returned to England on the news of Elizabeth's accession and was made Bishop of Salisbury in 1560. At S. Paul's Cross he preached in defence of the Anglican position and challenged the Romanists to produce a single proof of their claims from the first six centuries. This was to strike a characteristic note. Cooper, Bishop of Winchester, in replying to the Presbyterians, had refused to burke the title Catholic, and had definitely accepted it as descriptive of the Anglican position. Now Jewel, in his *Apologia pro Ecclesia Anglicana*, written in 1562 and quickly translated into English and other languages, maintained that the English Church had departed from the Roman communion, but not from primitive antiquity, from the Apostles or from Christ. The book was so well received in his own country that it was ordered to be set up in the parishes, and a copy may still be seen in some old village churches, as at Durnford in Wiltshire. It involved him in seven years' earnest controversy, during which the lines of English apologetic were fixed for all time. His old acquaintance, the Venetian Scipio, challenged him on the ground of England's non-participation in the Council of Trent, now recognised by Romanists as oecumenical. In an open letter Jewel replied that England sent no representatives to Trent precisely because it was not a General Council; there were no Germans present and no Greeks.

Perhaps Jewel's greatest work was his discovery and protection of a boy named Richard Hooker (1553–1600). He found Hooker a clerkship in his own college at Oxford, and was posthumously rewarded by the election of his protégé as Fellow and afterwards as Reader in Hebrew to the University. Hooker became preacher at S. Paul's Cross, and rewarded the kindness of his landlady by marrying her daughter, who brought him 'neither beauty nor portion, but many cares', amongst which not the least was the necessity to leave the comfort of his college for a country cure, where 'his old pupils found him tending sheep and reading Horace, and called in to rock the cradle'. He was made Master of the Temple in 1586, and his tender soul was there vexed with the controversy with Travers already described. Anxious to avoid the necessity of further quarrelling with a good but mistaken man, he got himself removed to a living near Salisbury, where, out of the experience gained in the controversy, he composed the greater part of his *Ecclesiastical Polity*. Of this book Hallam said that it was 'the first great original prose work in our language', and Pope Clement VIII that 'it had in it such seeds of eternity that it would abide till the last fire shall consume all learning'. The book is philosophical rather than theological, basing all not on Scripture—for even a divine law is not necessarily immutable—but on moral reason. As Hooker saw reason behind Scripture, so he saw the Catholic Church behind the English Church. The Genevan discipline is local and modern, whereas episcopacy, although not speculatively indispensable, is ancient and universal. Similarly he tried to preserve the values of current views on the sacraments. He used the simile of soul and body to illustrate the relation between the glorified Christ and the sacrament of the altar, but deprecated the endeavour to find the Presence theoretically in the external elements upon the altar rather than practically in the soul of the believer. Thus Hooker, like a wise householder, brought out of his treasury things new and old, and thus, 'his master mind checked and turned the tide of revolution'.

By such means, then, was the Elizabethan settlement carried through with the assistance of men who had their eyes wide open and knew what they were doing. It was not the thing of rents and patches that controversialists have tried to prove it. It was the work of men who refused to identify Catholicism with Romanism or Evangelicalism with Puritanism. They were almost alone in Europe in their effort to reconcile the results of the new learning with the age-long teaching of the Church. It has been said that the English Church came out of their hands with an Erastian clergy, a Calvinistic creed, and a Popish liturgy. These are less than half-truths, but there is enough truth in them to show that the effort of the times was not to find some *via media*, some devious path between conflicting opinions, but a real synthesis that should combine the truth of Scripture and of history. That there were losses is undeniable. The severance of England from the Continent made for an insularity that cramped the development of religious life for centuries. It was a thousand pities that Romanists should be driven into recusancy and Puritans into exile, but both were too intransigent to be brought within the limits of any comprehension. It was a great loss, too, that Rome should be left to the influence of narrow spirits who succeeded in piling dogma upon dogma without any warrant of Scripture or Christian antiquity. But it was a gain that both on its secular and its religious side the nation should be left free from foreign interference so that it might develop itself. It was a gain that the Bible should be open to all, and it was a still greater gain that Christian people should have had the opportunity to rediscover a Christian moral conscience. And it can be reckoned as a gain, too, that in spite of the close connexion between Church and State the Church's independence in the definition of doctrine should have been so explicitly recognised. In spite of all its imperfections it still remains true to say that of all the religious systems that issued from the conflicts of the sixteenth century the Elizabethan settlement was the most worthy.

CHAPTER VIII

THE BORDERS OF EUROPE

WE have now to consider the form taken by the Reformation in certain States of which hitherto we have said nothing. We begin with Scandinavia, where the reform represents the only victory obtained by Lutheranism outside Germany. In 1520 the three kingdoms of Sweden, Norway, and Denmark were held in an ill-defined union under Christian II. Their unity was broken as the result of the massacre known as the 'Stockholm blood-bath'. Christian had had to fight for his position in Sweden, and had been assisted by an excommunication pronounced against his enemies under the authority of Pope Leo X. When he had gained the victory and was actually being crowned, he broke the terms of an amnesty and imprisoned the leaders who had opposed him. At their trial they were asked the simple question whether men who had fought against the Pope and the Holy Roman Church were not heretics, and when they assented they were ruthlessly butchered to the number of about a hundred, including both ecclesiastics and laymen. The natural result was a revolt, which ended by placing its leader, Gustavus Vasa, on the throne of Sweden. Gustavus's need of money for the organisation of his kingdom led him to make repeated inroads on the wealth of the Church, which was the greatest landowner in the country. Matters came to a crisis in 1527 when the Diet of Westeras refused to permit this spoliation to continue. 'Then', said Gustavus, 'pay me back what I have expended in your service and I will never return to this ungrateful country of mine', and he suited his action to the words by striding out of the assembly. The Diet knew that they could not do without him and capitulated, leaving him a free hand.

In the meantime a good deal of Lutheran teaching had gone on, chiefly under the superintendence of Olaf Petersson (Olaus Petri) and his brother, who had both studied in Wittenberg. Gustavus had himself been attracted by their views on the proper relation between Church and State, and was consequently the more ready to use his power with this same Diet of Westeras to get himself put in charge of the ecclesiastical organisation. By the Recess of Westeras, all episcopal, capitular, and monastic property which was not absolutely required was put into the hands of the King, and by the ordinances of the same year (1527) no dignitaries were to be appointed until their names had been approved by the King, and compulsory confession was abolished. This, in effect, meant that Lutheranism had been accepted as the State religion. Olaf had accepted the Lutheran theory of consubstantiation, and this was made national doctrine when the Swedish Mass Book was published in 1531. The clergy for the most part accepted the change. There were no martyrs for religion. In 1524, during the early troubles, Peter Magnusson had actually been consecrated as Bishop of Westeras in Rome itself. In 1528 he consecrated three other bishops with all the old rites, and so the succession was preserved. During the reign of Gustavus's son, Eric XIV, it looked as if things might go much farther. He was himself a sincere Calvinist, and allowed a considerable laxity to develop both in the conduct of the services and in the lives of the clergy. But after nine years he was succeeded by John III, who was not only conservative in opinion himself, but was also under the influence of a Catholic wife. Now took place a series of efforts to make terms with the Papacy, in the course of which John actually went so far as to make his confession and receive communion after the Roman manner. Jesuit agents were active in trying to win back the people, and their common efforts might have succeeded if Pope Gregory XIII had taken a more conciliatory line and made a few concessions. However, the influence of the Romanising party declined after the death of the Queen, and matters returned to the more national conservative position of the early years of the reign. This was exemplified in the Church order (Kyrkoordning) of 1571, which retained confession and public penance and provided for the consecration of bishops. This order is the basis of the use of the Church of Sweden to-day. Although John's son Sigismund III was himself a Roman Catholic, he was unable to secure any advance on this position, and when, in fact, a great meeting was held at Upsala in 1593 to put an end to further religious questionings, it officially adopted the *Augsburg Confession* as the doctrinal standard and Luther's Catechism as the basis of instruction. Thus was concluded the most conservative of the Continental efforts at reformation. It is the only one that affords any parallel to the English settlement under Elizabeth.

Meanwhile, things had gone much farther in Denmark. Here, too, Christian II had been driven from his dominions in 1523, and had been succeeded by his uncle and rival, Frederick I, Duke of Schleswig-Holstein. He was a convinced Lutheran, but as Christian, by a curious mingling of reforms and papal obedience, had managed to preserve the support of Pope, Emperor, and Lutherans, he had to move with great caution. The bishops had united with the nobles to make him take an oath on his accession that he would not introduce Lutheranism, but things gradually drifted in that direction. The King drove a wedge between the bishops and the nobles by supporting the latter in their attacks on ecclesiastical property, and ensured the continuance of Lutheran teaching by appointing the reforming preacher Tausen as his own chaplain and so exempting him from episcopal control. After a quarrel with the Pope, Clement VII, about the succession to the Archbishopric of Lund, he freed the bishops-elect from the necessity of seeking papal confirmation, and by the Ordinance of the Diet of Odense, 1527, secured freedom of conscience, so that no one should henceforth ask whether a man was Lutheran or Catholic, and ordered that in future bishops should no more fetch the pall from Rome. After this the bishops got their confirmation, not from the Pope, but from the Archbishop of Lund. In the confusion that followed, this confirmation was looked upon as the only necessary requirement before entering upon office, and, consecration being disregarded, the succession was lost. After an abortive attempt at a disputation between the rival schools, the bishops lost heart and Lutheran teaching spread apace. Hopes were renewed, however, on the death of Frederick, but after much strife he was succeeded by Christian III, and the Church's cause was lost. The Copenhagen Decree of 1536 gave the Church lands in Denmark and Norway to the Crown Christian tried to get Luther and Melanchthon to come and evangelise his people, but, as they were both unable or unwilling, Bugenhagen was sent in their place. His first task was to crown Christian, and after this supersession of the bishops' rights a new ecclesiastical constitution was organised for Denmark, which divided out the Church under seven superintendents. A form of ordination was administered to the superintendents by Bugenhagen himself, although he was only in priest's orders. Norway, which had lost even the shadow of independence, and had been made subject to Denmark both politically and ecclesiastically, accepted similar changes in spite of the strenuous opposition of Olaf, Archbishop of Trondhjem. The whole was carried out with comparatively little confusion. The *Augsburg Confession* was adopted; the monasteries were flung open, although the monks were not compelled to leave them; the Cathedral Chapters ceased to exist as the old canons died off; one bishop was imprisoned, but others either left the country or became superintendents; and there was little iconoclasm. To this day many of the Danish churches retain the old ornaments both of the church and of the minister.

To turn now to the Netherlands. When Charles V handed over these seventeen provinces to his son Philip II in 1555, they were already riddled with heresy. Lutheranism and Calvinism had each its adherents, and the medieval Cathari and Beghards had produced a soil in which even Anabaptism grew more readily than elsewhere. Charles's expedients had been the introduction of the Inquisition and a proposal to divide the unwieldy dioceses into something more manageable. The latter proposal Philip obtained papal leave to carry into effect, but he increased his own personal unpopularity because his scheme was identified with Spanish dominance. Consequently, when he followed it up in 1566 with an edict enforcing the Decrees of Trent, disaffection broke into open revolt. Already Calvinism had become the predominant creed of those who desired change, and adherents to the number of a hundred thousand had rallied round the *Confessio Belgica*, which had been drawn up by a Walloon minister, Guido de Bres, and on the ground of its express repudiation of Anabaptism had claimed the sympathy of Philip. Needless to say, it did not win Philip, but it unified the opposition to his rule. To enforce his will he dispatched the Duke of Alva at the head of the finest troops in Europe. Alva proceeded to his task with a ruthless severity that alienated at least many of the middle classes. He was opposed by William of Nassau (the Silent), Prince of Orange, and the strife between them ended in the separation of the south from the north by both political and religious barriers, Belgium remaining Catholic and Holland becoming Calvinist. The work of reducing Belgium to papal obedience was completed by Alva's successor, the Duke of Parma, and by the Jesuits, who poured into the country and made Belgium one of the most solidly Roman Catholic territories in the world. The northern provinces, on the other hand, formed the Union of Utrecht (1579), which was the foundation of the Dutch Republic, and the religion they adopted became the foundation of the Dutch Reformed Church.

In 1571 the first national synod had met outside Dutch boundaries at Emden, and had adopted a constitution on the Genevan model; but William was anxious for as large a measure of toleration as possible, and the consequent problems that arose concerning the relation between Church and State form the most interesting part of the later history. The greatest controversy is associated with the name of Jacobus Arminius, a man of so great a talent that when a teacher at the University of Basel he had been offered the degree of doctor in divinity while still in his twenty-second year, an honour which his modesty had compelled him to decline. He represents a reaction from the strict Calvinism of the *Belgic Confession* with its insistence on the doctrine of predestination. The defenders of that doctrine had themselves become divided into 'sublapsarians' and 'supralapsarians'. It was his appointment in 1603 to the professorship of divinity in the new reformed University of Leyden that forced Arminius into a declaration of his own views. He charged the current Calvinism with making God the author of sin, and revealed on his own part such a belief in the power of man's free will as made him appear to many a teacher of doctrines very like those of the Council of Trent. He did not deny election, but based it on God's foreknowledge of man's perseverance in good. This involved Arminius in a controversy that embittered the remaining years of his life, and even waxed fiercer after his death. In the end a great synod was held at Dort in 1618 to decide the issue. The synod solemnly condemned the five articles in which the Remonstrants, as Arminius's followers were called, expressed their views, and two hundred Arminian clergy were compelled to leave the national Church. On the original theological controversy was grafted a political difference, the strict Calvinists belonging to the Stadtholder's, or Orange, party, while the Arminians became identified with provincialism. In this struggle the famous lawyer Grotius became involved on the side of the Remonstrants. He was imprisoned in 1619, but two years later his wife got permission to share his seclusion and managed to get him smuggled out in his own book-chest. He was accused of too much sympathy with Rome, but his great book, *De Jure Belli ac Pacis*, was placed on the Index. He was also accused of leanings towards Socinianism, but he himself wrote a book on the Atonement to vindicate the Remonstrants from that charge. His true sympathies are shown in his treatise on *The Truth of the Christian Religion*, to which were appended, in its English version, a number of testimonies to his affection for the Church of England. His widow actually became a communicant of that Church. In point of fact he aimed at a wide toleration, and taught that all believers in the fundamental truths of the Gospel should be admitted into the fellowship of Christ's religion.

Behind these controversies lay a profound uncertainty about the proper relation between Church and State. All parties were willing to accept the help of the State in times of stress when particular religious views needed to be enforced or protected. But who was to see that the State itself was kept in the straight path? If every king was a potential Josiah, how was his orthodoxy to be ensured?

The papal view had emphasised the superiority of the spiritual to the civil power. Luther was an opportunist who called in the State whenever necessary. Zwingli had gone still further in identifying spiritual and civil authority. Calvinism, on the other hand, had so carefully organised its Presbyterian system that it felt able to exercise ecclesiastical discipline without State interference. But the effort to compose a consistent theory has been associated, somewhat unnecessarily, with the name of Erastus. This distinguished scientist had become professor of medicine in the University of Heidelberg in 1558, and had done a good deal to free the world of his day from the superstitions of astrology and alchemy, without, however, losing a propensity for the burning of witches. He was vastly interested in theology and followed the views of Zwingli. He had resisted the imposition of the Presbyterian system in the Palatinate on the ground that it would introduce an Inquisition as bad as that of Spain, and his temerity had led to excommunication. As a result of this unpleasant personal experience, he had challenged the right of the ecclesiastical organisation to impose such a penalty. Since it included civil disabilities, there was something to be said for its imposition being left in the hands of the State. Only in this limited sense can Erastus be called an Erastian. But this seed grew until it produced the view that the Church was simply the State on its spiritual side, and made the ecclesiastical organisation a mere department of the civil Government. In any case, it was always presupposed that there was only one form of religion in each country; the toleration of many religions under one Government was not yet imaginable. The question was of particular importance in the Netherlands, which owed their very existence to their resistance to religious tyranny. Consequently the religious sense of the people was so strongly developed as to express itself in the fullest form of the Calvinistic system, which would admit no sharing of powers with the State. The Remonstrants, when they presented their five Arminian articles in 1610, asked for a national, as distinguished from an ecclesiastical, synod to deal with them. They lost their case at the Synod of Dort, but the logical precision with which the Calvinists pushed the victory of their views made clear the issues and produced a reaction. A few years later the Remonstrants were admitted into Holland, and during the seventeenth century Erastianism exercised much influence even in England. It cannot be said that the Christian world has yet solved the difficulties raised in the Netherlands during this period.

In speaking of Grotius we mentioned that he was once suspected of Socinianism. The country with which that particular heresy was most closely associated was Poland, during the sixteenth century perhaps the most important Catholic Power after Spain. Here we have a singular instance of Protestantism failing to secure a victory after having been given an almost complete freedom of entry. Lutheranism came in from Germany and Calvinism from the west in the early days of the Reformation movement. The ease with which this was effected was due to the independent spirit of the nobles, who held the ecclesiastical courts in derision, and by welcoming any men of learning, irrespective of their opinions, succeeded in making Poland a general refuge for free-thinkers. That there was already a certain familiarity with differences of religious opinion was due to the fact that some part of the people owed an allegiance to the Greek Church and also to the influence exercised by Hussite propaganda in the preceding century. The King, Sigismund I, made no protest until in 1525 the town of Danzig found its local government in the charge of Lutherans. Fearing that this would play into the hands of Albert of Brandenburg, his Lutheran neighbour, the King forcibly repressed the reform. In spite, however, of frequent Acts passed by the ecclesiastical synod, no further effective measures were taken, and in 1548 the Bohemian Brethren, expelled from their own homes, found a shelter in Poland. The same year Sigismund II succeeded to the throne and reforming opinions spread apace. To such an extent were they successful that in 1556 the Diet pressed the *cujus regio* principle to its utmost conclusion by enacting that every nobleman could introduce into his own household any religion that was according to the Scriptures. The King followed this up by demanding a comprehensive reform from the Pope, only to be refused with contumely. The first

Calvinist synod was held in 1550, and five years later the Calvinists effected a union with the Bohemian Brethren. Union with the other representatives of reform was not so easy, but the dissensions between them became so great a scandal as to threaten their common cause. Some hopes were placed in the pacific efforts of John à Lasco. This nobleman had sat at the feet of both Erasmus and Zwingli. He had been one of the foreigners to influence the mind of Cranmer during Edward's reign, when he had worked as pastor of the foreign congregation in London. He had fled from England on the accession of Mary and returned to his native land in 1556. However, although he was not personally objectionable to the Lutherans, he died after four years' efforts without bringing peace. In the meantime confusion had been worse confounded by the growth of anti-Trinitarian views. It is these that are specially associated with the Sozzini. The elder of them, Laelius Socinus, to use the Latin name, was a native of Siena, and had travelled over Europe in search of a religion until he had died penniless in Zürich at the age of thirty-seven. His nephew, Faustus, came to Zürich to collect his papers, and is said to have found in them the opinions that he propagated for the rest of his life.

Faustus Socinus came to Poland in 1572, and found that anti-Trinitarian views had already been established among a small community there. He was a thinker of a coldly intellectual type, and was well fitted to advance the disintegration of such Christian doctrine as was even still common to both Catholic and Reformed. He recognised the divinity of the Father alone, Christ being simply a human Messiah. Salvation was to be won simply by the virtuous following of the teaching of Jesus. He rejected the doctrine of original sin, and consequently believed in no objective Atonement. The sacraments were no more than outward signs. These opinions were warmly opposed by the other reformers, but the anti-Trinitarians found a home in Transylvania, and especially founded an important school at Racow, from which their declaration of faith, the Racovian Confession, takes its name. Their influence, and the consequent inability of the Protestants to form a common creed, explains the strongly Catholic reaction that set in.

Sigismund accepted the Tridentine Decrees and sought by pacific rather than violent means to persuade his people to follow his lead. The Papacy, under the influence of the counter-Reformation, ably seconded his efforts. The papal nuncios and the Jesuits accompanying them were men of exceptional character, who so strengthened their own faithful that even some of the nobles were won back, and the triumph of Protestantism was turned into defeat. At the Diet of 1569 the reformers asked for a union with the Catholics, but the reply was postponed until such time as the Protestants should have agreed among themselves what they really did believe. The next year Sigismund rejected a proposal of the Protestants that they should be placed on a statutory equality with the Catholics, and when he died in 1573 the cause of the Reformation in Poland was definitely lost.

It remains to trace the course of events in Scotland. The characteristic notes of the Reformation in this country are its thoroughness, its comparative freedom from bloodshed, and its entire lack of Royal patronage. The degradation of the medieval Church in Scotland was, if possible, more complete than in Rome itself. If the dignified Roman clergy could give an elaborate funeral to a well-known courtesan, the Scotch primate, Cardinal David Beaton, could attend the marriage of his illegitimate daughter and endow her out of Church lands 'beyond the dower of the richest nobleman's daughter'. But he was at least clever, courageous, and patriotic, while the utter supineness of his colleagues enabled the reformers to win their victory almost by default. It is true that there was at first some show of resistance. Lutheran books were prohibited by an Act of Parliament of 1525, and Patrick Hamilton, a Lutheran, was burnt at S. Andrews in 1528, to be followed by George Wishart, a Zwinglian, at the same place in 1546. But the fact that the movement for reform took on the character of a patriotic outburst against the intrusion of all foreigners made the nation utterly unwilling to support a policy of persecution, and the reformed teaching had already made great strides before the bishops, with their **Synods of Edinburgh** and with their *Catechism of John*

Hamilton (1552), stirred themselves to make a feeble attempt at a Catholic reform. The Scots began to suspect the French policy of the Queen-Regent, who sent her daughter, Mary Stuart, to be educated in France, and ultimately to marry the Dauphin. Thus Protestantism and patriotism became identified, and the combination helps to explain the veneration in which Scotchmen still hold the name of John Knox. Wishart had won over this young priest to the new opinions, and when, after Wishart's execution, Cardinal Beaton was murdered, Knox attached himself as chaplain to the desperadoes who had been guilty of the deed and had then shut themselves up in S. Andrews castle. On his capture he was sent to the galleys at Rouen, where he remained until he was released at the request of Edward VI. That king was so impressed by the fervency of his preaching that three years after, in 1552, he offered him the bishopric of Rochester, but Knox would not accept it on the ground that he could not abide the Second Prayer Book, published in that year. On the accession of Mary he found a refuge with Calvin in Geneva, but also acted as pastor to the exiles at Frankfort, among whom his vehemence aroused a host of quarrels. He returned to his own country in time for the stirring events of 1557, although he was absent again at Geneva when in that year the 'Lords of congregation', as the noblemen in sympathy with the Reformation began to be called, signed a Bond to renounce the 'congregation of Satan' and set up a provisional reform of their own. This was in accordance with a custom of signing bonds which appears in Scotch secular history, but this is its first appearance in religious history, and is important as the precedent for the later covenants. The course of reform thus set afoot was hastened by the burning of another Protestant, the aged Walter Mylne, the next year, and the people showed which way their sympathies were set by breaking in pieces the image of S. Giles when it was being carried in procession on his festival in Edinburgh. In 1559 Knox, having bitterly offended Elizabeth by writing his *Monstrous Regiment of Women* in defence of the Salic law, had to come round by sea to arrive in Scotland. He was immediately outlawed, but went to Perth. After his sermon there a stone thrown by a boy broke an image at the altar.

where a priest was just beginning Mass, and started an iconoclastic outburst on the part of what Knox himself describes as 'the raschal multitude', which did not end until every ornament in the church had been broken and the four great monasteries of the town had been ransacked to the very walls. The next year the insurgents, with help from England, forced all French troops to leave the country. Thus freed from foreign interference the Parliament adopted the Confession of Faith, abolished the Pope's authority, and made the saying of Mass punishable by death on the third offence. The bishops remained silent and uttered no word in defence of their faith.

The year 1560 was thus the turning-point in the Scotch Reformation. The new system was provisional, being neither episcopal nor yet presbyteral. Its main props were the Confession of Faith, the *First Book of Discipline*, and the *Book of Common Order*. The Confession was mainly the work of Knox and showed the strong influence of Geneva; but five others were concerned in it, and as their Christian name was John, it is often known as the work of the Six Johns. According to it the true Kirk is to be distinguished from 'the filthie Synagogues . . . the horrible harlot, the Kirk malignant' by the true preaching of the word of God, the right administration of the sacraments, and ecclesiastical discipline uprightly ministered. The Catholic Church is an invisible body, known only to God; controversies on the faith are to be settled by Scripture alone; and those are to be condemned who see in sacraments nothing but bare signs. The *First Book of Discipline* was also compiled by the Six Johns. It bears witness to the reformers' passion for sermons, not only by describing the bishops as 'dumb dogges', but by stating that no man could rightly administer the sacraments unless he were a preacher. Festivals, even Christmas and Easter, are abolished; the sacraments are reduced to two, and for the Lord's Supper people are to sit at table; all ecclesiastical buildings, except those used as parish churches or schools, are to be suppressed; ministers are to be appointed by the nomination of the people without ordination, and although they ought all to be equal they are to have superintendents set over them; and the old right of excommunication is as strictly preserved as it was in medieval days. This discipline was accepted by the Convention, to which it was presented in 1561, only on the condition that such members of the old hierarchy as joined the congregation should be allowed to retain their existing revenues. This preserved them a comfortable income while exempting them from all duties, and left the new ministers in poverty. The *Book of Common Order* had been used by Knox's congregation in Geneva, and reduced the services to the utmost simplicity. Characteristically, its models were taken from the Old Testament rather than from the New, and its greatest blot was that, as a violent reaction against popery, it allowed no service, not even a prayer or reading of Scripture, at the burial of the dead.

This compromise lasted till 1572, the old bishops and abbots still retaining their seats in Parliament in order, it was said, to preserve the balance of the constitution by maintaining the Three Estates of the realm. In that year, however, as the result of a Convention held at Leith, a return was made to the principle of episcopacy. Bishops were to be elected to the old sees under the sanction of the Crown by the Cathedral chapter, and were to be duly consecrated, although, as the consecrators were not themselves in episcopal orders, the historic succession was not preserved. Knox himself, who died in that year, lived long enough to signify his agreement with the measure. Effective leadership, however, remained in the hands of the ministers, of whom the best known was Andrew Melville. In 1581 they started experimental presbyteries, and held an Assembly which put out the *Second Book of Discipline*, restoring the laying-on of hands in ordination, but endeavouring to set up ecclesiastical courts independent of the civil power. But King James VI had a strong aversion to Presbyterianism, perhaps because he associated it with the Republicanism of his old tutor Buchanan. In 1584 he succeeded in checking its progress when he persuaded Parliament to pass the Black Acts of Edinburgh, ratifying the Three Estates, making the King supreme over all causes, forbidding Convocations except under his licence, and placing the chief ecclesiastical jurisdiction in the hands of the bishops. But eight years later he had to give way, and, the Black Acts being repealed, the power given to the bishops was handed over to the presbyteries, and permission was given for the annual holding of a General Assembly. Thus Melville triumphed. In 1592 true Presbyterianism was for the first time established in Scotland. Nevertheless, when he had become James I of England, the King made another attempt to get his own way. Three of the titular bishops were summoned to England, and, although they had not received priests' orders, were consecrated *per saltum* to the episcopate by three English bishops. When they returned, they consecrated the prelates already nominated to the remaining ten sees of the country.

This restoration of the episcopate was received with comparative indifference by nobles, ministers, and people. The dominating influence was still that of Calvin, who, without ever setting foot in Scotland, has had more to do than any other individual with the formation of the Scottish character.

CHAPTER IX

THE SEVENTEENTH CENTURY

EUROPE emerged from the Reformation with all its old unity broken. We have now to see how the various creeds and nationalities went their respective ways. The seventeenth century shows us the Thirty Years War in the Empire; the assimilation of the Huguenots, and a great revival in France; and in England the rise, eclipse, and resurrection of Anglicanism.

Bohemia was the storm-centre of the counter-Reformation. There we find not only the age-long racial strife between Slav and Teuton, but also the struggle between Catholics and the heirs of the Hussite propaganda. Lutheranism and Calvinism had both their adherents in this exchange-mart of religions, but the almost national faith that had sprung from John Huss was Utraquism, which expressed itself most characteristically in the custom of sharing the cup with the laity. By this time, however, success had deprived the Utraquists of living zeal, and the religious force of the nation was concentrated in the Bohemian Brethren, a strange, half-mystical sect, which eliminated the distinction between clergy and laity, looked for its happiness in another world, withdrew from towns to live an agricultural life, and yet did, perhaps, its greatest work in producing the famous educationist Comenius. The Brethren were banned in 1602, and their churches were handed over to the Catholics and Utraquists, but they lived on in secret, and their pacifism helped to leave Bohemia an almost inevitable prey to warring factions maintained by the Great Powers outside.

The Donauwörth affair first showed the Protestants that the Peace of Augsburg, which had secured them their religious liberties in 1555, was crumbling beneath the pressure of the counter-Reformation, and that they must prepare to defend themselves. Maximilian, Duke of Bavaria, was an ardent supporter of the new Catholic movement, and when in 1606 a religious procession at Donauwörth was assaulted and dispersed by the Protestants, he eagerly accepted the task of punishing the town. This he did with ruthless severity, and the town, which was definitely Protestant, had to admit a majority of Catholics to its council. This led to a demand on the part of the Protestants in the Diet that the Augsburg settlement should be re-affirmed, and when the Catholics replied that that settlement had been nullified by the Decrees of Trent, they organised an Evangelical Union, in which for once Lutherans and Calvinists made common cause. They were soon opposed by a Catholic League, and the train thus laid required only a spark to set Europe ablaze. This was contributed by the Defenestration of Prague in 1618. Protestant meetings had been forbidden in the city as a result of the war of pamphlets that had celebrated the first Protestant centenary in the previous year. In retaliation, some Protestant politicians threw three Catholics out of the window of the old palace. Only one was hurt, a fact which Catholics attributed to the support of angelic ministrants and Protestants to the fact that the men had alighted on a mattress in the shape of a heap of paper in the dry moat. This was the comic introduction to the most tragic war in modern history.

The Thirty Years War is divided into three parts, only the first two of which were waged for religious reasons. The first lasted from 1618 to 1629 and resulted in the complete collapse of German Protestantism. After the defenestration the Bohemian Protestants took to arms. They turned their local struggle into a universal conflagration by offering the crown of Bohemia on the death of the Emperor Matthias to the Elector Palatinate, Frederick. The importance of this was that it might have led to Frederick's election as Emperor, and that would have meant a Protestant Empire. Although Ferdinand had already been crowned King of Bohemia, and was later elected Emperor, Frederick accepted the offer of Bohemia, and the consequent strife ultimately affected the greatest Powers in Europe. In 1620, at the Battle of the White Hill, outside Prague,

THE SEVENTEENTH CENTURY 107

Maximilian of Bavaria, at the head of the troops of the Catholic League, crushed the Bohemians. Not only were they eliminated from the struggle, but the Protestant Union was broken up. Bohemia was subjected to a reign of terror, and finally merged in the Habsburg possessions. The war might have ended if it had not been for the intervention of Christian IV of Denmark, who wished to save Protestantism in the north by the secularisation and annexation of some of the bishoprics adjacent to his own territories. He, however, was balanced by Wallenstein, who came in on the Imperialist side. Christian was defeated at the Battle of Lutter in 1626, and compelled to withdraw from the fray. By the Peace of Lübeck (1629) he surrendered his claim to the Saxon bishoprics, although he was allowed to retain Schleswig-Holstein. The Palatinate had been handed over to the Catholics, Bohemia had lost its national existence, the Catholics had resumed control of several secularised bishoprics, and the Catholic Empire was stronger than ever. This was the result of the first part of the war.

The second part lasted from 1630 to 1635, and saw the restoration of Protestant prestige. This was due to the intervention of Gustavus Adolphus, the great King of Sweden. He was seriously determined to help the cause of Protestantism, but he also wished to make the Baltic into a Swedish lake, for which purpose it was essential to obtain a footing on its southern shore. In both aims he was assisted by his own military genius, which enabled him to use infantry to the full without losing mobility. He endeavoured to place himself at the head of a great German confederation, which should be strong enough to resist the Emperor and the counter-Reformation. He was roused to the most strenuous action when some of his troops were lost in the appalling sack of Magdeburg, wherein some 20,000 people perished at the hands of the Imperialist forces in 1631. He avenged himself on the two Imperialist leaders, Tilly and Pappenheim, in the great victory of Breitenfeld in the same year. After this he was able to subdue all the episcopal States on the Rhine, while his ally, the Elector of Saxony, invaded Bohemia. Thus he achieved his double purpose; the Empire lay at his feet and the tide of the counter-Reformation was definitely turned. The Catholic cause seemed lost, and the Imperialists could only save themselves by recalling Wallenstein, whom, from motives of jealousy, they had driven into retirement. This general, together with Pappenheim, faced Gustavus in the indecisive Battle of Lützen (1632). In the battle both Gustavus and Pappenheim were killed. The third of the protagonists was removed when Wallenstein was assasinated two years later. In the Battle of Nördlingen (1634) the Swedes lost their gains, but by the Peace of Prague of 1635 the Protestants made good their claim to a place in the sun and both Catholic and Protestant lands were restored to the position of 1627.

This closed the second part of the war, and the third part had no particular religious significance. It was lengthened out from 1635 to 1648 by the intervention of France, who hitherto had tried, under the diplomacy of Richelieu, to make gain for herself by playing off the two parties to the religious strife, but now, with the help of Sweden, she turned it into a dynastic war against Bavaria and Spain. It was of a dreariness beyond description, and interests us only because of its termination in the Peace of Westphalia (1648), by which the independence of the German States, the Swiss cantons, and the United Netherlands was recognised, and France and Sweden obtained certain territorial gains. But from the religious point of view its importance lies in the fact that at long last it terminated the strife engendered by the Reformation and gave to the Protestants the free exercise of religion and the right of admission to offices. The Papacy was overwhelmed. Innocent X, in the Bull *Zelo domus Dei* declared it 'null and void, accursed, and without any influence or result for the past, the present, or the future'; but his protest was ignored, and that fact marks the end of papal influence in European politics, and almost in religion, for an epoch.

In the meantime France had been preparing for a great revival Henry IV, having wavered in his own religious allegiance, having won his kingdom by a Mass, and given peace to the Huguenots by the Edict of Nantes, pursued his pacific course. To him has been attributed the Grand Design of a kind of primitive League of Nations, by which the three religions of Catholicism, Lutheranism, and

Calvinism should be allowed and war banished except as against the Turk. Within his own boundaries he refused to receive the Decrees of Trent, although his clergy accepted them, and they were never promulgated in France. At the same time he welcomed the influx of Jesuits, and in spite of opposition founded their college at La Flèche. He was ill-requited in that he was at last assassinated by the mad schoolmaster, Ravaillac, who, although not instigated by the Jesuits, was relying on the teaching of some Spanish members of that Order to the effect that a monarch could be slain if he did not serve the interests of the true religion.

Under Louis XIII (1610-1643) the Huguenots pursued their semi-independent career. This was opposed to the Catholic and centralising policy of Richelieu. When the Minister imposed Catholicism on Béarn they rose to arms, and at La Rochelle framed schemes for establishing an *imperium in imperio*. Apparently some of them, at least, relied on the support of England to build up a kind of republic. But in the meantime they organised themselves the more carefully in circles for mutual defence. In 1625 they took up arms again, but they suffered so severe a defeat that their leader, Soubise, had to find refuge in England. Two years later the English, under Buckingham, made a futile effort to assist them at La Rochelle, where they were besieged, and the capitulation of the town marked the end of their political independence. By the Peace of Alais they were guaranteed their religious liberty, but their municipal institutions were remodelled, and with the rest of the country they were subjected to the despotism that Richelieu was steadily building. But by his very absolutism the great Minister was able to protect the Huguenots from their Catholic enemies, and they developed into good citizens, perfectly loyal, and the most industrious members of the population.

The same national sense that had guided Richelieu in his relations with the Huguenots can be discerned in his dealings with the Papacy. He had no sympathy with the ultramontanes, and looked upon the Church in France as a national institution, compelling the bishops to recognise their position as servants of the State, while encouraging them to maintain their spiritual prerogatives. A Council of

Conscience advised the King on ecclesiastical appointments, and the General Assembly was kept under strict Government supervision. Thus was encouraged that Gallicanism which was to pervade the French Church for many generations, and even to give rise to the hope that it might one day unite itself with other national Churches, such as the English. The revival, of which this spirit was both a cause and a result, may be considered under the heads of learning, piety, and nationalism.

Under the first head it falls to mention a group of men who would have done honour to any Church in any period. The earliest of them, Francis de Sales (1567-1622), was of noble birth, and was brought up amid scenes where the conversion of the people to Protestantism most markedly stirred the current of daily life. Priested at the age of twenty-six, he began his work in Savoy, where the bulk of the population was Calvinist and Catholicism was represented by dissolute soldiery. He converted his own people first, and then set himself to the task of winning back the heretics, whom he treated with such winning gentleness as to gain almost the whole population. Anyone who has read his *Introduction to the Devout Life*, with its wealth of picturesque simile and its deep spirituality, can understand how fascinating his preaching must have been. As a preacher he was always welcome in Paris, and Henry IV tried to attach him permanently there with the offer of the highest dignities; but he remained at his post, and was made Bishop of Geneva in 1602, though, of course, he was not able to reside there. In 1604 he made the acquaintance of Mme. de Chantal, with whom afterwards he founded the Order of the Visitation. The temper of his piety can be best understood by recalling the resolution that he himself made at his ordination: 'to remember all day that he was preparing to say Mass the next morning.' An even more interesting career is that of S. Vincent de Paul (1576-1660). Brought up on a farm, his intellectual abilities led to his being trained for the priesthood. After his ordination he refused a benefice in order to devote himself to study, but on a journey to receive a much-needed legacy he was captured by Tunisian pirates and lived as a galley-slave for two years. He converted his last master, a renegade Italian,

THE SEVENTEENTH CENTURY 111

back to Christianity, and with him effected his escape. He became tutor to the de Retz family and was allowed freedom to put into execution the amazing philanthropic schemes that were the results of his own experience of misery. He founded fraternities of charity for the poor, which spread to many cities. He worked among the prisoners condemned to the galleys in Marseilles and Bordeaux with such success that Louis XIII made him Almoner-General. He then, at Chartres, founded the Congregation of Missions for training preachers to assist the spread of vital religion in the towns. He instituted hospitals for the sick and for foundlings—the tragic witnesses to the evil of the times. And greatest of all his benefits to humanity, he started the Sisters of Charity—the band of devoted ministrants to suffering and poverty who have brought comfort to many of the worst slums of Europe. As it never occurred to him that philanthropy could be of lasting value without the gospel, all this work of organised charity was backed up by continual preaching and evangelistic efforts. It is said that during the last twenty years of his life nearly twenty thousand persons attended his retreats at S. Lazare.

With these two apostolic men must be coupled M. Olier and Père Eudes. It was they who did more than any others to remedy the state of ignorance and neglect into which the clergy had fallen. It is said that even among the priests there were those who knew so little Latin that they would give the blessing in the words *Ave Maria*. The means by which this was ended was the founding of seminaries, in which the future priests and bishops could receive a proper training. The most famous of these institutions was Olier's foundation of S. Sulpice, which later developed the well-known method of catechetical instruction. Eudes founded the Congregation of Jesus and Mary, now known as the Eudists. Some of the new elements in Roman Catholicism come out in the teaching of these men. Eudes was really the founder of the cult of the Sacred Heart of Jesus and of the Heart of Mary, the Confraternity of the Heart of Jesus and His Mother being approved by Pope Alexander VII in 1666. Their evangelistic zeal was beyond all praise. Olier was responsible for successful missions in the Auvergne district, and Eudes between 1642 and 1672 conducted missions in Brittany which have left that province still one of the most ardently Catholic countries in the world.

Before we speak of the other giants of learning and piety in this great age of France it will be well to notice the development of nationalist aspirations in the French Church. Louis XIII was succeeded by the Grand Monarque (Louis XIV) in 1643, and Richelieu, who had died the previous year, was replaced by Mazarin. They pursued much the same policy as that already laid down. Louis found himself involved with Pope Innocent XI in a dispute over the *régale*, the right claimed by the King of France to draw the income of bishoprics during a vacancy and to appoint the new prelates. Although this right had only been claimed originally in the ancient domains of the Crown, Louis extended it in 1673 and 1675 until it included practically the whole realm. The Pope refused to admit the claim and declared the ministrations of bishops so appointed invalid. Even the Jesuits supported the King. In the General Assembly of 1681 the clergy as a whole followed suit, and in a letter to the Pope urged him to yield to the Royal claims, which involved only a question of discipline and not of faith. This was followed in 1682 by the famous *Gallican Declaration*, drawn up by Bossuet, the 'Eagle of Meaux'. This asserted that the Popes have a spiritual, not a temporal, power, and that they cannot release the subjects of a king from their allegiance; that local statutes and customs, such as those of the Gallican Church, should have their own inviolability; and that the Pope's judgment, even in matters of faith, is not irreversible unless it has the consent of the Church. This led to a prolonged literary warfare with the Roman champions, and the Pope reinforced the work of his theologians by refusing recognition to the regalist nominees. In a short time no fewer than thirty-five sees were without fully recognised bishops, those appointed managing the temporal affairs of their dioceses, but performing no spiritual functions. Five years later fuel was added to the fire by a dispute over the privileges of the French ambassador in Rome. To force the Pope's hand, Louis occupied Avignon, and was rumoured to threaten the formation of a French patriarchate. But this was at the moment when Louis' prestige stood higher than that of any other monarch in Europe. Later, when the English revolution of 1689 had destroyed his influence in this country and there was a new occupant of the papal throne, he restored Avignon, and in 1693 he retracted the Declaration. When they had made a similar recantation, the elected bishops were allowed to be consecrated, and formal peace reigned once more. But the French *Parlement*, consisting mostly of lawyers, remained fully determined to maintain what they regarded as the constitutional privileges of the national Church, and the clergy, agreeing with them, bided their time.

In spite of this somewhat intransigent attitude towards the Papacy, Louis was no supporter of heresy. Indeed, he delighted to show his orthodoxy by repressive measures against non-Catholics. Strenuous efforts were made by the great preachers of the day to win converts from the Huguenots, and Louis forwarded them by the infamous system of *dragonnades* (the quartering of violent and rapacious dragoons in the Protestant districts) and by many other methods of persecution, as a result of which considerable numbers fled the country. In 1685 the work was brought to a conclusion by the revocation of the Edict of Nantes. It has often been said that this was the result of the influence of the Jesuits working through Mme. de Maintenon, whom Louis had privately married. However this may be, the King must himself bear the blame for a mistake that was as stupid as it was criminal. A body that had long ceased to present any political danger and had become the most useful element in the life of the country was dispersed, and with this loss of religious freedom the State undid the work of Henry IV, and lost its own chance of attaining a liberal and parliamentary government, which might have saved it from the disasters of the following century.

The Waldenses, or the Vaudois, also suffered in this effort to make France the country of one religion only. Their home in Savoy offered a refuge for some of the Huguenots. Consequently they were involved in the same disaster. On Louis' demand their privileges were withdrawn and a massacre ensued. The survivors, however, remained in the fastnesses of the mountains and were able to descend to their valleys when a more peaceful day dawned. A more difficult task awaited the Government in its effort to put down Protestantism in the Cevennes. The revolt of the Camisards is one of the most extraordinary incidents in the history of religious persecution. Incensed by the repressive methods of the Roman clergy, and stirred up by the fanatical preaching of their own 'prophets,' the untutored peasants arose and, after murdering the archpriest Chayla, dared to face the skilled troops sent to reduce them to order. Seguier, their most violent leader, was captured and burnt, but under Laporte and Cavalier they carried on a guerilla warfare in their mountains that drove the Royal troops to desperation. Quarrels among the leaders led to their defeat. Cavalier, who had begun life as a baker's boy, made good terms for himself and for those of his companions who would accept the pledge of religious freedom. He was looked upon as a traitor by the rest, but made his way to England and rose to be a Major-General and Governor of Jersey. The others carried on the war without success and were almost exterminated.

It is clear that Frenchmen had sufficient excitements to stimulate their interest in religious questions. But these external incentives were as nothing compared with two profound problems that arose to agitate public opinion and to engage the ablest minds that even that age produced. The first was the question of Jansenism. Jansen himself had been Bishop of Ypres and had died in 1638. But he had been a great student of Augustine, and before his death had embodied his admiration for the great African in a book called *Augustinus*. In 1640 this book was discovered and published, and found a fruitful soil for its peculiar teaching at Port Royal, a Cistercian nunnery, which had been reformed by Mère Angélique. During the Reverend Mother's absence in Paris the convent was occupied by a band of earnest and able students, including Angélique's brother Arnauld, with Le Maistre and Pascal. When Angélique returned to the convent, of which she had become abbess at the age of seven, and which she had reformed at the age of seventeen, the students removed to a place near at hand, where they carried on that great work of evolving an educational method which was to make them the hated rivals of the Jesuits. These latter, perceiving a semi-Pro-

THE SEVENTEENTH CENTURY 115

testantism in Arnauld's writings which would serve their purpose well, extracted five propositions dealing with the doctrine of grace and obtained a condemnation of them from Innocent X. They were frustrated by Arnauld's capitulation. Thereupon they claimed that these propositions were contained in Jansen, and obtained a papal Bull to compel all religious communities in France to assent to the statement that the propositions were those of Jansen. This was to make the views thoroughly disreputable, for Jansenist theology differed little from that of another disciple of Augustine, Calvin; it made man an utterly irresponsible instrument in the hands of God and left no room for free-will. Arnauld and the nuns of Port Royal refused to agree to this ascription of his propositions to Jansen. The obvious test of submitting to a search of the dead bishop's works seems never to have been tried. The students were banished from the valley and the nuns dispersed. They returned when a temporary pacification was patched up in 1668, but the whole controversy flamed up again when Jesuit influence prevailed upon Clement XI to issue the Bull *Unigenitus*, condemning a book by the new 'director' of Port Royal, Père Quesnel. The nuns would give only a modified assent to the Bull, and the convent was finally dissolved. Many of the Jansenists were imprisoned, and the party was destroyed.

In spite of their apparent victory the Jesuits lost more than they gained in this struggle, for there was called out against them the amazing genius of Pascal. This young and delicate scholar, the full span of whose life was only thirty-nine years (1623-62), was the originator of modern French literary style, a founder of modern mathematics, and the precursor of much modern philosophical thought; and he was also the inventor of a calculating machine and of the first omnibus service in Paris. Science was the one absorbing passion of his life until he experienced a conversion in 1654, which enabled him to share fully in that personal religion which was the joy and occupation of his friends of Port Royal. It was two years later that Arnauld asked him to try his hand at writing something popular on their controversy with the Jesuits. The result was the eight-page pamphlet entitled, *A Letter written by an Inhabi-*

tant of Paris to a Provincial friend of his on the matter of the present quarrels in the University. That was the beginning of the Provincial Letters, in which Pascal exposed the Jesuits and their characteristic methods to the derision of half Europe. He saw that the immediate point at issue was the Jesuits' desire to get rid of Port Royal by branding it as heretical. But behind this there lay both a theological and a moral issue. In regard to the first—the belief that God's grace is at all times sufficient for all men, though it never forces any—Pascal was in closer agreement with medieval thought than with Port Royal, for he was never a Jansenist. But on the other question he was diametrically opposed to the Jesuits. By their theory of 'probabilism' they had laid it down that if a man were in doubt what course of action he should adopt he would be justified in adopting that which had been pointed out by any one serious theologian as probably right. This theory, of course, made it possible to adapt any rule to almost any circumstances, and the Jesuits had found it very useful in keeping attached to the Church men who still wished to retain their unspiritual life in the world. In the eyes of Pascal such a system of casuistry was a deliberate attempt to make religion easy, and he infinitely preferred the Jansenist view of religion as a hard and narrow way. Perhaps he himself erred in one direction as the Jesuits did in the other, but there is no doubt that in this period religion was being ever more widely divorced from ethics, and it was very needful that some prophet voice should proclaim the truth of the utter holiness of God. An even more famous publication of Blaise Pascal's is the *Thoughts*, a compilation of notes from which he had intended to write up a great Apology for the Christian faith. Descartes, who died in 1650, had dealt a blow to the position of Christianity by practically excluding it from his system of thought. He had set out on his search for truth by refusing to accept anything as true unless it were capable of being clearly proved. He had expressly put religion on one side in this inquiry, nominally regarding it as something that one could take for granted while a philosophical position was being built up. This was extremely abhorrent to Pascal who believed that 'religion's all or nothing', and he set himself specially to win back those who had learnt to treat Christianity as a matter of comparative indifference. It is impossible not to ask oneself whether God and eternity are realities, and if one has to rule one's life in accordance with the answer to the question, would not even a gambler realise that there were greater risks in giving a negative reply than an affirmative one? Try as you will, you must sometimes make an unprovable assumption, and it is better to make it on the safe side. But the decision, once made, must be carried to its full conclusion. No man dare be half a Christian; he must give himself wholly to faith and it must issue in a morally reformed character. It will thus be found that religion is a personal experience, which, having its rise in the emotions, embraces the reason and justifies the authority which has handed down religious truth. Pascal thus threw himself against the current French thought, which looked upon religion as a kind of social cement, and staked his all on a personal experience which sprang from the heart and was very different from the placid intellectual assent that was expected of most men in his day. If he did not succeed in converting his own generation, his thought has reappeared in that intuitionalism which is the best-known form of French philosophy to-day.

If Jansenism gave rise to much controversy, Quietism was responsible for much more. This was a question about the right method of approaching God. In prayer and meditation the exercise of man's own faculties plays a necessary part. But S. Teresa with her careful introspective psychology had discovered that she often had the most intimate experience of God when she made no effort of her own, but let herself rest completely quiescent without any conscious thought or feeling. This foundation had been built upon by her fellow-countryman Miguel de Molinos, who, in his *Spiritual Guide*, published in 1675, seemed to advocate the extension of this quiescence, not only over the moments of prayer, but over the whole active life of man. This was to destroy all effort and exercise of the will. Strangely enough, the danger of this teaching was not at first perceived, and the Jesuit who first attacked it found his book put on the Index. The matter was taken up by Louis XIV, always ready to atone for his many vices by a strident orthodoxy. He caused Molinos to be denounced to the Inquisition. The Quietist teacher was condemned in 1687 and died in prison in 1696.

Molinos's teaching was spread in France by the wealthy lady, Mme. Guyon, who became the founder of a type of mysticism which had as its most characteristic notes contemplation and absorption in the divine. In 1688 she was imprisoned, but the influence of great ladies gained her release, and even Mme. de Maintenon fell under her sway for a time. More important was the hold she gained over Fénelon, who was in attendance at the Court as tutor to the King's grandson, the Duke of Burgundy. Fénelon was a most attractive figure. He had already shown the temper of his mind by refusing to accept the aid of the dragoons when he had been sent on a mission to the Protestants. He had had experience of female education, and had produced a book on the subject when he was in charge of a society for the instruction of Protestant women; and now he was showing considerable genius in the education of the young Duke, which was to issue in his *Telemachus*, a writing which inculcated as many virtues in the typical prince as Machiavelli had sought to eliminate. But Fénelon did not please the King, who appointed him Archbishop of Cambrai as a step towards getting rid of him from the Court. The opportunity to banish him came when Mme. de Guyon was again imprisoned. Bossuet had taken a violent dislike to her teaching and wrote a book on *Prayer* against her. Fénelon defended her. His views were published in his *Maximes des Saints*, which was really intended to distinguish her teaching from that of the Quietists, and was described by himself as 'a sort of dictionary of mystical theology, to prevent righteous souls passing beyond the limits laid down by our fathers'. Louis demanded its condemnation, but Pope Innocent XII delayed as long as possible, and then only gave his official view in the grudging form: 'He erred through excess of Divine love, you through want of love to your neighbour.' But, indeed, the teaching of the book was incomprehensible to the multitude. Its aim was to exalt a disinterested love of God above one inspired by fear of punishment or hope of reward, and the difficulties of the subject were such that even the Bull against him did not speak of him as a heretic nor condemn the book to the flames. Fénelon submitted, and spent the rest of his life in earnest and self-sacrificing work in his diocese. But he sought to prove his orthodoxy by the sternness of his denunciations of the Jansenists in the final stage of their struggle and by opposing Bossuet in his efforts on behalf of Gallican liberties. However, his influence was henceforth confined to his own see, while that of his rival continued to be felt throughout the French Church and even beyond its borders. Bossuet had greater influence with the King than Fénelon, and this combined with his extraordinary powers as a preacher to give him a commanding position. Like Fénelon he had been unwilling to use force to compel the conversion of Protestants, but he was so successful with them as to win back to Catholicism the great Turenne. For some time he carried on a correspondence with the philosopher-politician Leibniz, on the possibility of a union between the Catholic and Lutheran Churches, and showed himself willing to concede the cup to the laity and marriage to the clergy. But Leibniz was obliged to abandon the project for political reasons. Bossuet was able to detect beneath all the magnificence of Louis' reign the seeds of decay. He prevailed with the King to suspend for a time his connexion with Mme. de Montespan; if he had been successful in getting Louis to accept his other advice to pay more attention to relieving the miseries of the populace, the future history of France might have been very different.

CHAPTER X

THE SEVENTEENTH CENTURY IN ENGLAND

THE seventeenth century in England gives us the story of the rise, eclipse, and resurrection of Anglicanism. This fluctuation was very largely due to the close association of the Church and Crown under the Stuarts. The members of that dynasty were often essentially foreigners with Roman Catholic queens, and their disasters were largely due to that double fact, together with a certain infatuated and obstinate temperament that seemed characteristic and ineradicable. The Church accepted their theory of divine right, which logically included legitimism, absolutism, and passive obedience, and identified the seat of authority in the Church with the throne itself. The Stuarts on their side saw in the Church the mainstay of their rule. 'No bishop, no king', seemed an obvious truism. James, indeed, when he came from Scotland in 1603, was welcomed both by Presbyterians and by recusants. The former thought him one of themselves, but they did not know that his early upbringing had taught him to hate Presbyterianism, which, he said, 'agreeth as well with monarchy as God and the devil!' On his way south he was presented with the Millenary Petition, so called because it was exaggeratedly supposed to represent the views of a thousand clergy. It asked for the abolition of certain 'abuses' in public worship, such as the use of the ring in marriage and the sign of the cross at baptism, the wearing of the surplice, and the rite of confirmation. It also proposed a conference, which was promised for the next year. On the other hand the recusants thought that in view of his upbringing and experience they would be likely to win more toleration from James than they had from the authoress of the settlement. Perhaps the King would have found that course agreeable had it not been for the fact that his hand was forced by the occurrence, first of the Main Plot, as the result of which Lord Cobham and Sir Walter Raleigh were imprisoned, and the Bye Plot, after which the priest William Watson was executed. Consequently he was compelled, in spite of himself, to issue a Proclamation ordering all Jesuits and seminarists to quit the kingdom.

The promised conference was held at Hampton Court in 1604. It marks the end of the first great Puritan effort to obtain ascendency in England. On the first day there was a Privy Council meeting at which the King discussed with nine bishops and five deans the questions at issue. On the second day, four representatives of the petitioners were present. They went beyond the subjects mentioned in the Petition and asked in addition for a recasting of the Articles and Catechism and a new translation of the Bible. Also, a significant addition, they wished the presbyters to be associated with the bishops in the administration of discipline. The King was thoroughly alarmed. He saw that the real problem was whether England should or should not cut itself off from historical Christianity. Consequently few concessions were made. When the parties met on the third day, a new Bible was promised and the changes in the Prayer Book were explained to the Puritans; but they accepted the position with a bad grace, and the cross and surplice remained a serious difficulty. However, the Prayer Book was issued with a few explanations, and conformity was ordered by a Royal Proclamation. Nevertheless from this point the bishops did try to recognise the claims of the presbytery by associating with themselves a number of priests in the acts both of excommunication and ordination.

The same year a number of canons were drawn up by Convocation and confirmed by the King, which with some amendments made in 1865 are still binding. The thirty-sixth of these canons required subscription to the Supremacy, the Prayer Book, and Articles. As a result of their refusal to obey this a number of Puritan clergy were ejected from their cures. Their number has often been reckoned as three hundred, but has lately been estimated to be not more than fifty or sixty. In any case it must be remembered that they were actually failing to carry out the vow made at their institution. The next year saw the Gunpowder Plot miscarry. It was due to the disappointment of the recusants at failure of the King's support. No doubt they had suffered great provocation. There had been six thousand convictions for recusancy and several executions. But the magnitude of the plot, and the moral turpitude that could act upon a doctrine of equivocation which was indistinguishable from plain lying, justified the repressive measures adopted by the Government. A new Oath of Allegiance was now framed condemning as 'impious and heretical the damnable doctrine and position' that the Pope could excommunicate princes and thus expose them to the danger of being deposed or murdered. In 1606 it was further enacted that henceforth no Roman Catholic might act as guardian or trustee or follow the profession of barrister or doctor.

The promise of a new translation of the Bible was fulfilled by the issue of the Authorised Version of 1611. Since Henry VIII's reign there had been put forth the Bishops' Bible of 1568, in which Parker had had a share; the Genevan Bible (1557–60), which had been completed by the Protestants of Frankfort; and the Douai or Rheims Version for the Roman Catholics (1582–1610). But the trouble with all these was that they were tendencious, and, either in the translation or in the notes appended to the text, tried to commend some partisan interpretation to the reader. The Authorised Version had the great merit of leaving the reader to form his own judgment. It combines the work of about fifty revisers sitting in companies at Oxford, Cambridge, and Westminster, and it has done more than any other book to form both the English language and character. In spite of its title there is no evidence of formal authorisation; for some time the Genevan version was used side by side with it; in the end the Authorised Version won its way into the nation's affections, not by regulation, but on its merits.

During the rest of the reign Puritanism grew in influence, partly because its clergy were the more earnest, but also because the definitely Anglican clergy, leaning upon the High Commission Court and so upon the King, became more closely identified with his absolutist aims. A sign of the times was seen in the hostile reception that was given in 1618 to the *Book of Sports*. It seems strange that in the very year when Europe was rent by the outbreak of the Thirty Years War, England should be so agitated over the question of Sunday observance. But the Puritans, identifying Sunday with the Sabbath, and applying to it all the Old Testament regulations, had reduced the medieval Sunday to a day of gloom. As late as 1611 the Wardens of the Taylors' Company at Salisbury had been imprisoned for allowing morris dancing on Sunday. Elsewhere there had been great opposition to the Puritan views, and James sought to strengthen the opposition by issuing his Declaration of Sports. But he made the mistake of ordering all clergy to read it from the pulpit. So many refused that he gave way and withdrew the Declaration. Another method by which the King was circumvented had more important consequences. A number of Puritans who could not accept the established services in any wise had escaped to join their like-minded friends already settled in Holland. This was in 1608. Twelve years later they formed a project to extend their search for a suitable home still farther. They arranged for the expedition to start from England, and on September 6, 1620, 101 of these Pilgrim Fathers set sail from Plymouth, arriving two months later in Massachusetts.

The man who had done more than any other to strengthen the organisation of the Church after the Hampton Court Conference was Richard Bancroft, who became Archbishop of Canterbury in the December of that year. It was he who had developed the High Commission Court for the purpose, and when his proposals were defeated in Parliament he carried them through by his visitatorial system organised with the power of this Court behind it. He was merciful to Puritans and maintained that the clergy were only Nonconformist through ignorance. If, on the one hand, he succeeded in placing coercive power in the hands of the bishops, he also showed considerable sympathy for the clergy, who at this time were in great poverty. They were mostly paid a servant's wage, a third of the livings being of the value of £5 or less, and ninety per cent. of them less than £26; and these stipends were to support married men. The remedies adopted were the uniting of benefices and the partial restoration of tithing in kind. The King himself was sympathetic, and did not rob the Church as his predecessors had done, but restored ecclesiastical property where he could in order to help. Bancroft's successor, Abbott, was a very different type of man. He was made Archbishop because James wanted someone whose episcopal pretensions would not be too high and who would therefore be able the more easily to win over the Scotch to his proposal for a revived episcopacy. Abbott was an excellent man for that purpose, but in other respects he did not fit in so well with James's schemes, and proved so fierce a Puritan that he refused to read the Declaration of Sports in 1618. But he was disliked even by the Puritans, and only widened the breach that Bancroft was beginning to heal. His position was made more difficult by a tragic accident in which he had the misfortune to kill a keeper with his cross-bow in 1621. He was extricated from his difficulties by James, who appointed a commission of bishops to inquire into the matter, and they restored him to all his functions. Some later nominees to bishoprics, however, found the position still so awkward as to refuse to be consecrated by him. But the leading figure in the Church of that day was undoubtedly Lancelot Andrewes, who would certainly have succeeded Bancroft as Archbishop if his views on the divine right of bishops had not been so exalted. Elizabeth had wanted to make him Bishop of Salisbury, but he had refused as a protest against the rapacity with which the Queen was confiscating the revenues of sees to fill her own pocket. Under James he became Bishop successively of Chichester, Ely, and Winchester. He loved everything pertaining to worship from the smallest prayer to the last candle. His *Preces Privatae* have become a classic of devotion, and in his private chapel he restored a dignified ceremonial which became a pattern for cathedrals. As a scholar he had no equal in the English Church. He knew fifteen languages, and attracted Isaac Casaubon, the best classical scholar in Europe, to England and converted him to Anglicanism. Andrewes was called upon to enter into a controversy with Roman scholars.

Cardinal Bellarmine had attacked the English Oath of Allegiance, and James, 'the wisest fool in Christendom', had seen fit to answer the attack himself. Bellarmine replied in the name of his chaplain Tortus. James could not answer a chaplain and Andrewes was called in. In his *Tortura Torti* he takes up the position that the Royal Supremacy is not a taking of papal authority and giving it to the King, and that in any case papal authority is not necessary to the Catholic faith, because it is not one of those things that have been held always, everywhere, and by all. Thus Andrewes helped to maintain English theology on that high level to which Jewel and Hooker had already raised it.

Charles I, who came to the throne in 1625, carried even further than his father the insistence on the divine right. The theological discussions of the Synod of Dort had their echoes in England, and the bulk of the superior clergy were both Arminian and Erastian. This coincided with Charles's own views, and the breach with the Puritans quickly widened. On the whole the poor people sympathised with the clergy, because they valued the old religious teaching and the frequency of the old saints' days and holidays. The middle classes, on the other hand, developed a gloomy religion, which enabled them to keep the poor more closely set upon their tasks, to amass wealth for themselves, and to exchange the old religious feasts for the sole enjoyment of the pleasures of the table. More and more dissatisfaction was expressed with the fixed hours and orderly services of the Church, and separatism increased by leaps and bounds. Charles was not the man to deal with such a situation. He had no power to conciliate opponents. He was reserved and obstinate, with an inordinate conceit of himself. He might have made an excellent country gentleman, and was at his best in the bosom of his family. But his peculiar views on the kingship encouraged him to aim at getting his own way at all costs, and he tried to play off opponents against each other by a tortuous diplomacy which ruined his credit, and made him in effect a really bad king.

His obstinacy was early shown in the case of Richard Montagu. This man had had difficulties in his parish with Roman controversialists, who had identified the Anglican theology with general Protestant teaching and attacked both in *A Gag for the New Gospel*. Montagu replied in *A New Gag for an Old Goose*, separating sharply between Anglicanism and Puritanism, and adopting the now common line of Anglican apologetic that while Rome was by no means to be identified with antichrist, she had nevertheless greatly erred. This defence was by no means pleasing to the well-to-do laity, who accused him of trying to restore Romanism in disguise, and the House of Commons imprisoned him. Charles must needs take the opportunity of making him his chaplain, and ultimately appointed him Bishop of Chichester. Thus the King was definitely at feud with Parliament and the Puritans, and he emphasised the difference by prefixing a declaration to the Articles in 1628 to prevent a Calvinist explanation being foisted upon them, demanding that they should be accepted in 'the plain and full meaning thereof'. This he followed up the next year by dissolving Parliament altogether, and for the next eleven years he ruled by a personal despotism. In this attitude he had no support from the Archbishop. Abbott was in disgrace because he would not accept the theory of divine right as embodied in the statement put out by another of the clergy that 'subjects must render a passive obedience when they could not give an active one'. In 1633 he was succeeded by Laud.

Much controversy has raged around the character of William Laud. Oxford, at least, always holds him in grateful remembrance as the President of S. John's who built a new quadrangle for his college, and as the Chancellor who gave new statutes to the University and proved a munificent benefactor to the Bodleian Library and the University Press. He had already achieved fame as the opponent of the Jesuit Fisher, against whom he appealed from the Pope to the present position of the Greek Church and to a future General Council, thus reinforcing the Anglo-Catholicism that was characteristic of the Caroline divines. He was the confessor and chief ecclesiastical adviser of Charles during Abbott's disgrace, and had been successively Bishop of S. David's, Bath and Wells, and London, before he succeeded to Canterbury. He was very successful in winning the adherence of Roman Catholics, and gives a list of twenty-two whom he brought over to the English Church, including Chillingworth, the author of *The Religion of Protestants*. As a result of his efforts after reunion the Pope offered him a cardinal's hat, but he refused 'until Rome should be other than she is'. The Roman agent, Dom Leander, suggested that the Pope would be willing to allow clerical marriage, communion in both kinds, the English liturgy, and conditional re-ordination. As Archbishop, Laud showed himself a sincere if somewhat harsh reformer, using the High Commission Court to press his ideas of moral and liturgical decency on rich and poor alike. He helped to drive the courtier bishops from London to reside in their dioceses, and restored to its proper condition S. Paul's Cathedral, which had become little more than an alley on Change. His strictness no doubt helped to hasten the coming disasters, but at least he tried to preserve Charles from some of his rash actions.

From 1633 the course of events was swift and dramatic. The re-issue of the *Book of Sports* aroused a fury of resentment, and the cropping of the ears of recalcitrant Puritans, like Prynne, did nothing to improve matters. In 1637 an ill-timed attempt was made to force the Prayer Book on Scotland, and the legend of Jenny Geddes hurling the stool at the head of the preacher in S. Giles's, Edinburgh, is sufficient indication of the way in which it was received. The next year the Scots signed a National Covenant to free themselves from foreign interference in religion, and by 1639 they were in open rebellion. In 1640 Charles was compelled to summon first the Short and then the Long Parliament, and lost considerable prestige through the impeachment and death of his friend Strafford. Against Laud's advice the King kept Convocation sitting after the dissolution of the Short Parliament, and passed new canons and the notorious Etcetera Oath, which tried to retain the principle of episcopacy by pledging people to preserve the government of the Church by 'archbishops, bishops, deans, and archdeacons, etc.' The canons were naturally declared illegal by the Long Parliament, and Laud, whose share in them gave an opportunity for the expression of all the pent-up animosity he had aroused, was impeached and sent to the Tower. In 1641 came the Grand Remonstrance.

Pym in this appeal to the nation presented a long recital of the illegal acts of the King and desired the exclusion of the bishops from the House of Lords. Some went farther, and demanded the total abolition, root and branch, of the episcopacy. This produced a division in the ranks, nearly half of the members resenting the attack on the Church and going over to the King's side. The Royalists were dubbed Cavaliers, and the Puritans, from their close-cropped heads, Roundheads. The debate on the Remonstrance was indecisive, but the High Commission Court was abolished, and in the next year, by the Clerical Disabilities Act, the clergy were excluded from Parliament. In 1642 the Civil War began. Parliament, in order to gain the support of the Scotch troops, was constrained to accept the Solemn League and Covenant, and in accordance with its terms passed an Act for the abolition of episcopacy in 1643. Two years later an Assembly met at Westminster, drew up a Confession of Faith and a Catechism, and a *Directory of Worship*. The Prayer Book was forbidden, and for fifteen years the Church of England had no legal rights. Cromwell rose to power as the ablest cavalry leader of his time, being more than a match even for Prince Rupert at Marston Moor. Charles was completely beaten, and by a political blunder of the first magnitude was executed in 1649. The next day appeared the *Eikon Basilike*, which displayed to the world the truly religious character of the King and his inward life of devotion. Its actual author was John Gauden, the Dean of Bocking, one of Charles's chaplains, who by its means started a revulsion of feeling that worked slowly to its inevitable conclusion during the time of the Commonwealth.

The rise of Oliver Cromwell marks a change from the period of religious controversy to that of trade rivalry. He was himself a deeply religious man, permitting no outrages on the part of his troops and inflicting a fine for every oath. But when, by his building up of the fleet, he had constituted himself the European champion of Protestantism and had terrified even the Pope by his threat to bring English guns against the castle of S. Angelo, his scheme for a great Protestant alliance was defeated by the English

SEVENTEENTH CENTURY IN ENGLAND

trade rivalry against the Dutch. Nor could he command universal Protestant adherence even at home. He himself was not a Presbyterian. His friend Milton had coined the famous phrase that 'new Presbyter is but old Priest writ large'. The Presbyterians had been glad of the support of his army, but had intended to punish his soldiers as sectaries, once the deliverance was secure. He was himself an Independent, desiring to separate the policy of Church and State and allowing each congregation its own self-government with no other bond between them than that of brotherly love. But 'he valued dogmatic nicety as little in religion as he valued constitutional precision in politics'. Consequently, when he was made Lord Protector in 1653, he was ready to grant religious liberty on a basis that included all Puritans and even Jews. By the Instrument of Government he granted toleration to all except Popery, Prelacy (i.e. the Church of England), and Licentiousness (i.e. the tenets of the Antinomians).

The lot of the Anglicans was hard. A Commission of Triers was instituted, consisting of thirty-eight persons, whose duty was to examine all candidates for benefices, and they were followed by others who examined those already in possession. By these means most of the clergy were dispossessed, and the Triers even managed to exclude Dr. Pococke, the greatest Orientalist in Europe. In 1655 appeared a Proclamation forbidding the ejected clergy to act as schoolmasters or chaplains, or to preach, administer the sacraments, or use the Prayer Book. Many of the clergy with their families were driven into destitution, many died in prison or on their way to slavery. By the Humble Petition and Advice the Protectorate became almost regal. Independency was practically established. The work of destruction in the churches, intermitted since Edward VI's reign, was renewed. S. Asaph Cathedral became a stable for the postmaster, the horses feeding from the bishop's throne and drinking from the font, while Cromwell's own troopers used the choir of S. Paul's as a stable. Christmas and other Church feasts were forbidden, dancing was punishable, marriage became a merely civil contract. Personal religion of the old sort was still kept alive through the publication of *The Whole Duty of Man* in 1658, a work probably written by Dr. Stern, Master of Jesus, Cambridge, and afterwards Archbishop of York. That year Cromwell died, and in many places the people began to fetch their parsons back into the church to pray straightway from the Book of Common Prayer.

Cromwell's son Richard proved unequal to the Protectorate, and after a year of anarchy Charles II was invited to the throne by a combination of Royalists, Presbyterians, and that part of the army which believed in the authority of the civil power. He was half-infidel, half-Romanist, but in the Declaration of Breda, 1660, he promised liberty to tender consciences, undertaking that 'no man shall be called in question for differences of opinion in matters of religion'. The rising tide of Royalism and Anglicanism made toleration impossible, but it is a thousand pities that the Church was persuaded to visit punishment for its recent sufferings on the head of its opponents. Laud's friend, Juxon, was made Archbishop of Canterbury. He was another ex-President of S. John's, who had become successively Bishop of Hereford and of London, and had ministered to Charles I at his execution. He crowned Charles II, and with his universally admired tact and gentleness tried to keep both Church and King in the path of the Laudian reform. But in the profligate character of the King he was bitterly disappointed.

The first care was to restore the *status quo*. The Convention Parliament of 1660 ordered the restoration of the deprived clergy. They came back to the number of about a thousand, and for the next century and a half squire and parson were to be the leading figures of English parochial life. The Commons would allow no toleration, refusing to accept a Declaration of Indulgence, and the same year the saintly but bigoted author of the *Pilgrim's Progress*, John Bunyan, was imprisoned. The bishops had returned to their sees without waiting for the authorisation of Parliament, but sixteen new ones had to be consecrated. They were restored to their position in the House of Lords, and Parliament assured the Church in the possession of all ecclesiastical lands as they were held before the outbreak of the Civil War. In 1661 another attempt was made at comprehension at the Savoy Conference, when twelve bishops met twelve

Puritans under the presidency of Sheldon, Bishop of London. It broke down under the extreme demands of the Puritans, who had forgotten nothing, but repeated all the old objections, Baxter showing how far they wished to go by producing in a few hours a *Directory of Worship* with which he proposed to supersede the Book of Common Prayer. Convocation, indeed, revised the Prayer Book, making about six hundred minor alterations, but leaving it in effect the same as it was in 1559. The slackness of the previous years necessitated the insertion of a form for the baptism 'of such as were of riper years', and the Black Rubric was reinserted with the significant change of a denial of a Corporal Presence in the Eucharist, rather than of a Real and Essential Presence. This meant the abandonment of the policy of comprehension. By the last of the Acts of Uniformity, issued the following year, all ministers were compelled to use the Prayer Book, those not episcopally ordained were to be so, and all were to make a declaration repudiating the Covenant and the bearing of arms against the King. The Puritan ministers remained staunch, and on S. Bartholomew's Day two thousand of them left their parishes and helped to form the Dissenting congregations that were to play so large a part in the English life of the future.

Dissent received a noteworthy accession at this time in the Society of Friends, sometimes called Quakers from the fact that they shivered and shook under religious excitement. Their leader was George Fox, who began his ministry in 1647. His teaching was a protest against the formalism into which he believed that the Reformation sects and the historic Church had alike fallen. For a purely spiritual religion it was necessary to reject all creeds, sacraments, liturgies, and professional ministries, and to rely solely upon the inner light from God shining in the heart of the individual. The Friends had their headquarters at Swarthmore Hall, the home of Margaret Fell, a well-to-do widow, whom Fox married. Their most important convert was William Penn, who, obtaining the grant of Pennsylvania from Charles II in recognition of the services performed by his father, the Admiral Sir William Penn, established there in 1682 a colony where might be found that freedom of worship which England denied.

For the churchmen a period of intellectual and spiritual revival set in, which made of the Caroline divines a galaxy of all the talents and of the period a kind of Golden Age for the English Church. Two saintly friends had been removed by death before the late troubles began Of these George Herbert is the better known, both for some of his hymns and for the *Priest to the Temple*, in which he stored for future generations the wealth of spiritual wisdom that he had garnered in his little cure of Bemerton, near Salisbury. Here the tiny church still stands to remind one of the time when even the ploughmen would wait a moment at their work while 'Mr. Herbert's saint's-bell rang to prayers', and when most of his parishioners and many gentlemen of the neighbourhood would join the congregation each day at ten and four. His friend, Nicholas Ferrar, was showing himself a good business man in the Virginia Company, when plague drove his family to Little Gidding in Huntingdonshire and they settled down to a kind of family monastic life, combining mysticism with ordered hours of prayer and work. After the death of Nicholas in 1637, the family continued their semi-conventual life, but they were bitterly attacked in a pamphlet on 'the Arminian Nunnery'. Perhaps the fact that Nicholas had once been a member of the Royalist Parliament, and that the King himself had honoured Little Gidding by more than one visit, increased the animosity against them and led to the attack on the house by the Parliamentary soldiers in 1646, which ended in its pillage and the destruction of his voluminous writings. These two men show the Laudian revival on its most spiritual side, and it says much for the work of Laud that after the Restoration there were enough good and able men to carry on the work. We have no space to dwell on the work of men like Sheldon, who succeeded Juxon as Archbishop of Canterbury and built the Sheldonian Theatre at Oxford; nor of Pearson, Bishop of Chester, who wrote the *Exposition of the Creed;* nor of Bull of S. David's, whose work in the *Harmonia Apostolica* was so warmly praised by Bossuet. But perhaps the greatest of them was Jeremy Taylor (1613-67), who, after being chaplain to Charles I and a prisoner during the Commonwealth, became Bishop of Down and Connor at the Restoration. It is said that there has been 'no greater master of rhetoric in English literature'. He wrote the *Liberty of Prophesying*, and his deep spirituality appears in the *Holy Living* and *Holy Dying*. In the *Ductor Dubitantium* he gave us practically the only systematic treatise on spiritual direction that has appeared in Anglican circles until recent times.

But while the reign was thus glorious for the Church, it had a dark side for the Puritans and Romanists. Against the former was published the notorious Clarendon Code, a series of three Acts intended to put down Nonconformity and receiving their name from the fact that they were issued under the Lord Chancellor Clarendon. The Corporation Act (1661) compelled all members of Corporations to take an oath against the Covenant and to receive Holy Communion according to the Anglican rite. This was the beginning of an appalling abuse of the Sacrament for test purposes. The Conventicle Act (1664) forbade more than five people above the number of the household to assemble for worship outside the church. This was due to Parliament's fear that such gatherings might help in fomenting insurrection, and was enforced by giving the Justices of the Peace power to enter private houses and arrest inmates. The Five Mile Act (1665) forbade preachers to come within five miles of any town where they had formerly worked, unless they had taken the oath against arms. These Acts comprise the Clarendon Code. The measures against Romanists were affected by the growing fear of Parliament that the King intended to introduce Roman Catholicism into the country. In 1670, by the secret Treaty of Dover with Louis XIV, he agreed to establish the Pope in England with French aid. This was the culmination of a long intrigue and was dictated by Charles's hope that Rome would be his best assistant in fastening despotism upon the country. Two years later he issued a new Declaration of Indulgence. It was said that this was a mere fulfilment of the promise made in the Declaration of Breda. It ordered that, since the penal statutes against the Puritans had failed, they were to be allowed to worship as they wished and that Roman Catholics were to have the privilege of carrying on their own worship in their houses. But even the Protestants suspected this as a concession to the Romanists, and on the protest of the Commons the Declaration was withdrawn. Parliament pursued its advantage. The Test Act of 1673 represents the triumph of the Commons. By this all holders of civil and military office were ordered to take the Oath of Supremacy, to declare against transubstantiation, and to receive Holy Communion according to the Anglican rite. The rest of the reign was an attempt to prevent a Romanist succession to the throne. It was during this time that the opposition earned the title of Whigs, and the supporters of the King were called Tories. Through an alleged Popish Plot, revealed by Titus Oates in 1678, the Whigs stirred up popular frenzy and procured the execution of many Roman Catholics. The Tories retaliated by producing the story of the Rye-house Plot and persecuting the Whigs. The King won in these intrigues. He secured the succession to his brother, and on his deathbed professed his adherence to the Roman Church.

CHAPTER XI

THE EXPANSION OF CHRISTENDOM

It has often happened in the history of the Church that the greatest progress has been made in the times of greatest tumult. As a witty divine has said, 'the Church, like some political parties, is at her best in opposition'. Even when the tumult has been of her own creating it has often given her an impulse to fresh endeavour. This was clearly exemplified in the sixteenth and seventeenth centuries, when, in spite of the conflicts in Europe, more converts were being won to the faith than at any time since the conversion of the barbarians. During the intervening thousand years the world had presented itself in the guise of a battlefield, with Christians on one side and Mohammedans on the other, and in such circumstances little missionary work was possible. But in the new age discoveries had been made which dwarfed the significance of the old division and opened new worlds for the Church to conquer.

The glory of the successful seizure of this opportunity must be awarded to the followers of the counter-Reformation. There are, indeed, some clear reasons why the Protestants were long in taking up any share in this task. The original discoveries of new lands were made by the great Catholic countries of Spain and Portugal. Protestants were busy consolidating their conquests at home and spreading the knowledge of the Bible in their immediate neighbourhood. They did not begin to come into contact with the heathen until the development of overseas trade by the Dutch and English. But there was a deeper and sadder reason in the fact that the Reformers were not themselves convinced either of the value or of the necessity of foreign missionary work. It is true that Erasmus could sigh: 'Would that God had accounted me worthy to die in such a holy work,' and Grotius could urge young men to take up a missionary calling; but most of the men who accepted whole-heartedly the reformed opinions believed that the heathen had had their chance of receiving the gospel in the Apostolic Age, and that, having rejected it then, they had lost it for ever. Melanchthon, Zwingli, Calvin, Beza, Bucer, seemed to look forward to a gradual narrowing of the evangelical limits until at last the end of the world should come. And in this they but followed Luther, who thought that the Moslems were irreclaimable enemies by means of whom God visited His wrath upon the sins of Christendom. 'Nor do I go about with the notion that the Jews can ever be converted; that is impossible.'

If the earlier period had been the age when missionary work was done by great apostolic men, often working with little support from their home base, this period is to be regarded as the age when Christian Governments interested themselves in the work and made themselves, at least to some extent, responsible for it. This, indeed, was one of the incentives with which they sent out their costly expeditions of discovery. If the inspiring motive was commerce, that of evangelisation was not far behind. The explorers who found the new route to India were crusaders, coming upon the Moslem from behind and wresting his conquests from him. The crosses with which they had marked the slow stages of their advance along the west coast of Africa claimed the land for Christ. Even when Henry the Navigator, finding it impossible otherwise to pay his way, started the dreadful slave-trade, the Pope who commissioned him to the task believed that it would end in the conversion of the negroes. Columbus believed that he had more to offer than the conversion of a few slaves, though that incentive was not omitted. He would be answering the invitation of the Grand Khan, who had explicitly asked for missionaries to teach his people the doctrines of Christianity: thus Spain, taking advantage of papal slackness, would meet the rapidly approaching end of the world with the conversion of Tartary as the brightest jewel in her crown. That is how Columbus won the help

THE EXPANSION OF CHRISTENDOM 187

of Queen Isabella, and why Franciscans accompanied him on his voyages.

The conversion of America thus begins with its discovery. The missionaries appear as the champions of the natives. Las Casas, a Dominican, arriving in the West Indies and seeing how the natives wilted and died under the conditions of the slavery to which they were exposed, resorted to the Spanish Court and got it made illegal to enslave any Indians other than those who had levied an unrighteous war. Later he tried to save them by suggesting the importation of negroes, an expedient he was soon bitterly to regret. That was in 1511. Ten years later Cortez conquered Mexico. Great as he was, not merely in his character of conqueror, but in that of statesman and cultivator of the new lands, his ability in the work of civilisation was easily out-distanced by that of the missionaries. In Paraguay the Jesuits settled in 1586, and, protecting the Indians both from the vices of the settlers and from their raids, succeeded in building up a family life of which religion was the centre and industry the characteristic. The Fathers were looked up to as the heads of the community; there was no private property, but the lives of the people were passed amid beautiful common gardens and immense ranches. In 1648 permission was given from Madrid for the natives to carry arms, and henceforth they were free from molestation. The colony grew until it included thirty-three garden cities and a territory about the size of Great Britain. But the system contained the germs of evil. The Jesuits tried to conceal from Europe the immense wealth that they were accumulating, but the Portuguese knew in 1731 that it amounted to four million ducats a year. Naturally the jealousy of both Spain and Portugal was aroused; it seemed absurd to have this rich and upstart state growing in semi-independence under Jesuit government within their territories. In 1750 they resolved to drive the Jesuits out and govern the country between them. The missionaries encouraged their converts to resist, which they did with marked courage for six years. In the end the Jesuits were recalled. The Indians, who had been so closely shepherded, proved to be utterly unstable without the support of their masters, and the complete collapse of this fine work forms, perhaps, the most melancholy tragedy of missionary history. Although Franciscans and Dominicans, as well as the Jesuits, had already done great work in Mexico, Peru, and other parts of South America, the same weakness seems to have been inherent in the methods employed. This weakness may account for the general estimation that the Church in South America is still the least satisfactory part of the Roman communion.

It was the French who introduced Christianity to North America. Champlain explored the S. Lawrence in 1603 and founded Quebec in 1608. He regarded the conversion of the Indians as his prime duty, and was assisted in his efforts by Franciscans and Jesuits. Difficulties arose out of the jealousy of the Iroquois against the Hurons, whom the French had made their friends. The first missions among the Hurons were almost destroyed by the Iroquois in 1649. The bravery of the missionaries among these tribes could not be surpassed. 'I could not have believed', said Bressani of his sufferings at the hands of the Iroquois, 'that a man was so hard to kill.' Yet when Dutch traders ransomed him and sent him back to France, he only waited for his wounds to heal and then returned, maimed and disfigured, to the work. Père Marquette worked among the Illinois; a see was founded at Montreal in 1658, and the Ursulines did a great educational work among the women and girls. The Roman Church among the French Canadians is still a witness to the apostolic zeal of the early workers for religion, who inherited the ideals of the counter-Reformation. But already, in 1620, the Pilgrim Fathers had arrived in New Plymouth, and Massachusetts was to be the scene of Protestant missions. Their religion was Congregationalist and their theology strongly Calvinistic. One of their ministers, John Eliot, earned for himself the title 'Apostle of the Indians', translating the Bible for them and establishing schools where they might learn agriculture and various crafts. His work attracted the attention of the Long Parliament in 1647, and Cromwell himself made a scheme for the training of missionaries, but died before carrying it into effect. The Church of England planted its first mission in Virginia, and £100, given by Sir Walter Raleigh to spread the gospel there, is the first recorded

THE EXPANSION OF CHRISTENDOM 189

missionary subscription. The Rev. Robert Hunt, who had resigned his living at Reculver to accompany the colonists, was the first Anglican priest to celebrate the Divine Mysteries in those parts, which he did at Jamestown in 1607. The first college was opened there in 1700, in buildings erected after designs by Sir Christopher Wren. The work was also developing in New York, and Laud in 1638 had intended to send a bishop, but was prevented by the troubles in which he became involved. In 1686 King James tried to regularise the position of the clergy by ordering that every officiating minister should obtain a certificate from Canterbury, but two years later the supervision of the clerical duties in the American colonies was put into the hands of the Bishop of London. It was not until there had been a revival of religion in Europe that really great progress was made in the evangelisation of North America by members of the reformed churches.

In India the natives received the explorers as friends, and Vasco da Gama at first thought that the Hindu gods were Christian saints. Yet the Portuguese soon learned to believe that a Christian has no duties towards a pagan, and to destroy the natural force of international law by opening a way for their missionaries and merchants with fire and sword. Goa was their principal settlement and thither Francis Xavier came in 1541. Franciscans and Dominicans had arrived before him, a see had been founded in 1534, and a fine cathedral with a seminary for training native priests had been already built. He soon pressed on to the unevangelised pearl fisheries. His methods were of the simplest. Not having learnt the language, he worked through interpreters. On arriving at a village he would ring a bell to summon the inhabitants, and proceed to teach them the Lord's Prayer, Hail Mary, Creed, and Commandments in the vulgar tongue; and then he would baptise as many as were willing, going on till sheer fatigue compelled him to desist. Unfortunately the Inquisition was introduced, and they had it working, complete with triennial *auto-da-fé*, in Goa by the seventeenth century. Xavier's own phrase, *feci Christianos*, is sufficiently suggestive of his short and wholesale way of converting the heathen. No wonder that he professed his despair of ever making real Christians in India. In 1654 the Inquisitors actually went so far as to burn the Metropolitan of the Syrian Christians. It was not altogether a bad thing when the Dutch tried to deprive the Portuguese of their Goanese possessions.

Farther south there was no such secular assistance, and the Jesuits proceeded by other methods. In 1606 Robert de Nobili aimed at getting hold of the highest caste by living in Madura as a Brahmin. He adopted native dress, and for a year lived in a grass hut on herbs and water. He pushed this method so far as to incorporate the caste system into Christianity and to forge a deed in which evidence was given that the Jesuits were descended from the god Brahma. He died in 1656, but the method was still pursued in 1673 by John de Britto. Its results were seen when the same dancers accompanied the processions of the heathen goddess and of the Blessed Virgin. An even worse consequence was that the missionaries, in order not to offend the Brahmins, had to refuse the consolations of religion to the pariahs. The French Capuchins were naturally incensed at this absurd and dishonest syncretism, and strife with the Jesuits grew strong at Pondicherry. At length Pope Benedict XIV interfered, and in 1744 condemned all resort to artifice, and finally the Jesuit mission was formally suppressed.

In Malabar a peculiar position arose on account of the presence there of the Syrian Christians, who were a relic of the old Nestorian Church. In 1599 they had submitted to the Roman missionaries at the Synod of Diamper. The Romans adopted their usual custom in attempting to suppress the Syrian liturgy. When the Dutch captured Ceylon in 1656, the Syrians applied to Jerusalem and Cairo for bishops. The result was a split between the two creeds of Nestorianism and Monophysitism. The Lutherans, who now came into the country, tried to effect a union with them, but were repulsed, and thereupon set up independent missions.

Internecine quarrels among the missionaries marred the story of individual heroism in the Far East. Cochin China

THE EXPANSION OF CHRISTENDOM 141

was the scene of French efforts. Alexandre de Rhodes arrived in 1627, and within seven years converted 30,000 people. Jesuits joined in the work and drove out the French mission by their jealousy, but bishops were appointed, and in 1684 Louis XIV officially invited the King of Siam to accept Christianity. He agreed to the sending of a mission, but after four years the natives, who resented foreign intrusion, revolted, and the King and his Minister lost their lives. Nevertheless the work continued and still had its native seminary at the end of the century.

In China itself the Jesuit Ricci practised much the same methods as had been used by his brethren in India. From 1578 to 1610 he set himself to understand the Chinese and to win their confidence. Knowing the reverence they paid to learning, he made himself thoroughly familiar with their language and literature, and then showed them how much he was in advance of them in astronomy and mathematics. Thus he came in time to win the confidence of the Emperor himself, who gave him every facility for spreading his faith. But Ricci tried to make that faith acceptable by allowing his converts to retain their ancestor-worship, finding in it an easy path to the veneration of the saints. Ricci's successors were joined by Dominicans, Franciscans, and Capuchins, and this led to quarrels, for the Dominicans referred the question of countenancing Chinese customs to the Inquisition at Rome. The judgment given was indecisive, but the matter came up repeatedly in later years, and was made a subject of sharp contention between the Jesuits on the one side, and the French missionaries backed up by the Sorbonne on the other. Successive Popes gave conflicting decisions, and the matter roused great debate in Europe. In the meantime the number of Chinese converts increased, till by the end of the seventeenth century there were as many as 300,000. But this caused the officials of Fuh-kien to complain to the Emperor, and in 1746 he ordered that the missionaries should be collected together and transported. This was the beginning of a proscription of Christianity that lasted till the middle of the nineteenth century.

The greatest triumph of the Jesuits was in Japan, where they were said to have gained nearly a million converts

142 HISTORY OF THE MODERN CHURCH

in fifty years, a number which some of them regarded as compensating for the loss of England. Francis Xavier landed at Kagoshima in 1549, and although he never learnt the language he managed to spend two years persuading people in considerable numbers to be baptised. One of his companions, Juan Fernandez, a rich silk merchant of Cordova, who had given up everything to undertake mission work as a layman, was more successful as a linguist, and it is to him that the early conversions were largely due. Dominicans and Franciscans here also share in the glory of having won many thousands to believe in Christ. It was a suspicion of disloyalty that brought about the beginning of the end. The Japanese officials were led to believe that the work of the missionaries might be only a preliminary to an attempt on the part of Spain or Portugal to annex their country. 'First the missionary, then the trader, then the soldier': this was to become a common argument against missions. In 1598 a persecution began with the crucifixion of twenty-six Christians and culminated in 1638 with the slaughter of 17,000 others who had tried to defend themselves in the castle of Shimabara. It was against Portugal especially that the fiercest part of this persecution was levelled, and that fact is a sufficient indication of the evil that may result from too close an association of a Government with missionary propaganda.

But the day of Government interest in missions for selfish purposes of exploitation was not to last much longer, and another method in missionary organisation was already waiting to make itself felt. The new period would be one in which the initiative would be taken, not by Governments, but by societies. Voluntary associations with this end in view, as distinct from the religious Orders, began with the founding in 1622 of the Congregation *de Propaganda Fide*, by Pope Gregory XV. This is the great organisation in Rome which still directs the missionary enterprise of that Church. To this was added, in 1627, the College of the Propaganda to act as a seminary for the training of missionaries. This did not prevent the French from establishing their own society, the *Société des Missions Etrangères*, which they did in 1658. The object was both national and evangelistic. De la Motte Lambert, one of its two founders, spent his life in the Cochin China mission. The other, François Pallu, extended French trade, as well as the gospel, by persuading the Ministers Mazarin and Colbert to found a French East India Company and give the missionaries free passages in its vessels. The first English society to be formed was the New England Company, founded by the Long Parliament in 1649, which still maintains its work in the Indian reserve in Canada. But the most important step in the history of English missions was taken in 1698, when the Society for Promoting Christian Knowledge was founded by the zeal of Dr. Bray, with the object of providing Christian literature and promoting Christian education both at home and abroad. In 1701 Dr. Bray was also instrumental in getting founded a daughter society, the Society for the Propagation of the Gospel in Foreign Parts, with the two-fold aim of ministering to English settlers across the seas and of spreading the gospel among the heathen with whom the settlers came in contact. As the only English colonies at that time were in North America and the West Indies, this meant, in effect, that the Society would work on behalf of the settlers in those parts, their negro slaves, and the Red Indians. It was these societies that inaugurated the era of modern missionary effort, but the time when they were to do their best work was not yet.

CHAPTER XII

THE EASTERN CHURCH

IN the last chapter we spoke only of missions undertaken by the Western half of Christendom, but it must not be forgotten that considerable missionary work was accomplished by at least some branches of the Eastern Church. In order to understand the opportunities and limitations of this work it will be necessary to sketch the history of the Eastern Church from the sixteenth to the eighteenth centuries.

Even before the Great Schism between East and West in 1054, Eastern Christendom was not itself united. The greater part of it was Orthodox, but there were considerable sections which for nationalist and theological reasons had broken off from the Church of the old Eastern Empire. Thus the Assyrians (East Syrian) were Nestorian, while the Armenians, the Jacobites (West Syrians), the Copts (Egyptian), and the Abyssinians were Monophysite. These had no dealings with the Orthodox, and for the present must be left out of our consideration. After the fall of Constantinople in 1453, the great Orthodox Church of the East found itself soon divided politically into two parts, as it fell within the Turkish Empire or the Russian. This vast body of believers never possessed the compact unity of jurisdiction which the Western Church enjoyed under the highly centralised authority of the Pope and the Roman Curia. It consisted of a number of autocephalous or independent Churches, with common beliefs and customs, all looking upon the Patriarch of Constantinople as their leading or oecumenical bishop. It was characteristic of these Churches that they associated themselves very closely with the secular government, and it is therefore convenient to consider them as they came under the civil jurisdiction of Turkey or Russia.

It seems strange at first sight that the Turks, with their well-known animosity to all non-Moslems, should have tolerated a Christian organisation in their territories at all. But the Turks drew a distinction between complete unbelievers, whom they called Kaffirs and condemned to extermination or conversion, and half-believers, like the Jews and Christians, who reverenced the Scriptures and, being 'People of the Book', might be given some modified protection. Among the Christians the Turks disdained to recognise differences of creed, but only of nationality. Consequently they regarded the Orthodox as the Rum-millet, or Roman nation—that is, the representatives of the old Byzantine Empire. The Turkish Government quickly realised that the clergy might be of considerable service to it in organising this conquered empire and reducing it to taxation. When Mohammed II entered Constantinople the Patriarchate was vacant. He insisted upon an immediate election, and himself invested the chosen prelate with the crozier and confirmed him in the privileges of his office. To these were added a certain secular authority, for the Oecumenical Patriarch became the intermediary between the Turkish Government and his co-religionists, having authority even over his fellow-patriarchs of Alexandria, Antioch, and Jerusalem. Naturally he had to pay dearly for the privilege, and simony became a besetting sin of the whole hierarchy, for each tried to recoup himself for his own payments out of the pockets of the rest. This meant that ultimately the burden fell upon the people. The evil was increased by the fact that the Patriarchate became closely associated with the Phanar, as the Greek quarter in Constantinople was called, after the old lighthouse near the site of which was the cathedral church. It was only the wealthy Phanariot Greeks who had enough money to buy ecclesiastical offices, and they used the opportunity to send members of their own close corporation to occupy responsible posts far and near. This involved a process of Hellenisation that embittered many of the Balkan peoples.

The sufferings of the subject nations were increased by the Turkish habit of taking Christian boys and training them as Janizaries or New Soldiery. Once every four years all the boys between six and nine years of age were paraded before the officers, and a fifth of the number were taken to Constantinople to be brought up as Mohammedans and to be enlisted in the Janizaries. Although they did not always forget their homes, the boys seem to have remained faithful to their new religion, as they certainly did to their masters. Thus was produced the flower of the Turkish Army until 1676, when the Central Government grew too slack to collect this human tribute.

The Latin Church was not slow to take advantage of the disabilities under which the Orthodox were suffering, and their designs were ably seconded by French diplomacy. The French had long been on good terms with the Turks, seeing in them a useful ally who could take their Austrian foes in the rear. It has already been pointed out that the Turks could take no cognisance of differences in Christian creeds, but only of nationalities. Nevertheless they were quite ready to strengthen their own position by fostering animosities among their Christian subjects, and were very willing to afford special protection to religious persons and places favoured by the French King. In the time of Louis XIV this protection was extended, not only to the holy places in Palestine and to the Jesuits and Capuchins acting as the King's chaplains, but also to such widely separated native bodies owning spiritual allegiance to the Pope as the Maronites, a body of Lebanon natives who had accepted Catholicism in the days of the Crusades, and the Mirdites, a warrior clan of Roman Catholics in northern Albania. Thus developed the Uniate Churches, which, as the generations passed, assumed considerable proportions.

In such circumstances as these it was natural that there should be some dealings between the Orthodox and the Protestants. In 1559, at the time when Elizabeth was helping to fix the form of the English settlement, we find Melanchthon trying to promote a union between the Lutherans and the Greek Church, and from 1573 to 1581 the same effort was being carried on by the theologians of

THE EASTERN CHURCH 147

Tübingen. But reformed opinions found little place in Orthodox theology before the days of the great Patriarch of Constantinople, Cyril Lucar. He it was who presented Charles I with the *Codex Alexandrinus*, the famous manuscript of the Bible, dating from the middle of the fifth century, which is now in the British Museum. He was attracted by the teaching of Calvin and drew up a Confession of a strongly Calvinistic tone. He was circumvented, not only by the opposition of his own people, but also by the hatred of the Jesuits, who, as we have seen, had French support. Calvinism was at the moment spreading in Russia, and Cyril was accused of stirring up the Cossacks against the Turks. He was strangled by the Janizaries in 1637, and his body thrown into the sea. His views produced a strong reaction in Russia, while in the East itself they were directly responsible for the great Council of Jerusalem in 1672. This Council was actually held at Bethlehem under Dositheos, the Patriarch of Jerusalem. It disowned the Confession of Cyril Lucar, trying to prove that he did not write it and that in any case it could not be called the Confession of the Eastern Church. In its place there was accepted a Confession written by Dositheos himself. Calvinism was repudiated and the doctrine of Transubstantiation was accepted. This 'represents the high-water mark of Roman influence on Greek doctrine'. Soon after this there was some relief from the Turkish oppression. In 1683 John Sobieski broke the long tale of Turkish victories by inflicting upon them a severe defeat when they had besieged Vienna. Venice, which was the great rival of the Turks at sea, took advantage of this to attack the Morea, of which they gained possession in 1687. This was confirmed to them by the Treaty of Carlowitz (1699), which also compelled the Turks to relinquish their hold on Hungary and Transylvania. For the next twenty years Venetian influence was all powerful. Again the Roman Church took advantage of the situation. A Latin hierarchy was introduced, and although it helped further to break up the Orthodox administration, the higher standard set by the clergy of the Roman communion did much to raise the tone of the Orthodox. However, when the Turks returned in force in 1699, the Greeks were unwilling to give their support to the Venetians, and consequently relapsed again under Turkish dominance.

The history of the Church in the Balkan states is taken up with their varying relations to the Patriarch of Constantinople and to the Turkish Government. Bulgaria had lost its national autonomy as long ago as 1393, when the Turks had taken its capital of Tirnovo. It continued to have its own autocephalous Archbishop at Ochrida, but this was of little use to the Bulgars, since none but the Phanariot Greeks could pay enough to the Turks for the post. Consequently they were ecclesiastically as much under the Greeks as they were civilly under the Turks. At last even the semblance of independence was lost, when in 1767 the autocephalous archbishopric was destroyed and the Bulgarian Church was placed under the immediate supervision of Constantinople. Hellenisation was now carried on extensively; the Greek language was enforced in schools and churches, and thence arose the cordial hatred of the Bulgar for the Greek.

In Rumania the process of Hellenisation was carried on with equal vigour, for the Turks, not able to trust the native Hospodars, sold the offices to the Greeks, and as the Rumanians were ecclesiastically subject to the Archbishop of Ochrida they had no protection. In such circumstances they were subjected to a continual fire of temptation from the Roman Catholics of Austria on the one side, and from the Unitarians of Bohemia and Poland on the other. In 1643 George Rakoczy I, of the autonomous principality of Transylvania, tried to turn the whole country Protestant, but failed. In 1685, when Transylvania was united with Roman Catholic Austria, Leopold tried to make the Rumanians accept the papal claims. A synod held in 1697 agreed to do so, and actual union with the Papacy was effected by the Synod of Karlsburg in 1700. But many of the clergy and laity refused to become parties to this defection from the Orthodox faith. The Austrians thereupon started a persecution to drive the people into the Catholic fold, but this was at last stopped by Maria Teresa in 1761, and in the next two centuries the Rumanians at last won the victory in a long drawn-out struggle for freedom.

The Orthodox dislike of Roman Catholicism was most bitterly illustrated in Serbia, where the people in the fifteenth century accepted Turkish rule rather than submit to the Pope. During the period of the great Turkish victories of Belgrade and Mohacs, the Serbians were submitted to the ecclesiastical rule of the Archbishop of Ochrida. They were delivered from this position of dependence by one of their own sons, who had experienced a romantic career. This was Mechmed Sokolovic (Mohammed Sokoli), who had been taken as a boy for the corps of Janizaries and brought up as a Moslem. His abilities won for him the post of Grand Vizier. In his glory he did not forget his old people, but was able to restore to his ancestral Church its independence by giving it a patriarch of its own at Pec. This was in 1557, and for a century the Turks respected the arrangement. But in 1689 the Patriarch was so ill-advised as to listen to the blandishments of Leopold and throw in his lot with the Austrians. The Sultan thereupon destroyed the Patriarchate of Pec, and placed the Serbian Church directly under the Patriarch of Constantinople. From that time the Serbians felt the full force of the exactions of the Phanar, and experienced that process of Hellenisation which was not content with putting Greeks into all the more lucrative posts, but substituted the Greek language for the Old Slavonic in teaching and worship. It says much for the stubbornness of the human will that throughout the period of Turkish domination so large a proportion of the people in the Balkans maintained any semblance of Christianity at all. Only in Bosnia and Montenegro were there conversions to Islam on a large scale, but the results of them still remain.

Throughout this period the true centre of Orthodoxy was not in the Turkish Empire but in Russia. That state of affairs had come about very largely through feminine influence. Just before the end of the fifteenth century, the Russian King, Ivan III, had won for himself an unique influence by triumphing over the Tatars and Lithuanians, and thus reducing to something like order the chaos of rival princedoms that had hitherto prevailed. He was married to Zoe, the daughter of Constantine XIII, the last of the Eastern Roman Emperors. The old Roman Empire had disappeared before the Turk, but Zoe inspired her husband with the idea of resuscitating its fallen glories in Russia. This, in effect, he did. Having made himself the Grand Prince of Moscow, supreme over all the other princes, he united the princedoms into one monarchy, and then acted on the assumption that this monarchy was the heir of the Byzantine Empire and the natural defender of the Orthodox Church. This was a great disappointment to the Papacy, for Zoe had been educated in Rome and it was hoped that with her marriage Roman influence in Moscow would become paramount. But the papal legate, who had intended to make a triumphal procession into the city with a Latin cross borne before him, had to be content with smuggling the obnoxious symbol in a sledge, and Zoe disappointed his expectations by urging on the independent policy of her husband. After the marriage Ivan assumed the title of Tsar (Caesar), and appropriated the double-headed eagle of Byzantium as the Russian emblem. His son, Vassili (Basil), who succeeded him in 1506, was the first to assume the title 'Tsar and Autocrat of all the Russias'. He was, indeed, an autocrat somewhat after the fashion of our own Henry VIII, for having no issue by his first marriage he desired greatly to take a new wife, and at length found a Metropolitan who was willing to pronounce a divorce and to marry him again on condition that the first wife entered a convent. During this time the Russian Church was spiritually subject to Constantinople. Its greatest work was to begin the evangelisation of the north by building monasteries among the wild tribes of those parts. But its condition was backward; it had no interest in the Renaissance or the Reformation, and the only learning it possessed lay between the covers of the books brought in with Zoe.

The one child of Vassili's second marriage became known to history as Ivan the Terrible. He was brought up in the wildest courses by unscrupulous courtiers who wished to keep him a nonentity. But at the age of eighteen he asserted himself and was crowned in 1547. He was checked in his wild career by a prophet-priest, who on the occasion of a terrible fire in Moscow appeared before the prince and told him that it was the scourge of God for his evil deeds. Then for fourteen years he ruled as an enlightened monarch, seeking his country's good. He endeavoured to establish some order in local administration, but the difficulty of obtaining qualified officials made it inevitable that the business should fall into the hands of the central bureaucracy at Moscow. To set in order the Church he summoned the Council of the Hundred Chapters in 1551. This Council tried to do something for education, but the graver question was that of the Church lands. Most of the ecclesiastical property was in the hands of the monasteries. Of these there were two sorts, the Urban, which were set up in the centres of population, and the Desert, which, beginning in solitary places, often attracted population to share in the benefits of their agricultural schemes. Both of these had accumulated considerable properties, until in the middle of the sixteenth century they owned a third of all the available land in Russia. The usual result of increased wealth was seen in the debased lives of the monks. Ivan was desirous of relieving them of some of the means of temptation. All he was able to secure, however, was the annulling of gifts made to the Church during his minority and the restitution of lands ceded without his consent. He was more successful in war, wresting Kazan from the Tatars in 1553, and so turning back the tide of Mohammedan invasion that had so long threatened north-eastern Europe. It is at this point that England enters Russian history, for in that year the English, finding the path of discovery closed to them in the south, had rounded the North Cape, and to their surprise had discovered Russia. The hero of this exploit was Richard Chancellor, who not only negotiated the formation of a trading company between Ivan and Edward VI, but left to posterity a lively account of the religious condition of Russia, noting already the glaring contrast between its fervent religiousness and its debased morality. An even worse contrast is seen in Ivan himself, for the rest of his reign is taken up with accounts of fiendish punishments inflicted upon his people for fancied wrongs, and repeated again and again until one is sick with reading. He seems to have become melancholy mad after the death of his wife. Already suspicious of his *boyars* or nobles, he accused them of poisoning her, and proceeded to take a terrible revenge that spread and widened till it included most of his kingdom.

During the next reign Russia was freed from dependence on Constantinople. This happened in curious circumstances. The Patriarch of Constantinople was in Moscow soliciting alms for his church, whose coffers were so depleted that it could not pay its tribute to the Sultan and had been threatened with suppression. Boris Godounov, the friend of the reigning Tsar Feodor, wished himself to succeed to the throne, and with the assistance of Feodor hit upon a scheme to gain popular favour. This was to obtain the Patriarchate for Russia by inducing the poor prelate to stay in the country and set up his throne at Vladimir. When this plan proved unacceptable, they induced him to yield so far as to consent to the formation of a separate Patriarchate at Moscow. Thus, by the authority of Constantinople itself, Russia was recognised as an autocephalous Church in 1589. Other ecclesiastical events, however, did not run so smoothly. In Poland and the parts of Russia adjacent to it, Jesuit influence was very strong, and was increased by the inefficiency of the Orthodox clergy. Aided by Royal encouragement in Poland itself, the Catholic cause gained in prestige until the Metropolitan of Kiev and other Orthodox bishops were induced to hold a synod at Brest Litovsk in 1595, and make the submission of their Church to the Pope on condition that they were allowed to keep their doctrine, ceremonies, and discipline as aforetime. This was the beginning of a Uniate Church, but it did not carry all the Orthodox with it. The bishops and others who remained faithful excommunicated those who had submitted, and there existed side by side two Churches identical in every respect except their allegiance. The Polish king pressed his advantage and tried to win the rest of Russia by supporting the claims of a usurper, the false Dimitri. Godounov, who had succeeded Feodor, himself died, and a flood of Polish soldiers and Catholic priests poured into the country to support the claims of Dimitri. Everywhere they were successful until a stand was made by the Orthodox in the greatest of the Russian monasteries, the Troitski Lavra. Here they successfully resisted a siege by

30,000 men with ninety guns, and turned the tide of invasion. The country gradually rallied to the cause, the Poles were driven out, and in 1612 the Polish garrison was compelled to evacuate the Kremlin. These events had much the same effect in Russia as the sailing of the Armada had in England: they made Roman Catholicism synonymous with treason. Henceforth the Orthodox clergy were the bulwark of national defence, and any heresy or departure from their fellowship was the most serious of crimes.

Out of these troubles the first of the Romanov dynasty came to the throne. In the absence of a direct heir, Michael Romanov was elected, chiefly by the voice of the lower gentry and the common people. He was only a youth of sixteen, but he adopted the title of Autocrat and restored that hereditary autocracy, which was the only form of government the Russians were yet able to understand. But in the terrible state of the country the reign might have gone badly had it not been for Michael's father, Philaret, who was appointed Patriarch, and, till death parted them in 1633, shared the government with him. Thus the medieval ideal of a unified State with secular and ecclesiastical heads representing the two sides of one shield was realised. On the secular side the reign is important for the peaceful settlement made both with Poland and with Gustavus Adolphus of Sweden, and also for the census, which, necessary as it was in order to form a basis for a just taxation, nevertheless had the effect of binding the peasants to the soil and reducing them to the level of serfs. On the ecclesiastical side it is important for the emergence of those questions of heresy which were to form so sinister a feature of the later history. This happened through the action of Dionysius, the heroic archimandrite of the Troitski Lavra, who had saved his country by defending the monastery against the Poles. He was President of a Commission set up by Michael to revise the liturgy, and had the temerity to condemn as an interpolation the latter part of the phrase used in the Blessing of the Waters: 'Come, O Lord, and sanctify this water with Thy Holy Spirit and with fire.' His almost illiterate enemies asserted that he denied the descent of the Holy Spirit with fire, and the populace believed an alarming rumour that he wished to banish fire from Russia. In 1618 he was condemned and imprisoned amid circumstances of the greatest indignity. In Kiev, on the other hand, sympathy with Roman Catholicism was still very strong. As a reaction against the teaching of Cyril Lucar, the Metropolitan, Peter Mogila, put out his famous *Orthodox Confession*, which was as strongly Latin in tone as Lucar's had been Calvinistic. It was this that gave the lead to the Council of Jerusalem in 1672. Since that Council the theology of the Eastern Church has been based upon the Bible, the Seven Oecumenical Councils, the Council of Jerusalem, (including the Confession of Dositheos), and Peter Mogila's Confession. But in Russia events were still to show how different an idea of the proportion of faith prevailed there from that which was characteristic of the rest of Christendom.

In the next reign, that of Alexis, the remarkable Nikon was Patriarch. He had had an extraordinary career. He had been born in 1605 of a peasant family and had received his education in the village school. At the age of twelve he became a monk, but after eight years in the monastery his parents persuaded him to leave it and marry. For ten years he had charge of a Moscow church, but the death of his three children made him believe that he was intended after all for a monastic life, and he once again became a monk, while his wife entered a convent. When he had become *hegumen* and was attending a council, he made the acquaintance of Alexis, who was impressed by his business ability and in 1649 made him Archbishop of Novgorod. In many respects Nikon reminds us of the English Becket. It is significant that on his appointment he insisted that he should be left severely alone in the legal as well as the spiritual management of his diocese. But he was also a practical reformer, and he made the parish priests, or popes, subject to the control of the bishop. Hitherto they had been inclined to submit only to the orders of the people who elected and paid them; and this had led both to cheapness and a lowering of the standard. Nikon's reform was resented by both parties. This resentment was increased when he refused to ordain any who could not read at sight. He also reformed the manner of conducting the services. Owing to their inordinate length and the discomfort of the unheated churches, the custom had arisen of dividing the liturgy into parts and having the different parts taken simultaneously by different officials. Nikon effectually reduced the babel by ordering that only one voice should be heard at a time. He was also responsible for that reform of the music by introducing choirs singing in harmony, which has made the Russian Church music one of the most impressive exercises that can be heard to-day. In 1652 he was made Patriarch of Moscow, but with characteristic determination he refused to accept the office till he had extracted a promise from the assembled multitude that they would obey him in everything he should teach them concerning the divine dogmas and canons. He now entered upon an adventure in the way of liturgical reform that rent his Church in twain. It was not his fault if the work was not well done, for he took the greatest pains in the collection of the necessary manuscripts. But the people he employed were careless and made unnecessary alterations that were calculated to exacerbate conservative feeling without procuring much benefit. It seems incredible that so much disturbance could be caused over the questions whether the Hallelujah should be sung twice or thrice, whether processions should go the way of the sun or against it, and whether two or three fingers should be used in giving the blessing. Yet this was the kind of thing over which the Old Believers, as they were called, broke off and left the Church. In 1666, the year when Londoners were battling with the Great Fire that burnt S. Paul's, the Russians were sending a whole army of soldiers into the northern snows to compel the monks of the great monastery of Solovetski to accept the changes, an effort which failed for ten years and only succeeded when all the inhabitants had been massacred and new monks had been drafted in. Before that consummation Nikon himself had been sacrificed to the jealousy of his enemies. There was a question of real importance at issue. Nikon had claimed that in ecclesiastical matters he stood to the Tsar as the sun to the moon, that the Tsar received his consecration and coronation from the bishop as the moon receives its light from the sun, and that therefore the Tsar had no right to the title or authority of head of the Church. To accept this would have been to put an end to all autocratic government, and in spite of his personal predilection for Nikon, Alexis found himself obliged to listen to the Synod, which proclaimed that the King was free from law and from all necessity of accountability, and to appoint a new Patriarch, who explained that with the single exception of officiating in sacred things all the other episcopal privileges are clearly represented in the Tsar. Nikon was deprived in 1666. In the struggle with the civil power he had lost, and the Church remained bound in subservience to the State until the Bolshevists cut the knot. But in his liturgical reforms he triumphed, and the results of his work abide to-day.

During the reigns of Feodor II and Sophia the persecution of the Old Believers continued, rising at times to the pitch of the greatest ferocity, and resulting in the production of grotesque forms of fanaticism. The Fire Baptists were originally persecuted members of the sect who, finding themselves cut off from possibility of escape, burnt the buildings in which they sheltered and perished with them. As many as 2,700 destroyed themselves at one time in this fashion on an island of Lake Ladoga in 1688. Doctrinal justification for such self-immolation was found in the corrupt text, 'There is one baptism by fire for the remission of sins.' The thing became a habit and continued at intervals till the end of the nineteenth century. Owing to the difficulty of replacing their priests as they died off, many new sects of more or less extravagant beliefs arose, but the bulk of the Old Believers clung together and, ultimately obtaining the services of a Bosnian bishop, maintained themselves to the number of four millions at the outbreak of the Great War.

The main stream of Russian Church life was closely affected by the reign of Peter the Great. This is not the place to speak of the young epileptic's savagery; of his visits to England and other countries to examine the latest amenities of civilisation; of his interest in mechanical contrivances, shown by his personal experiments in dentistry on the members of his suite; of his determination to turn his people from an Oriental nation into a Western

THE EASTERN CHURCH 157

one, evinced most dramatically in clipping off the beards of the nobles with his own hands; of his blood-lust displayed in his personal share in the work of the executioner when he butchered the Streltsi guard after they rebelled against him; or of his iniquities that have no name. He has been compared to a chimpanzee apeing civilisation. But the fact that has caught hold of later imagination is that he definitely strove to make his people look West instead of East and thus inaugurated an epoch-making period of change. The difficulties that met him in this attempt can be judged from the outcry when he ordered a general system of education, and from the horror when he changed the beginning of the year to the first of January from the first of September, which had always been regarded as the day of creation, because then the fruit would be ripe in the Garden of Eden. Ecclesiastically he played with the idea of introducing Lutheran reforms, of securing union with the English Church through the non-Jurors, and with the Roman Church through the Sorbonne. But he did carry through his scheme for reducing the Church to a department of State. The Patriarchate became vacant in 1700. For a time he kept a creature of his own as guardian of the Chair, but later he suppressed the Patriarch, and in 1721 put the office into commission by the appointment of the Holy Synod. This was a kind of committee for Church affairs, and was presided over by a Procurator, who was appointed by the Tsar and regulated all its business. Under this management the Russian Church conducted its affairs till our own time. Peter also turned his attention to the wealth of the Church and particularly of the monasteries. How great that was can be judged from the fact that the Troitski Lavra alone possessed 92,000 serfs. The Tsar ordered that the monasteries should be cleared of all who were not regularly tonsured monks, and that no new members should be enrolled under thirty years of age. Their revenues he took entirely into his own hands, giving each monk henceforth a meagre annual allowance. In spite of all his effort to Westernise his Church and country, Peter did not prevent its spiritual effect in the East. During his reign its missions spread widely through Siberia and southwards to Irkutsk. It was the only branch of the

Eastern Church that could attempt missionary work at the time, and it proved itself the only Church that could convert Mohammedans. This tradition was ably sustained during the nineteenth century in the work of Bishop Innocent, who converted Kamtchatka; and of Professor Ilminski, who laboured among the Moslem Tatars. In China the Cossacks effected a settlement and were allowed to have their own Church. Russian missionaries conducted a successful mission at the beginning of the eighteenth century in Peking itself. In modern times Archbishop Nicolai built up in Japan a Church of 36,000 communicants with a complete native ministry of its own.

CHAPTER XIII

NATIONALISM AND TOLERATION

WE return now to the story of events in Western Christendom. The seventeenth century had accepted the principle of nationalism accompanied by religious intolerance. The idea that one nation must have only one religion was as strong in the minds of the reformers as had been the idea that the world itself could have only one form of Christianity in the mind of S. Augustine. There was no spirit of tolerance inherent in Protestantism, but the logic of events ultimately produced it. To have three mutually intolerant religions established side by side was already a step forward. In the eighteenth century, while nationalism still grew in strength, it was accompanied by the dawning realisation that people of differing creeds might live together with mutual forbearance under the same Government. We shall see how this came about, first in Germany and Austria, and then in England.

The Thirty Years War had left Germany completely exhausted, with her population fallen from sixteen millions to six. With exhaustion came toleration. The powerlessness of the Papacy to affect the Peace of Westphalia marks the end of the counter-Reformation, and the lines then drawn between Catholicism and Protestantism remained roughly permanent. Within the borders of Protestantism Calvinism had won equal rights with Lutheranism, but this was a liberty for the State rather than for the individual. The prince had the right to fix the religion of his subjects and to see that all observed the same religion. Thus in 1727 Firmian, Archbishop of Salzburg, whom the Treaty had made Primate of Germany, began to restore order within his territories in such a fashion as to expel 20,000 of his subjects who adhered to their Protestant profession. This was the last definite expression of the *cujus regio, ejus religio* principle, and its folly from the point of view of the nation became evident when other States, such as Prussia, who received the refugees, found their communal life greatly enriched in consequence. To many it seemed that Catholicism was at last dying. The Seven Years War (1756-63) served to give colour to the impression, since it resulted in the shifting of the centre of power from Catholic Austria to Protestant Prussia. Frederick the Great himself told Voltaire that he would live to see the end of Catholicism. In these circumstances it was natural that Catholic nations should begin to sit rather loose to the Papacy, and to cherish thoughts of a semi-independent Church of their own. What Gallicanism had already been to France, that Febronianism was to be to Germany and Josephism to Austria.

Febronius is the name under which Nicholas von Hontheim, coadjutor to the Archbishop of Trier, had put out his book, *De statu Ecclesiae*, in 1763. This was an examination of the proper constitution of the Church in the light of antiquity. The conclusions reached are practically those of the Gallicans. S. Peter was the first among equals, and as the bishops derive their commission direct from Christ, so the Pope only receives his special primacy from the Church. Nevertheless he is the head of the Church, and on him devolves the duty of seeing that the canons are observed, and his judgment is binding unless the whole Church or a General Council declare to the contrary. But all the privileges that have been heaped on him since the publication of the False Decretals should be withdrawn, and princes should set about the reform of their national Churches with the advice of their own episcopate. The book was placed on the Index the very next year, and von Hontheim protected himself by denying its authorship. But he was at the head of a reforming movement, and in 1769 presided at a meeting in Coblenz representative of the Archbishops-Electors, which drew up thirty Articles in agreement with the teaching of the book. One result of the type of thought thus engendered is seen in the growing antagonism towards the Jesuits, who had always stood out as the champions of papal power. This antagonism resulted in their suppression in 1773 by Pope Clement XIV, an event to which we must refer again. Yet it is significant of the changing spirit of the times that when the Jesuits were excluded from the Catholic States they were offered a refuge within his Protestant dominions by Frederick the Great, who thus became responsible for an epoch-making act of real toleration. Febronianism went through some vicissitudes. Rome was still capable of exerting enough pressure on von Hontheim to make him recant in 1778, but three years later he published a Latin commentary on his book which took up the same ground. His teaching spread, and in 1786 the Archbishops-Electors felt strong enough to arrange another meeting at Ems, which presented Twenty-seven Articles to Rome. The Pope refused to accept them, and owing to the jealousy of other bishops no efforts were made to force them into effect.

In the meantime, however, a similar movement had been spreading in Austria. Maria Teresa had prepared the way by her tactful firmness towards Roman pretensions. She had ordered that no papal briefs should run in her dominions without her express sanction; she had raised the age of admission into monasteries to twenty-five; she had brought the clergy under national taxation; she had stopped the Inquisition and religious persecution within her borders; and she had helped to expel the Jesuits. For the last part of her reign her son, Joseph II, had been associated with her. When in 1780 he began to reign alone, he proceeded to carry things much farther. He had long been looked upon as a possible leader by those who desired to secure some measure of ecclesiastical independence, for he had been asked to help in effecting the freedom of the German Church at the time when the Articles of Coblenz were drawn up. He also held unusually enlightened views on the subject of religious tolerance. A visit to France had convinced him of the harm done by the expulsion of the Huguenots, and, while preserving his own Catholicism, he found it possible to give a large measure of civil liberty in his own dominions to both Protestants and Eastern Orthodox, not only granting them leave to practise their religion, but also opening to them all offices in the State. These privileges were embodied in the Toleration Edict of 1781. He turned his attention to the monasteries, and within twelve years dissolved nearly eight hundred of the two thousand then existing. From the bishops he exacted, not only the ordinary Oath of Allegiance, but also a promise to report any seditious meetings to the Emperor. In all this his object seemed to be not merely to free the Church from external interference, but definitely to put it under Government control. This drove Pope Pius VI to the extraordinary course of visiting Vienna in person, to prevent matters going to further extremes. The result of the visit was indeterminate, but in the next year, 1783, the Emperor returned the compliment at Rome, and from that time his reform took on a more moderate character. There is little doubt that Joseph's somewhat autocratic liberalism offended many of his people. The ultramontanes naturally disliked him, but even the growing school of philosophers disdained him, and Frederick the Great spoke of him as 'my brother the sacristan'. But when he died, broken-hearted, in 1790, he at least left behind the memory of the great Toleration Act of 1781. After that the French Revolution brought new factors into these problems.

In England national rights had already been secured for the Church, but, owing to the very circumstances of its struggle for existence, Anglicans were slow to learn the lesson of toleration. The governing classes were even less tolerant than the clergy; if the Tories were in power the Nonconformists were in jeopardy, and if the Whigs were uppermost it was the Romanists who were more likely to be made the scapegoats of any trouble. The mass of the people found it quite impossible to forget the Armada, the Jesuit mission, and the Gunpowder Plot, and were therefore definitely anti-Roman. Toleration was not likely to proceed apace in such circumstances. The tentative efforts of Charles II were not well received, and the first sure beginnings of the struggle towards religious freedom must be placed in the reign of his brother, James II. The latter was a convinced Roman Catholic; it was obviously impossible to keep in being repressive measures against other members of that Church, and consequently, although in the end his reign proved a serious set-back for Roman interests, it did furnish the beginnings of toleration. The reason for James's failure is that he pitched his aims too high. He would be content with nothing less than the restoration of Roman Catholicism as the national religion and of personal autocracy as the form of government. Late events, especially the outcry about the Popish Plot, had made both aims impossible of achievement. But it is questionable whether under the most favourable auspices an obstinate bigot like James could have accomplished them. Even Innocent XI distrusted his zeal, and hoped more for the papal cause from the tolerance of William of Orange. It is indeed asserted that the Pope actually persuaded King Leopold to lend his assistance to William—not the first instance we have had of a pope striving to gain his end by helping Protestant against Catholic.

James set about his self-appointed task at the earliest possible moment. In the year of his accession (1685) he began appointing Roman Catholics to commissions in the new army that was being formed against Monmouth. This, in effect, was to claim a dispensing power over the Test Act, and Parliament at once protested against the illegality of the action. The next year, however, the King made an attempt to achieve the same end in the Universities. In order to force his will on recalcitrant clergymen, James had already appointed an Ecclesiastical Commission, which is variously described as a new court and as a revival of the old High Commission Court. It acted in virtue of the powers bestowed upon the Crown by the Supremacy Act. James had made the mistake of appointing the notorious Judge Jeffreys, the Lord Chancellor, as its president. This had brought the refusal of Sancroft, Archbishop of Canterbury, to serve on it at all, on the ground that he would not share in a spiritual commission of which a layman was the head. The King now set a turncoat as his own nominee over Christ Church, Oxford, and then proceeded to do the same at Magdalen. But the Fellows of the latter college refused to be overawed, and elected one of their own society. The Ecclesiastical Commission thereupon quashed the election. The King appeared at Oxford in person, and, summoning the Fellows before him, ordered them to do his bidding. When they refused, the King's nominee was intruded, and ultimately the college was filled with members of the Roman communion. But when the King at last began to be afraid of the revolution that he was stirring up, the legal President and Fellows were restored to their places amid universal acclaim. Cambridge also had its difficulties. At that university Isaac Newton was among those who were punished for their refusal to grant the degree of M.A. to a Romanist.

While this was going on England was being aroused to sympathy with the Huguenots, who were now pouring into the country after the revocation of the Edict of Nantes. James tried to take advantage of this feeling to publish a new Declaration of Indulgence. This Declaration was wider than that of 1672, in that it gave full right of public worship to Roman Catholics as well as to Protestants and arranged for dispensations to be given to place-holders who refused to take the oaths. It was issued in 1688 with instructions to the clergy to read it in church. This was too much. The clergy might not have been unwilling to promote toleration in Parliament, but everyone knew that this Declaration was a direct affront to the rights and dignity of Parliament, and to bid the clergy publish so unconstitutional a decree in the house of God was to mock at their sacred office. Sancroft hastily summoned a meeting of such bishops as were in the neighbourhood of London. Seven of them drew up and presented a petition to the King explaining the reason why they must refuse to publish the Declaration. The bishops were put on trial for their action. They became the heroes of the people: 'never before or since', it has been said, 'has the Church so gloriously represented a united nation.' Even the Whigs refused toleration on such terms, and when the bishops were acquitted of the charge of publishing a seditious libel—which was the way in which the Crown lawyers described their petition—a medal was struck and bonfires were lighted to mark the victory of freedom. After this James was warned of the coming invasion on the part of William of Orange. Left unsupported even by the Pope, he found no course open but to flee the country. With William and Mary toleration came in.

William himself was no lover of the Church, and gave

NATIONALISM AND TOLERATION

great offence because he wore his hat during service, but he was helped to maintain some semblance of sympathy with churchmanship by the divisions into which the different schools of thought in the Anglican communion now fell. On two points all churchmen were united as the result of the long struggles under the Stuarts—love of the Prayer Book and determination to preserve the episcopacy. But beyond these points of agreement there were wide differences of opinion. Men who followed the school of Laud were called High; Puritans who conformed were called Low; and a third class who were weary of strife and did not value theological nicety were called Latitude-men or Latitudinarians. It was these last who approximated most closely to William's Dutch Calvinism, which, since the Synod of Dort, had become much less strict than the original Genevan type. These men were of the Whig persuasion in politics, and on this ground, too, they found a natural friend in William by way of opposition to James's Toryism. It followed as a matter of course that the bishops were chosen from this school of thought. Tillotson and Tenison of Canterbury, Stillingfleet of Worcester, and Burnet of Salisbury were all of this type. But the rank and file of the clergy remained High Church and Tory, and that led to a regrettable divorce between the diocesans and their clergy, between the Upper and Lower Houses of Convocation.

The reign of William and Mary began with one more effort at comprehension, the last of the endeavours to unite Puritans to the Church on the basis of one Prayer Book. The Lower House of Convocation defeated this project before it became serious. In its place there was passed, in 1689, the Toleration Act, which has been described as the 'great charter of religious freedom, and the triumph of common sense'. This was not so ambitious as the abortive Declarations had been. It did not go beyond the reach of public opinion, but granted complete liberty of worship to all except Roman Catholics and Unitarians. Unhappily, this instalment of toleration to those outside the Church came simultaneously with a serious schism within the Church. On the accession of William and Mary many of the clergy felt in conscience bound by the Oath of Allegiance that they had taken to James, and were therefore unable to take the oath demanded of them to the new rulers. This position was the natural result of the doctrine of divine right, with its corollary of passive obedience or non-resistance to the will of the sovereign, which had been developed in the time of the early Stuarts. Five of the bishops who felt this conscientious scruple had taken part among the famous seven in their opposition to James. They had thus made it evident that the doctrine did not compel them to share in unlawful acts at the dictation of the sovereign. Nevertheless their deprivation was decided upon; and this created a further difficulty for many loyal churchmen. Such men held the High Church view of the self-sufficing spiritual authority of the Church, and bitterly resented the arbitrary action of the State in deposing bishops at its will. Consequently they clung to the ministrations of the deposed prelates. The schism thus created grew to considerable proportions. In 1690 Archbishop Sancroft, eight other bishops, and four hundred clergy were ejected, and a considerable number of the laity followed them. They were united on two points: the State point—that they were bound by their oath, since James had not released them; and the Church point—that since the clergy, who were deprived in 1690, were ejected by the authority of Parliament alone, those who were put in to succeed them were uncanonically appointed and merited no obedience. But as so often happens, other questions soon arose to rend the schism itself. When the deprived bishops died out, would it not be right to return to the State Church and to accept the ministrations of the others who had been put into their places, or must those ministrations still be refused and a succession of non-juring bishops maintained? Some followed the former line of action, but others carried on an episcopal succession until 1805, when the last of the non-juring bishops, Charles Booth, who was carrying on business as a watch-maker in Long Millgate, Manchester, died, and the schism ended. One effect of their separation was, curiously enough, to keep alive the tradition of 'Catholic' worship in the English Church, for they had more freedom for experiment than they would have had if they had remained bound by the liturgical formularies of the national Church; and as their leaning was entirely in the direction of historic customs they preserved ideals that might have been lost during the eighteenth century, and so influenced the progress of liturgical enrichment in Scotland, America, and other Churches of the Anglican communion. The mixed chalice, prayers for the faithful departed, the *epiklesis*, and the rejoining of the prayer of oblation to the consecration prayer are all 'usages' over which, indeed, they quarrelled, but which nevertheless they preserved for future use in a wider circle. Perhaps the best known of the non-jurors was Bishop Ken. He had been a ward of Isaac Walton and a scholar of Winchester. After his ordination he became chaplain to the Princess Mary at the Hague, where he was not afraid to rebuke William for his ill-treatment of her. He became Bishop of Bath and Wells in 1684, and was one of the seven bishops who figured in the famous trial. After the non-juring schism had continued for some time, he consented with the greatest reluctance to the proposal to perpetuate its succession of bishops. Queen Anne wished to restore him to his see. To this he would not consent, but voluntarily surrendered his rights to his friend Hooper, who was appointed in his place. The Queen gave expression to the universal esteem in which he was held by appointing him a pension in 1704. The gentle piety that was his chief characteristic is well seen in his best-known hymn, 'All praise to Thee, my God, this night.'

The difficulty felt by so many of the bishops about their attitude to William had a more serious effect upon the fortunes of the Scottish Church. There the Presbyterians had been making things very hard for the adherents of episcopacy, and moreover they were ardent supporters of the Revolution. Nevertheless William had discovered, when he came over, that 'the great body of the nobility and gentry are for Episcopacy, and it is the trading and inferior sort that are for Presbytery'. He therefore took the opportunity of a meeting with Rose, Bishop of Edinburgh, to try to win the Scotch bishops to his side. But Rose could not commit himself or his colleagues, and that sealed the fate of episcopacy in Scotland. In 1689 the Scotch Parliament passed an Act to disestablish episcopacy, and next year the Presbyterian ministers were restored and the Westminster Confession of Faith accepted as the creed of the Church.

168 HISTORY OF THE MODERN CHURCH

In England efforts were directed mainly against the Roman Catholics. These culminated in 1700 in an Act for preventing the growth of popery. Roman Catholics were forbidden to inherit or purchase land, and their children could receive no education except in their own homes. But William grew more and more out of favour with the Anglicans. He found Convocation so intractable that he did not summon it for eleven years, but attempted to govern the Church by issuing injunctions. Ecclesiastical patronage was exercised by a commission of Whig bishops. In 1701 an Act of Abjuration, passed after the death of James to make all the clergy abjure his son and descendants, brought an accession of some numbers to the ranks of the non-jurors, and when at last Convocation was allowed to meet, tne Lower House asserted its independence of the proceedings of the bishops by continuing in session after the prorogation. Nevertheless the life of the Church developed with considerable vigour, as is shown by the growth of societies which had for their object the extension of its work or the deepening of its spirituality. Of the most important of these the hero was Dr. Bray, the Rector of Sheldon. He had a great belief in the value of libraries, and devoted the profits of his *Discourse concerning Baptismal and Spiritual Regeneration* to help founding them. It is surprising to learn that this enabled him to start an organisation which resulted in the founding of eighty libraries in England and thirty-nine in North America. In 1698 he started the S.P.C.K., as already described, to develop this educational work. He went to America as the commissary of the Bishop of London, and although he failed in his ambition to obtain a bishop for America, he did get a charter in 1701 for a new society, the S.P.G., to supplement the work of the earlier one. In 1723 he formed the organisation known as Dr. Bray's Associates for founding clerical libraries and supporting negro schools. His libraries are still an immense boon to the parochial clergy.

Queen Anne's reign was the Golden Age for Church societies of all kinds. The Church was now at the height of its popularity, and vigorous efforts were made to raise the standard of life among the people. The Society for the Reformation of Manners, which had already been founded in 1692, carried on its work of bringing vice to justice, and many local societies joined clergy and laity together for encouraging more frequent attendance at the services of the Church and for devotional exercises. Charity expressed itself in the foundation of schools for the poor and for orphans. In London alone there were 120 Bluecoat Schools. The Corporation of Sons of the Clergy met the needs of clerical families. The Queen herself aided the work by assigning the Annates, which had been appropriated to the Crown by Henry VIII, to a fund for augmenting the stipends of the smaller livings. This was started on her birthday in 1704 with assets to the extent of £16,000 per annum, and has ever since been known as Queen Anne's Bounty. Together with this went great proposals for the building of churches. The Great Fire in London had destroyed eighty-three of the old churches, and it is to this that we owe the great activity of Sir Christopher Wren (1632-1723), who was responsible for fifty-three parish churches in London, as well as the new S. Paul's. An Act was passed for the building of fifty additional churches, but only twelve of them were carried through. The churches were filled for the Sunday services, many of the devout laity also finding opportunity to attend the daily services and the weekly celebrations of the Eucharist.

This revival was accompanied by a rather curious state of affairs in the Government. During the first part of her reign the Queen was much under the influence of Sarah Churchill, wife of the Duke of Marlborough, and the Duke's Whig friends were in power. This led to considerable friction on the subject of 'occasional conformity'. The intention of the Test Acts had been to secure that the country should be governed only by Church of England men. But in point of fact many who continued to attend dissenting worship qualified for office by an occasional communion in the church. From 1703 to 1706 the Commons repeatedly passed Bills which sought to end the anomalies of such occasional conformity by levying a fine of £100 upon any official who should resort to a conventicle and £5 for every day that he continued in office afterwards. The Lords as repeatedly threw out the Bill, but the clergy united with the Commons to arouse the country with the cry 'the Church in danger'. In 1710 the Lords tried to make an example of one of the leaders in this outcry, a certain Dr. Sacheverell, a Fellow of Magdalen College, Oxford. In his sermons he had alleged that whereas 'formerly the Whigs tried to bring the Church into the conventicle, now they labour to bring the conventicle into the Church'. He was, as Hearne, the non-juring antiquary, said, 'a man of much noise but little sincerity'. Nevertheless he was impeached. The trial caused much excitement, the mob actually stopping the Queen's coach and crying, 'We hope your Majesty is for High Church and Dr. Sacheverell', and all the punishment the Lords dared inflict upon him was to inhibit him from preaching for three years, and to order two of his sermons to be burnt by the public hangman. There followed a great High Church reaction. The Queen freed herself from the Duchess, dissolved Parliament, and the Tory tide swept in. Scotland, where the Act of Union of 1707 had guaranteed the establishment of the Presbyterian Kirk, was saved from the consequent persecution of episcopalians by an Act of Toleration in 1712, which gave freedom of worship to those of the episcopal communion. In England, on the other hand, the Occasional Conformity Act was at last passed (1711), and in 1714 the Schism Act prevented dissenters founding schools. But the positions were reversed in the next reign, persecution beginning again in Scotland, while in England the Schism Act was repealed in 1719, and the Occasional Conformity Act was repealed the same year.

CHAPTER XIV

DEISM AND THE ENLIGHTENMENT

IT is clear from what has been said in the last chapter that the principle of religious toleration had not yet gone far. Its progress was to be considerably accelerated in the later part of the eighteenth century by a loosening of the old bonds of strict credal definition that had hitherto bound all profession of Christianity. In this respect the Reformation had been just as medieval as scholasticism. Although Luther had girded at Aristotle he had not been able to cast off his shackles, and from the point of view of *a priori* arbitrariness there was nothing to choose between Calvin's *Institutes* and the *Summa* of S. Thomas Aquinas. The Reformation had broken to pieces the external system of Rome, but it had brought in exchange several other systems equally deduced from a number of data which were regarded as authoritatively bestowed by divine revelation. Its scholars were not as near akin to modern students as was Erasmus. None of them as yet had been able to institute a scientific method of inquiry into the bases of religious belief. It is this that divides them from our own day. The truly modern age did not begin until the historic method of inquiry had been built up. What separates us from the Middle Ages and the Reformation period is not any necessary difference in the conclusions at which we arrive, but the whole mental atmosphere in which our thinking is done. The three characteristic notes of modern thought may be taken to be its emphasis upon reason, its refusal to be bound by tradition, and its acceptance of the method pursued in natural science as the norm for all inquiry. The system was begun in the early seventeenth century when Lord Bacon of Verulam let nature reveal to him her secrets by applying a method which was purely inductive.

It was developed in Holland when the French Catholic Descartes 'grappled with the greatest problems of thought as from a *tabula rasa*'. No doubt it is capable of exaggerations and mistakes, as Pascal, Descartes' contemporary, pointed out, and it possesses very little hope of finality, but such as it is the method is woven into the fibre of all our thought, at least for those of us who are outside the Roman communion. That communion might have developed it from seed sown in the Renaissance, but the counter-Reformation made that impossible, and the seed germinated in later Protestantism, which was unfortunately less capable of checking its exaggerated tendencies. In England it resulted in Deism, a type of thought which spread to Germany and produced the Enlightenment (*Aufklärung*, Illumination). This exchange between the two countries was balanced by another, in which England was the debtor. From Germany came Pietism, which had meanwhile developed there, to replace Deism in England by Methodism. In this chapter we shall follow only the fortunes of the deistic movement as it passes into the Enlightenment.

In England thought had been profoundly stirred by the discoveries of men who followed the Baconian method of allowing observation and inductive experiment to become the basis of generalisation. Had it not been for the growing popularity of this method, the heliocentric system of the Polish scientist, Copernicus, would have remained in the obscurity which had hitherto enveloped it from the moment of its publication in 1543, the year of his death. But it was supported by the observations of Tycho Brahe, the generalisations of Johann Kepler, the explanations of Galileo, and the mathematical demonstrations of Isaac Newton. It dawned upon the minds of the age that the universe was subject, not to arbitrary action, divine or other, but to immutable law, and men began to look upon the world in which they lived, not as the centre of this universe, but as a moving speck in a great stream of being. England was in a condition peculiarly suitable for a free and somewhat irresponsible consideration of these new and disturbing thoughts, owing to the fact that the Government of the day was interested in the preservation of as much freedom as possible. The Hanoverian King, George I, knew no English,

DEISM AND THE ENLIGHTENMENT 173

and his Minister Walpole knew no German. They could only communicate with each other through the medium of bad Latin, and the consequence was that the administration of the Church was left almost entirely in the hands of Walpole, who used it simply as a valuable instrument for rewarding services to his own party in the State. Wake, the Archbishop of Canterbury, who was a sound churchman and acute theologian, the historian of Convocation and organiser of attempts at reunion with the Gallican Church, was driven into retirement; and religion was made as latitudinarian and unchurchly as possible. Three controversies resulted.

As was natural in this country, the first dealt with practical subjects. Hickes, the non-juring Bishop of Thetford, had been responsible for some papers posthumously published on the *Constitution of the Christian Church*, which had the effect of unchurching all who were not non-jurors. He was answered by Hoadly, the Bishop of Bangor, in his *Preservative against the Principles and the Practices of the Non-Jurors*, which had the opposite effect of recommending an extreme Erastianism and destroying the very theory of a visible Church. The Lower House of Convocation reported against him, and was in consequence temporarily prorogued. Then, when the question threatened to come before the Upper House, Convocation was permanently prorogued in May 1717, and was not allowed to meet again for the discussion of business for 135 years. The dispute thus summarily settled is known as the Bangorian Controversy, and its hero, who had never set foot in his diocese of Bangor, was rewarded with successive appointments to the bishoprics of Hereford, Salisbury, and Winchester.

The outer defences having been thus overthrown, the way was open for more serious questioning of fundamental belief. The original impetus had come from the Continent. Descartes, beginning by doubting everything of set purpose, and regarding clearness as the sole test of truth, had set aside practical religion as being a provisional something to live by while he conducted his inquiry. Then he had established that the only thing he could not doubt was his own existence as a thinking being. 'I think, therefore I am.' But from this unpromising beginning he had been able to build up an Ontological Argument for the existence of God. Leibniz, the librarian of Hanover and the diligent seeker after a union between Catholicism and Protestantism, went farther and proceeded to ask how men could know anything at all, answering that they have the seeds of knowledge in themselves, and that they acquire knowledge, not by gathering information from outside, but by the elucidation of their innate ideas. The Englishman Locke would have none of this. In his *Essay concerning Human Understanding*, he denied the existence of any innate ideas, the human mind is like a white paper on which sensation writes impressions and so gives rise to ideas. Everything must therefore be subject to the criticism of reason. The existence of God he found reasonably demonstrated by the argument from cause and effect. But when he came to the rest of the Christian creed he did not find things so easy. In his *Reasonableness of Christianity*, published in 1695, he wished to jettison the creeds and fall back upon the New Testament with a simple declaration of belief in Jesus as the Messiah. Thus there was general agreement about the existence of God, but none about His character. This led to the Trinitarian Controversy between Samuel Clarke and Daniel Waterland. The former was Rector of S. James's, Piccadilly, and published a book on the *Scripture Doctrine of the Trinity*, in which he took up a position very similar to that of Arius in the fourth century. Jesus was only divine with a communicated divinity; He was the Son of God rather than God the Son; and the Holy Spirit was similarly inferior to both Father and Son in dominion and authority. Waterland, who answered him, was Master of Magdalene, Cambridge. In a number of works, the first of which was published in 1719 and the last in 1734, he defended the historic faith of the Church, and did it so effectively as to make it impossible for any to take up the Arian position again. Henceforth there was found no half-way house between Trinitarianism and complete Unitarianism. But how far the movement went when there was no such staunch defence can be gathered from the complaints about the number of Presbyterians who relapsed into Socinianism during this century. The value of a close connexion with historic Christianity for preserving the faith of the creeds comes out in Waterland's devotion to the Fathers: 'We think that Christ never sits more secure or easy on His throne than when He has His most faithful guards about Him. . . . I follow the Fathers as far as reason requires and no farther; therefore this is following our own reason.'

These arguments prepared the way for the Deistic Controversy. It flowed directly out of the presuppositions of Protestantism. The Reformers had swept away tradition and had made the Bible the sole basis of belief. Hobbes, who died in 1679, had said that the Scripture itself must be subject to human reason. From this many had gone on to the assumption that there must be one common form of religious inheritance that could be discovered by reason at the back of all known creeds. It was the English form of Rousseau's cry, 'Back to Nature', and resulted in a rejection of all 'revealed' religion and a reliance upon a supposed original stock of 'natural' religion. It is obvious that no proper historic method had as yet been discovered by philosophers who could make such claims. They only knew that the early history of religion was not as it had hitherto been written, but their own reconstruction of primitive conditions was as imaginative as Rousseau's dream of an original 'social contract'. Nevertheless it was a very serious challenge to the religious leaders of the day, and it produced replies that have made the eighteenth century the classic age of Christian apologetic.

Sherlock, the opponent of Bishop Hoadly, whom he succeeded at Bangor and at Salisbury before he refused Canterbury and finally settled down as Bishop of London, spent his skill in defending the credibility of the resurrection of Jesus. His book, *The Tryal of the Witnesses of the Resurrection of Jesus Christ*, published in 1729, was a reply to Woolston, who had made an attack on all miracles. It represents the examination of the witnesses as being conducted in court, and reaches a dramatic moment when the guards are questioned about their statement that the Lord's body had been taken away by the disciples, evidence which is summarily dismissed as worthless on the guards' own confession that they were asleep at the time.

A more philosophic defence of Christianity was undertaken by the Irishman, George Berkeley, who became

Bishop of Cloyne in 1734. He was an idealist who inherited and carried farther the teaching of the Cambridge Platonists, a group of thinkers in the seventeenth century of whom Benjamin Whichcote, John Smith, and Henry More are the best known. They had used the philosophic system of Plato as the best background for their Christianity, and had developed a broad-minded tolerance tinged with mysticism that found its best expression in Sir Thomas Browne's *Religio Medici*. Berkeley pushed the teaching to its logical conclusion in a denial that matter can exist without mind, of which Dr. Johnson's famous kicking of a stone was no adequate refutation. His religious sensibility was shocked by the essentially irreligious rationalism of the Deists, and when he was on a mission to Rhode Island he wrote his *Alciphron, or the Minute Philosopher*, which was published on his return in 1732. It is a dialogue intended to defend a definite Christian belief against the whittling methods of the 'minute philosophers', as he calls the Deists. Christian beliefs are not only necessary to promote the highest good of man, but are also necessary to reason. Without them we cannot explain the universe as we know it. He makes a bold comparison between the faculty by which religious truth is apprehended, and the physical vision. We actually *see* in nature the handiwork of God.

One of the most influential of the Deist writers was John Toland, who visited Hanover and sowed seed there that was to spring up in the Enlightenment. In 1696 he published his work, *Christianity not Mysterious*, which took the characteristic line that only that is true which is clearly demonstrable. So long as a thing is only probable our judgment must remain in suspense. It was this that formed the starting-point for the argument of the famous *Analogy* of Bishop Butler. This great philosophic theologian was the son of a Wantage linen-draper, and had been intended, like Archbishop Secker, for the Presbyterian ministry before he was ordained and became successively Rector of Stanhope and Bishop of Durham. He possessed all the heavy common sense and dislike of enthusiasm which was characteristic of the eighteenth century, and he was not likely to push an argument farther than it would go. But this statement about probability was just suited to arouse

DEISM AND THE ENLIGHTENMENT

his peculiar genius. In *The Analogy of Religion, Natural and Revealed, to the Constitution and Course of Nature*, he had no difficulty in pointing out that probability is, in point of fact, the very guide of life. Starting from the theistic position he builds up the whole system of Christianity on inductive lines—the opposite direction to that in which apology had been wont to proceed. 'For solid structure and logical precision', it has been said, 'it stands almost unrivalled in the English language.'

The ablest of the Deists was a Fellow of All Souls, named Matthew Tindal, who in 1730 published his *Christianity as old as the Creation*. This was a shrewd thrust at those who believed, as orthodox Christians must believe, that their faith is in some sense the absolute religion. The belief rests upon the unchanging character of God. But Tindal turns the argument against the believers. What God has said, He has said once for all; what, therefore, in Christianity is new is not true, and what is true is not new. That throws us back again upon reason, the universal common sense, as the basis for natural religion. The argument was answered by William Law in his *Case of Reason*, in which he argues that reason has no case at all. Here we see the real reaction against all that was typical of eighteenth-century thought. Law has learnt of the Cambridge Platonists; he has also listened to the great German theosophical mystic, Jacob Boehme. He sounds the death-knell of reason as the guide in religion. Man has other instincts and other means of reaching at truth besides the rationalising intellect. Faith involves a movement of the whole personality, and not of one part of it only. Thus as cold common sense proves insufficient, enthusiasm comes back once more to make religion a living and throbbing reality. Law became the parent of much that was best in the different schools of the next century. He was himself a non-juror who had forfeited a fellowship at Emmanuel rather than take the oath to George I, and his high sacramental doctrine is shown in his argument against Hoadly that the sacrament is based, not simply upon a positive ordinance, but upon the very nature of things as they are. Yet his mysticism and his evangelical piety made him the teacher of the Methodists; and his books, *Christian Perfection*, the *Serious Call*, the

Spirit of Prayer, and the *Spirit of Love* formed a school of piety for many for whom the lifeless churches had almost ceased to have any message.

In the meantime English Deism was driving evangelical piety out of Germany. This was partly due to the fact that German Lutherans had developed a kind of Protestant scholasticism that presented a dry, official orthodoxy to the shafts of philosophic inquirers. It was also due in part to the influence of the French Encyclopedists. In 1751 Frederick the Great invited Voltaire to Potsdam, and although they presently quarrelled, the brilliant and cynical Frenchman had considerably affected the minds of the scholars with whom he had been brought in contact. A noticeable fact about the trend of inquiry in Germany was the interest that was taken in other religions. In 1721 Christian Wolff delivered a speech on the 'Practical Philosophy of the Chinese', in which he found opportunity to lavish praises on the morality inculcated by Confucius. This was added fuel to the argument now becoming common, to the effect that if other people could be so good without Christianity there must be some fundamental natural religion which was the common inheritance of the race. Wolff was banished, but later returned in triumph, bringing with him that combination of the teaching of Leibniz and Toland, which in the Enlightenment produced a Christianity without Christ and a Protestantism that 'still remained Protestant when it was no longer Christian'. Of this the greatest figure is Kant, who replaced religion by morality, and Christ by the Categorical Imperative. Nevertheless his work is both a criticism and a synthesis of the characteristic German and British positions upon which later systems could be built. With Leibniz he held that the mind has certain innate qualities which give form to that which comes from without; with Locke he held that the actual content of our knowledge comes from without. Knowledge, being the product of the two elements, is not knowledge of the things in themselves, but of what our minds make of them. In his *Critique of Pure Reason* (1781) he shows that a demonstration of God and natural religion from pure reason alone is impossible. But where

DEISM AND THE ENLIGHTENMENT

the purely intellectual process fails the 'practical reason' may succeed. Men inevitably feel within themselves the command of the moral law, the 'categorical imperative', and for this to be effective there must necessarily be postulated freedom, immortality, and God. What the pure reason thus leaves as a hypothesis only becomes a conviction of the practical reason. Kant, at least, gave a basis for a fundamentally religious conviction and for moral conduct. Unlike their French and English colleagues, these German Deists could find a shelter within their ecclesiastical organisation.

The best-known literary exponent of the ideals of the Enlightenment was Goethe, who passed a youth of considerable licence, and found his artistic temperament unsatisfied by the dryness of the current Lutheranism. In spite of that he lived to realise the shortcomings of rationalist teaching, and in the end saw that Christianity is 'far above all philosophy'. Lessing, in his *Nathan the Wise*, took for his hero a liberal Jew, thus clearly showing the type of thought that seemed to him ideal. He had a curious influence on future Biblical criticism by editing some fragments discovered in the Duke of Brunswick's library at Wolfenbüttel, of which he was librarian. These were some tracts of Reimarus, in which Christ was painted as a deluded eschatologist. The interest in Biblical studies thus aroused was maintained by Semler, a professor at Halle, who taught that revelation is not equally expressed in all parts of Scripture, and regarded the creeds as a later growth. From this moment dogma began to be studied historically, and that method was at last originated which has governed all subsequent thinking.

This development took place in a spirit of sharp antagonism to the stiff legalism of the 'fundamentalist' Lutherans. But it was not all gain to the rationalists, for now the influence of the French Revolution began to be felt, and in the light of that conflagration rationalism began to appear in the colour of avowed atheism. Reaction was inevitable. While some were destroying all traditions, others were achieving a sense of history and beginning to feel some admiration even for the Middle Ages. Thus there developed a Romantic Movement. Jacobi taught that reason is not enough, and that human activity really springs from belief. This led to idealism in the teaching of Fichte, Schelling, and, above all, of Hegel. The last named was a professor in Berlin when he died of cholera in 1831. He saw the universe as a development of the Absolute through effort. In this struggle there are three movements, the logical movements of thought—namely, thesis, antithesis, and synthesis. Christianity is the best representation of God's effort to reveal Himself. In the Trinity the Father represents the thesis of the divine unity; He is objectified in His antithesis, the Son; and the uniting love or synthesis is the Holy Spirit. So in the doctrine of the Incarnation; the Father is the thesis, finite humanity is the antithesis, and the synthesis is the God-man. Here is at least no contemptuous rejection of Christianity, but an effort to catch up its meaning into a philosophical form.

The movement was helped on its way by a practical measure, which was taken as a result of the need for Christian forces to strengthen themselves against Atheism. This was the compulsory union of the Lutheran and Calvinist (Reformed) Churches in Prussia by the order of Frederick William III in 1817. As was natural, the resultant 'Evangelical Church' had little regard for the niceties of credal definition. Even the Apostles' Creed was only retained by a later king's intervention. And philosophy was free to develop on its lines of a reduced Christianity. Schleiermacher held that religion consists, not in belief, but in feeling. The true aim of all religions is to unite man with God. All religions do this more or less adequately, but Christianity is the best of all. Its dogmas are simply the temporal expression of great experiences, but so long as the experiences remain the dogmas may change. As Christ succeeded supremely in reconciling the temporal and the eternal, man and God, He is to be regarded as the very centre of religion, and it should be the effort of all to repeat His experience for themselves. Ritschl improved on this by pointing out that the essential experience is not that of the individual, but of the Church, and as this is an experience of a definite personal relationship with God, 'natural' or speculative theology is worthless. To this he added a theory of knowledge which accepted as fundamentally true the view that it is impossible to know things in abstraction. But what one may know is their value. The piece of wood upon which I sit is known to me adequately as a chair. So Christ was truly a revelation to the primitive Church of God, but to ask what He was in His metaphysical nature is to put a question to which there can be no reply. This was to introduce a new and profoundly stimulating element into the consideration of theological problems. The question of the validity of 'value judgments' is one which is still agitating the minds of thinkers to-day, and its far-reaching effect is to be felt in every modern contribution to theological thought.

CHAPTER XV

PIETISM AND METHODISM

WE must now retrace our steps a little to notice how in the same way that Deism in England was preceded by Puritanism, so the Enlightenment in Germany, of which we have just been tracing the course, was preceded by Pietism. Like the Enlightenment itself, Pietism represents a reaction against the stiff orthodoxy of contemporary Lutheranism, but whereas the Enlightenment was a reaction of the head, Pietism was a reaction of the heart. It appealed to emotions to which neither legalism nor intellectualism had any access. It was very like the later evangelicalism of England, for the origin of which it was, indeed, partly responsible, and like the evangelicals the pietists were looked upon with some disdain. The name was attached to them from the *collegia pietatis*, or societies for mutual spiritual improvement, in which the early representatives of the movement were wont to gather together. Hence it has been described as 'German conventicle Christianity'. Theologically it was due to an overflowing of the Calvinist spirit into the sphere of Lutheranism—in which point again it is not unlike evangelicalism. Historically, its origin is international, and springs from a number of devotional writings, mostly English, that had a great vogue at the period. Bunyan's *Pilgrim's Progress*, Baxter's *Saints' Everlasting Rest*, Molinos's *Spiritual Guide*, Arndt's *True Christianity*, Bayly's *Practice of Piety*, have all been mentioned in this connexion.

The earliest home of this type of thought was really Holland, where, since the Synod of Dort, opinion had become so favourable to toleration as to allow the growth of a puritanical piety in conventicles. Gisbert Voet, the 'Pope of Utrecht', encouraged this form of piety, in spite of the fact that he was the leader of Dutch Calvinistic orthodoxy; and the mystical element in him found congenial matter in the teaching of his contemporary and fellow-countryman, Teelinck, who had lived among English Puritans. But Pietism was never truly mystical. It laid more stress on sin and the need of atonement and much less emphasis on the possibility of union with God than the mystics did. If Bethlehem is the centre of the mystic's religion, Calvary was the centre of the pietist's. Puritanical elements were discernible in their avoidance of plays and public games, their strictness in Sunday observance and Bible reading, and their plain dress. When England's ruling family was the same as that of Hanover, it became more than ever easy for this kind of religion to establish itself in Germany.

The founder of German Pietism was Philip Spener. He was the principal pastor in Frankfort, who in 1670 began to gather his people together into groups or *collegia* for mutual edification. He set forth his aims in a book, *Pia Desideria*, in which he showed his despair of the Lutheran Church as a whole, but sought to raise the spiritual standard of as large a number as possible by forming circles which represented a kind of true Church of real 'heart Christians' within the ecclesiastical organisation. The not unnatural result was that some of his faithful began to show their disdain of ordinary church worship and the sacraments, and this called forth Government interference, from which Spener was glad to escape by becoming Court preacher at Dresden. Spener's influence was shown to have spread to the University of Leipzig, where three young students, of whom the best known was August Hermann Francke, started Bible classes, *collegia philobiblica*, for the study of the Bible on practical and devotional lines. This aroused the wrath of the authorities, and the friends were driven out. Spener, too, was further harassed. In Dresden, the Elector took umbrage at being rebuked by his Court preacher for his drunkenness, and Spener moved on to Berlin. Here he had an unexpected opportunity of influence, for when the Elector founded the new University of Halle in 1691, he was able to get Francke appointed to a professorship, from which he dominated all the theological teaching.

Halle thus became, from the first, a centre of Pietism. Under the spur of Francke's unbounded energy many good works were started there, of which three deserve special mention. The first is the *Paedogogium*, the school in which were trained the many children who were sent to him from all quarters. It is said that at the time of his death over two thousand children were under instruction in his institutions. The second is his Orphan House, and the third is the Bible Institute for the publication and cheap circulation of the Scriptures, which, though not founded directly by him, still remains as a monument to the pious zeal of the group of which he was the leader. But more important than any of these things is the fact that Francke was at last able to roll away the greatest reproach under which Lutheranism suffered, and to awake in his people that zeal for missions which is of the essence of an effective Christianity. His death in 1727 marks the turn of the tide of pietistic influence in the main stream of German Lutheranism.

But in a quiet backwater a remarkable work was to be done by the pious nobleman Nicolaus von Zinzendorf. He had been a scholar in Francke's *Paedogogium*, and when he settled down on his estate it was with the determination to do all in his power to encourage spiritual religion. Here he found himself in contact with a branch of the old Hussite Church or *Unitas Fratrum*, which had been driven out of Bohemia and Moravia by the Thirty Years War. The German-speaking Moravians had sought a refuge in Saxony, and Zinzendorf allowed them to settle on his own estate, where they built themselves a village afterwards to become famous as Herrnhut. Zinzendorf was a godson of Spener, with much admiration for that leader's methods, and when he became interested in the religion of these tenants of his he tried to persuade them to organise themselves as *collegia pietatis* within the Lutheran Church. The Moravians, however, with their hardly maintained episcopal organisation, were much more anxious to remain a separate body. A compromise was arrived at by which the emigrants appointed elders for their secular organisation, and Zinzendorf himself, as owner of the estate, was made responsible for the society as a whole. These arrangements were ratified at a Communion service on August 13, 1727, from which the

Moravian Church dates its new beginning. The community soon began to develop its common life on the lines of a Protestant monasticism without vows. The children were brought up apart from their parents and marriages were regulated. This secured a measure of mobility in this little army of the Lord, and it was used in a noble furthering of the missionary cause. Every member of this Church was a potential missionary, and as there was no Government axe to grind, it was possible for missions to be looked upon, not as some part of a scheme of colonisation, but as a necessary obedience to the Lord's command to preach the gospel. Their work spread into most quarters of the globe, but the most important section of it was in America, where the settlement in Pennsylvania was named Bethlehem on Christmas Day, 1741, by Zinzendorf himself. Curiously enough, a collateral organisation, more definitely mystical and monastic in character, had already been established in the same country, at Ephrata. There, towards the end of the seventeenth century, John Kelpius, a native of Transylvania, had retired to a cave with some companions to await the return of the heavenly Bridegroom. He was succeeded by Conrad Beissel, an ex-baker of Ehrbach and now a Seventh-day Baptist, who established the first coenobitic institution, named Kedar, in 1735. To him there flocked many ascetics to join his 'Order of the Solitary', wearing a monastic habit and striving after ecstatic union with God through Christ with the aid of many hymns, in which an intensely erotic vocabulary was employed. Zinzendorf himself used similar language. His religion was thoroughly Christocentric, and he is responsible for much of the 'Jesus-worship' which loses sight of God the Father in clouds of sentimentalism. The effect was heightened by his ascription of the title Mother to the Holy Spirit who effects the new birth of the believer through Christ. He had many differences with his own Government at home, but he was able to secure the recognition of the Moravians as a branch of the Saxon State Church in 1749, after they had agreed to to take the Augsburg Confession for their Creed. Nevertheless they clung to their episcopate. A Calvinist Court-preacher in Berlin, who had received his early training in the Polish section of the Hussite Church, had been admitted to episcopal consecration in 1699, and he consecrated Nitschmann as missionary bishop in 1735, and Zinzendorf himself in 1737. Financial stress necessitated a further step in the direction of independence. Zinzendorf had been completely ruined by his expenditure for his Church. The Moravians formed a Board of Control, took over his debts and discharged them, and, taxation leading to representation, formed a synod that united their several congregations in one general governing body.

In the meantime the Pietism of the Lutheran Church, by contenting itself with its work among small *collegia* and holding aloof from the wider human interests of the people, had lost its power. Its influence was to reappear later in the sublimated form of Schleiermacher's philosophic emphasis upon the importance of the feelings in religion, but, as Zinzendorf himself spent most of his declining years in England, so the particular form of piety generated by the Moravians was to have its greatest influence in a rising school of English preachers.

In England the Evangelical Movement came as a reaction against the Deists. How Christianity had come to be regarded by the Deists is best expressed in Bishop Butler's words as they occur in the advertisement to his *Analogy*: 'It is come, I know not how, to be taken for granted, by many persons, that Christianity is not so much as a subject for inquiry; but that it is, now at length, discovered to be fictitious.' The defence that he himself and the other apologists of the period had set up justified religion at the bar of the intellect, but it had not warmed the heart. There was now to be a period in which practical Christianity succeeded to theoretic apology. The beginning was made in a resuscitation of those societies for deepening the spiritual life, of which we noticed the importance in the reign of Queen Anne. The particular society that is our immediate concern consisted of a group of Oxford men, the most eminent of whom were the brothers John and Charles Wesley. They were the sons of a Lincolnshire parson, the Rector of Epworth. Both parents were of gentle birth, and both had been brought up in Nonconformity, but had come over to the Church of England from motives of conviction.

Perhaps they were too earnest in their task, for they do not seem to have earned the good will of their parishioners, and it has been suggested that their house had been purposely set aflame on the occasion when John was rescued from such imminent peril that he ever afterwards looked upon himself as a brand plucked from the burning. During his course at Charterhouse and Christ Church, John showed no specially serious leanings; but the reading of Thomas à Kempis's *De Imitatione* at the age of twenty-two and the suggestion that he might take Holy Orders produced a marked change in him. He was ordained in 1725, and the next year was elected a Fellow of Lincoln College. The range of his interests at this time can be judged from the course of studies he then set for himself. Sunday was to be devoted to theology, Monday and Tuesday to the classics, Wednesday to logic and ethics, Thursday to Hebrew and Arabic, Friday to philosophy, and Saturday to oratory and poetry. This programme he was destined to attempt for only a year. For the two following years he was helping his father as Curate of Epworth, his sole experience of parochial work, and one that he does not seem to have found specially congenial. He was recalled to his college in 1729. At Oxford he found that his younger brother, Charles, had already gathered round him a band of serious young men who met together regularly in Christ Church to improve their studies and their religion. John took the lead in this society, and the members began to meet at Lincoln for the reading of the Greek Testament. They began to visit the prisoners at the Castle, and the sick in the parishes, and their methodical observance of the practices of a sacramental and High Churchly religion earned them the nickname of Methodists. They were joined by a poor servitor of Pembroke, George Whitefield, who was later to become as famous as John Wesley himself. The chief formative influences on the latter's mind at this time seem to have been the Early Fathers and William Law.

In 1736 he embraced an opportunity to go out to the new colony of Georgia as a missionary working under the Society for the Propagation of the Gospel. On the journey out he made the acquaintance of a number of Moravians bound for the same colony, and in order to converse with them he achieved the task of learning German while on shipboard. He was not unsuccessful in his work in the colony, but he maintained his acquaintance with his new Moravian friends, and their emphasis on an emotional conversion helped to make him feel unsettled about his own spiritual state. Real harm was done by his association with Sophia Hopkey, who in pique because he did not offer her a proposal of marriage consoled herself by marrying his rival. Wesley then, having doubts about the lady's religious convictions, made the incredible mistake of repelling her from communion. The husband prosecuted him in the civil court, and the disastrous business ended in Wesley leaving Georgia for ever. He was now quite assured that all was not well with his own spiritual condition. Arrived once again in England he immediately resorted to the Moravians, and was introduced to Peter Bohler, from whom he learnt that a man may be turned on an instant from the misery of sin to a consciousness of righteousness and joy in the Holy Spirit. This experience happened to Wesley at a meeting in Aldersgate Street on May 24, 1738, when someone was reading Luther's Preface to the Romans: 'I felt my heart strangely warmed. I felt I did trust in Christ, Christ alone, for salvation; and an assurance was given me that He had taken away my sins.' This led to a pilgrimage to Herrnhut, where the Moravians treated him as a child, Zinzendorf made him dig in his garden, and they all taught him simplicity without admitting him to Communion. He brought back mixed feelings, and was saved from joining the United Brethren. From this time begins his great preaching career. Taking the whole country as his parish, he went from end to end of the land, bringing to people for whom it had never yet been a reality the good news of the Gospel. It was the time when a great industrial population was multiplying in England and concentrating itself in large towns where the Church organisation was incapable of providing for them. Wesley gathered the people in thousands in the open air and preached to them with such force that many broke out into hysterical expressions of their terror at the certain punishment for sin, but on reaching an assurance of the love of God in Christ began to lead new and sober lives. The cardinal principle of Wesley's

PIETISM AND METHODISM 189

own religion was an ardent love for God, but the peculiarity of his experience made him emphasise two things that were in that proportion new elements in Christian preaching. The first was the 'new birth' as a result of the emotional experience of conversion, which in the teaching of his followers, though not in his own, became virtually a substitute for baptism; and the second was the possibility of Christian perfection, which was in essence nothing but the old belief in the practicability of a sanctified life, but was pushed to the extreme of denying the possibility of sin to the converted Christian. The success of this preaching was so great that some organisation became necessary. Lay preachers assisted in the work which the clergy were too suspicious to take up, and 'class meetings' were organised for the shepherding of those who had been affected by the preaching. While he lived Wesley was himself the life and centre of the vast and growing movement. The fact of his gentle birth helped his agents to support his natural autocracy, while his own brother Charles, whose strong sacramentalism is still preserved for us in his beautiful hymns, held him fast in his allegiance to the Church. He himself said to his followers, 'Be Church of England men still; do not cast away the peculiar glory which God hath put upon you'; but of him his elder brother Samuel said, 'I am not afraid that the Church will excommunicate him (discipline is at too low an ebb for that), but that he will excommunicate the Church.' In point of fact, he was generally on good terms with the bishops, although he once received a characteristically heavy rebuke from Bishop Butler: 'Sir, the pretending to extraordinary revelations and gifts of the Holy Ghost is a horrid thing, a very horrid thing.' But the mischief was that the bishops always dealt with him separately, and the abeyance of Convocation prevented the Church from taking any united action in regard to his societies. Consequently there was no wise guidance to keep the movement within such bounds as were consonant with membership of the Church. In 1760 his lay preachers at Norwich celebrated the Communion; in 1764 he persuaded a Greek prelate, Erasmus, Bishop of Arcadia, to ordain some of his preachers; and in 1784, impatient at the delay to get things done for America, he himself ordained Dr. Coke as superintendent and two others as presbyters for the work in that continent, following up this fatal step by ordinations for Scotland. He was now an old man, and his brother Charles put down his defection to the infirmities of age. He died in 1791, and his work has spread till there are now as many as twenty-eight million Methodists in various parts of the world.

The effect of all this was to weaken rather than to strengthen the Church of England. Nevertheless out of it there sprang that definitely evangelical movement which was to find a permanent home within the ecclesiastical organisation. The author of this movement was George Whitefield, whom we have already mentioned as being one of the Wesleys' early friends. He had gone as a servitor to Pembroke College from assisting his father at the Bell Inn, Gloucester. He had felt to the full the influence of the Wesleys' society in Oxford, and had been ordained at the early age of twenty-one. He had no learning, but possessed a marvellous gift of oratory. His first sermon is said to have driven fifteen persons mad, but that is the only occasion upon which we hear of hysterical phenomena following his preaching. He retained his superb voice in spite of forty to sixty hours' preaching a week, and in America even Benjamin Franklin could be moved to empty his pockets at his appeal. His theological views involved him in a breach with Wesley. While Wesley was Arminian, Whitefield was a thorough Calvinist. Wesley challenged Whitefield's teaching on Free Grace, and Whitefield would have nothing to do with Wesley's belief in the possibility of a sinless perfection on this side of the grave. Hence arose the two types of Methodism—the Wesleyan Methodist following Wesley's Arminianism, and the Calvinistic Methodist following Whitefield's Calvinism. Whitefield had a powerful friend in Selina, Countess of Huntingdon. She was responsible for introducing his teaching to the upper classes. She had a chapel, called the Surrey Chapel, in Westminster, where lecturers published the Methodist gospel, and in it there was a 'Nicodemus Corner', where important people could listen without themselves being seen. From this beginning she proceeded to spend her large fortune in the building and maintenance of many chapels throughout the country, where Whitefield's views were propagated. Eventually it was seen that these could not be recognised as Church of England chapels, and they were formed into a separate association under the name of 'Lady Huntingdon's Connexion'. To provide ministers she established a training college in Wales, which was afterwards moved to Cheshunt, and has since fallen into the hands of the Church of England. On the separation of her Connexion from the Establishment, most of the ordained ministers of her chapels dropped back into the ordinary parochial life of the Church from which they had come. They took their own views with them, and thus strengthened that type of thought in the English Church which is known as evangelical. Many of the most earnest parochial clergy were already friends of Wesley, such as Fletcher of Madely, of whom Voltaire said that he was a character as perfect as our Lord; Walker of Truro, who remonstrated in vain with Wesley for planting his societies in parishes where there were already evangelical incumbents; and Venn of Huddersfield, who after himself doing a certain amount of itinerating settled down to be the first preacher of Evangelicalism as distinct from Methodism in the North. But such men, with the exception of Fletcher, took little interest in the Arminian dispute, and the greater influence among the evangelicals was really wielded by those who were much more definitely Calvinist in their views. Toplady, the author of the beautiful hymn 'Rock of Ages', was a vigorous defender of the Calvinism of the English Church, and, indeed, if one started, as he did, with the assumption that the Church of England began at the Reformation, it would be easily possible to trace a strain of Calvinism in her doctrine. At any rate, on this occasion Calvinism was victorious: whereas the Arminian Wesleyans left the Church, Calvinism has coloured the views of the evangelicals within the Church until almost our own day.

CHAPTER XVI

VICISSITUDES OF ROMAN CATHOLICISM

DURING the eighteenth and nineteenth centuries the Roman Catholic Church suffered some extraordinary changes of fortune. These changes involved the loss of practically the whole of the territory over which she ruled as a temporal power and the loss of quite the whole of her political influence. They were losses against which she struggled with all her force, and the consequences of which she is unwilling even now to acknowledge; but they were accompanied by a great increase in her spiritual influence, and gave her a wider range of purely religious activity than she had enjoyed at any moment since the close of the Reformation.

In England her story was one of a continual, and at last successful, struggle towards emancipation. Long before the laws against them were repealed Roman Catholics had been allowed to carry on their worship with impunity. A more definite measure of relief seemed to be impending when in 1737 some of the disabilities of Irish Roman Catholics were removed. Hitherto the English followers of the Papacy had been under the ecclesiastical guidance of Vicars-Apostolic from Rome, but in 1740 the Pope took a step in advance by consecrating Richard Challoner as Bishop of Debra for work as his vicar in London. The influence of so saintly a man was badly needed by his flock, for Roman Catholicism in London was barely kept alive by the chapels attached to the foreign embassies. In Lancashire and Yorkshire it still held out, but in Scotland it had been practically exterminated, except in the Western Highlands, during the reign of George I, because of the complicity of the Roman Catholics in the Jacobite plots. In England many of the great families joined the Anglican Church when it was seen that the Jacobite cause was hopeless. Challoner did everything that a good and self-sacrificing bishop could do in the way of ministering to individuals. In Ireland much of the repressive legislation that still remained in force was repealed in 1771, but Challoner's own flock was not so fortunate. He wrote his *Meditations* and his *Garden of the Soul* to preserve their piety in days when they were still politically outcast. In spite, however, of his precautions, when the Government repealed the Act of William III and allowed Roman Catholics once again to acquire land, public fanaticism broke out under Lord George Gordon, and led to the Gordon Riots of 1780. Challoner himself only escaped with difficulty from the clutches of the mob, and his experiences hastened his end, which took place the next year. Public opinion, however, refused to be stampeded by the riots, and under the stress of the war with America, France, and Spain, Roman Catholics were given commissions in the Army and Navy. The good feeling was strengthened in 1789 when the English Romanists, having consulted the foreign universities, drew up a Protestation, signed by all the Vicars-Apostolic acting in England, asserting their loyalty to the Crown, denying the power of their Church to absolve them from it, and declaring that they acknowledged no infallibility in the Pope. After the passing of the union between Great Britain and Ireland and the frequent evidence of the sympathy aroused in England for the sufferers under the French Revolution, Pitt, the Prime Minister, would gladly have brought in a measure for complete emancipation, but he was held in check by the conscientious scruples of the King, George III. After that king's death the work of effecting toleration went rapidly forward. The Test and Corporation Acts were repealed in 1828, and the next year the Catholic Emancipation Act was passed.

Even in Spain, the country where the Reformation had had least effect, the eighteenth century brought some differences between the Church and the Government. Philip V was jealous both of the wealth and the privileges of the Church. A plan was formed to reduce the privileges, but this led to a fierce conflict with the Inquisition, which denounced its authors, and it had to be dropped. A scheme to take all the uninvested capital of the religious foundations and to inaugurate with it a Bank of Spain did not get even so far. But in 1753 a Concordat was drawn up and ratified, by which the Pope agreed to share the patronage of the smaller benefices with the King. When Charles III came to the throne in 1759 he found over 80,000 monks and nuns in his country, and the Inquisition and the Jesuits the most important powers in the land. He was full of Gallican ideals, and, while remaining a faithful son of the Church, determined to be master in his own land. In 1761, after a dispute with the Inquisition, he issued an edict declaring that the inquisitors and prelates owed obedience to the Crown, prohibiting the publication of papal Bulls and Briefs without his consent, and forbidding the Inquisition to issue any edict without his knowledge and approval. As the papal jurisdiction was mostly exercised through the Jesuits, this was a definite blow against them, and events quickly occurred which filled their cup to overflowing. Suspicion had hardened against them on the ground of their missionary methods, their commercial operations, and their political principles. Pombal, the Portuguese Minister, led an attack against them because of their opposition to his schemes in Paraguay. He had a strange ally in Pope Benedict XIV, who strongly disliked their pandering to heathenism in the mission-field. An inquiry was ordered, and the report was definitely adverse to the Society. In Portugal their leader was tried by the Inquisition and burnt, and they were expelled from Portuguese territory in 1759. There followed a wave of hatred against them everywhere, their end being hastened by the fact that an attempt had been made to assassinate the Portuguese King, Joseph, and they were being implicated in the plot. Similar suspicion had fallen upon them in France owing to an attempt on the life of Louis XV. But what stirred France against them even more than this was the gigantic failure of a business house which was run as part of their concerns in the mission-field at Martinique. The *Parlement* of Paris decided in 1761 that the Society must bear the responsibility, and followed this up the next year by publishing a volume which described the shortcomings of the Jesuits in the strongest language,

VICISSITUDES OF ROMAN CATHOLICISM 195

and ordered their dispersal. The Pope bade the clergy to protest against this, but the only result was that in 1764 the Society was expelled from France altogether. These events were not without their influence on Charles III in Spain. He had been much disturbed by an insurrection at Madrid, and strongly suspected the Jesuits of being at the bottom of it. He became convinced that the doctrine of regicide advocated by some of their number was the teaching of the Society as a whole, and in 1767 followed the example of Portugal and France by expelling them from his dominions. A concerted attack was now made by the Catholic powers upon the very existence of the society. A demand for its abolition was made in 1769, and, after a process that dragged on for four years, Pope Clement XIV published his famous bull *Dominus ac Redemptor Noster*, totally suppressing the Order. But the members, whose sole original purpose of existence was to support the Papacy, disobeyed the papal command. They defied the Pope, not only by accepting the shelter of the Protestant Frederick in Prussia and the Orthodox Catherine in Russia, but by continuing to elect their Vicar-General, and, worse still, by forging a papal brief in 1774 recounting the Pope's joy at their continued existence in Russia. In any case the harm that they had done to Catholic doctrine remained in the teaching of one who was not indeed of their number, but had drunk deep of their spirit and may be regarded as the founder of modern Roman Catholicism, S. Alphonsus Liguori.

It was in Italy that the influence of Liguori found a favourable opportunity. There the effect of the War of the Spanish Succession had been to demonstrate the complete political powerlessness of the Papacy. The impression was heightened by the terrible state of misrule into which the papal states had fallen. In the consequent torpor of religion S. Alphonsus did a work that has been compared to the revival produced by Wesley in England. He had begun life as a barrister, but had abandoned that profession after discovering that in pleading a particular case he had omitted to notice an all-important document. He was ordained priest in 1726 and at once began work as a mission preacher in and around Naples, using a simple style of oratory that was the opposite of the pompous rhetoric of the day. Those whom he influenced were gathered together in associations that remind one strongly of the Methodist societies, but instead of Wesley's lay preachers he founded the Redemptorists (Congregation of the Most Holy Redeemer), an organisation of priests living together under the control of the bishop and working among the slums. In this way he not only affected the laity, but also did much for the raising of the standard of clerical life. Naples at that time possessed eighty odd thousand of clergy, who all absorbed money, but few of whom did parochial work. Their state of morals was such that the Government had to interfere, and King Charles III effected a concordat by which their property was brought under taxation, and the number of ordinations was limited to ten for every thousand of the population. This meddling on the part of the State did not suit Alphonsus Liguori, but he realised that no Church is likely to be better than its clergy, and used all his influence with the Conclave of 1774 to get a reforming pope elected. As a moralist, Alphonsus desired to make the transition from vice to virtue as easy as possible. He had himself been brought up in a rigorist school, but in his *Moral Theology* he shows himself in reaction from Tutiorism, which is the principle that a course of action must not be pursued if its morality is at all doubtful, and on the way towards Probabilism, which is the principle that a man may follow a course of action in favour of which probable arguments may be brought forward, although the balance of evidence is on the other side. It is true that he rejects that view in favour of his own Aequiprobabilism, which is the principle that the easier path may be followed if the authorities in its favour are as good as those against it; but in practice many people have found it impossible to distinguish between his principle and that of the Jesuits, and there is no doubt that he often shows a leniency in moral judgment which is shocking to northern minds. In other departments of his theology Liguori shows a regrettable departure from primitive standards. He carried on the Jesuit practice of worshipping the Heart of Jesus as the early Church worshipped the Person of the Redeemer, and gave to Mary the position that the Arians had ascribed to Christ, making her a semi-divine mediatrix between God

VICISSITUDES OF ROMAN CATHOLICISM

and man, and not fearing to think that 'as the Son is Almighty by nature, so is the Mother by grace'. To all this the Roman Church has lent the weight of its authority by canonising him in 1839 and declaring him a doctor of the Church in 1871.

This kind of influence was opposed by Pope Benedict XIV, who earned for himself the title of the 'Protestant Pope', but was nevertheless a scholar and the historian of canonisation. He did good work for the Church by reconciling the Catholic powers, to whom he made much needed concessions. In Italy especially the states were gradually freeing themselves from the oppressive claims of the Papacy. The length to which the most earnest prelates were willing to go in the way of concession was seen in Tuscany, where Ricci, Bishop of Pistoia, persuaded a synod in his cathedral city to accept the Gallican Articles of 1682, and a Synod of Florence in 1787 to start a practical reform among the clergy. But the reactionary forces were too strong, and he was driven to resignation on a charge of Jansenism. Thus the influence of the Jesuits and of Alphonsus Liguori triumphed. Even the storm which swept over the country from France at the end of the century only changed the external features of the Papacy and left the heart of it untouched.

The suppression of the Jesuits brought no improvement in the condition of the Church in France. The bishops were aristocratic and wealthy, but they had neither spirituality nor ability. The rationalism of the Encyclopedists had brought forth no great apology for Christianity as Deism did in England. The profligacy of the Court found no adequate check in an ascetic clergy. The only startling impetus that religion received was the news in 1770 that Louis XV's daughter, Louise, had taken the veil as a Carmelite. As events moved towards the Revolution some sop was thrown to the Protestants in the way of an exemption from persecution accorded in 1787 by Louis XVI. But when the Revolution did come, the Church was identified with aristocracy and suffered accordingly. The first attack was naturally upon the enormous property held by ecclesiastical institutions. Talleyrand paid the deficit in the Treasury from the clerical revenues. In 1789 the Assembly confiscated ecclesiastical property and reduced the clergy to the position of servants of the State. The next year this was fixed by the Civil Constitution of the Clergy. The religious Orders were suppressed and the hundred and fifty bishoprics were reduced to eighty-three; and both the bishops and parochial clergy were to be elected by the people. This was too drastic; all but four of the bishops refused to take the required oath of obedience to the new constitution. Others were consecrated in their places, even Talleyrand, who had renounced his orders taking part in the consecrations. This produced a non-juring schism and was more potent than any other factor in making it impossible for the nation to settle down to the new regime. The next year complete religious freedom was announced, but in 1792 the non-juring clergy were compelled to leave the country, no fewer than forty thousand people thus being expelled. Jacobinism broke out in massacres the same year. The mob broke into the prisons and in one week despatched twelve hundred persons, of whom three hundred were priests. Atheism replaced religion. The Goddess of Reason was enthroned on the altar of Notre Dame, and in 1793 all religion was declared abolished. There followed the period of the Terror in which even constitutional bishops were executed. Sixteen Carmelite nuns were sentenced to death because they remained together and clung to their rule after they had been driven from their convent. The Visitation nuns of Rouen were more fortunate in that they were able to wander from place to place and keep their vows, until at last they were reunited under their Mother when the storm was past. The worship of reason was soon seen to be a failure and was replaced by a form of Deism called Theophilanthropy, which was not so intolerant. Religious freedom was restored in 1795, and Christian worship was allowed, first in private houses and then in churches. Steps were taken to reunite the Church and heal the schism between the constitutional and the non-juring clergy. A national council of the clergy was summoned to meet at Notre Dame in 1797. It passed canons admitting the supremacy of the Pope, but rejecting his jurisdiction over the Church in France. It stood upon the Gallican Articles of 1682, and at last there seemed a chance that the national aspirations of the French Church would be fulfilled.

VICISSITUDES OF ROMAN CATHOLICISM 199

But then a new factor in affairs appeared in the person of Napoleon.

Bonaparte was at the head of the French Army that came to Rome to avenge the murder of the French Republic's envoy there in 1796. If Pius VI had been willing to recognise the Civil Constitution of the Clergy all might have been well, but he preferred to rely on Austrian help, and when that failed he was driven to the humiliating Peace of Tolentino in 1797, by which he was compelled to cede more than a third of his territory and to refrain from further alliances against France. This sounded the death-knell of the temporal power of the Papacy. Rome was forced to turn itself into a republic, which the Pope refused to recognise. Thereupon, after the French troops had occupied Rome on the excuse of another murder, he was ordered to leave the city and was later taken to France, where he died in 1799. That year Napoleon was declared the First Consul of France, and became, in effect, its despot. His own religious views amounted probably to no more than a vague theism, but he had a firm belief in the Catholic faith and organisation as a social cement and a basis for secure government. Consequently he was very ready to enlist the support of the Papacy, and, as a preliminary, to effect a firm union between Rome and the Church in France. That would involve an ending of the discord among the Catholics of France. There still existed the difficulty between the constitutional and the non-juring clergy. The best plan seemed to be to make a clean sweep of all existing appointments, and begin all over again with a new body who should possess the papal guarantee and yet be subservient to himself. Napoleon was able to begin his negotiations after his great victory at Marengo in 1800. They issued in the Concordat of 1801, in which the Government of the French Republic recognised 'that the Catholic Apostolic and Roman religion is the religion of the great majority of French citizens'. By a Bull issued the same year the Pope 'suppressed, annulled, and for ever extinguished' all the French sees and deprived the bishops of all jurisdiction. New dioceses were delimited and bishops nominated to them by the First Consul were instituted by the Pope. Some of them were the old bishops restored, others were new. They nominated the parochial clergy, and all alike took an Oath of Allegiance to the Republic. Thus was a new Church created for France. Thirteen of the old bishops refused to resign and were excommunicated by the Pope, but with a few of the faithful formed a schism, *La Petite Église*, which did not die out for a hundred years. As a result of this bargain Pius VII, the new Pope with whom it had been effected, recovered the papal states from which his predecessor had been ejected. But Napoleon added to the Concordat certain Organic Articles, by which, under the head of police regulations, the Gallican Articles of 1682 were enforced, and the Pope was precluded from publishing any Bull in France or interfering in the affairs of the French Church without the authorisation of the Government. But in actual fact, though Napoleon seemed to have won a complete victory, the effect of the new creation was to make the clergy look upon the Pope as the source of their being and consequently to encourage the growth of that ultramontane spirit which it was designed to destroy, but which is the most marked feature of the modern Church of France. To the Protestants full religious rights were accorded, and their ministers were paid and controlled as servants of the State.

As a result of Napoleon's schemes in Europe the ecclesiastical condition of the Empire suffered great changes. In Germany the great archbishop-electorates were secularised, and Talleyrand used their territories to compensate the princes who had suffered under the French conquests. The archbishops themselves were left nothing but their spiritual privileges. The secularisation was ratified by a Diet of the Empire in 1803, and Prussia was the chief gainer by the division of the spoils. Three years later another venerable institution passed away when Francis II gave up the title of Holy Roman Emperor, and a break was made with the history of the last thousand years. Napoleon had himself usurped the last vestiges of the old imperial rule when he had himself crowned as Emperor of the French in Paris. On that occasion the Pope anointed and hallowed him while he himself placed the crown upon his own head. By this acquiescence Pius VII did not save himself from further slights, for in 1808 French troops entered Rome, the papal estates were annexed to France, and the Pope himself was carried off as a prisoner and kept as such till 1814. But the Emperor could not compel his prisoner to recognise the Gallican Articles, and when the Russian campaign failed he had to set the Pope at liberty. Napoleon signed his abdication while Pius entered Rome in triumph.

The Restoration of 1815 meant more than a resuscitation of local governments after the shackles of Napoleon had been cast off. A new spirit was in the air. The rationalism of the eighteenth century was discredited. Romanticism brought with it a new interest in the age of faith. At the Congress of Vienna Pius VII obtained a restoration of some part of the papal property, and he had already given a direction to the progress of Roman Catholicism by a Bull of 1814, in which he brought back the Jesuits. They soon resumed their place in papal councils and their world-wide activities, and, aided by the posthumous influence of Alphonsus Liguori, they set the tone of the revived Romanism. French ultramontanism was encouraged by the literary Catholic revival of which Le Maistre, Lamenais, and Chateaubriand were the heroes. It seemed that in the new world the Papacy might become the final arbiter of all vexed questions. A beginning was made in the sphere of dogma. In 1854 Pius IX, after consulting the Roman Catholic bishops, promulgated the dogma of the Immaculate Conception to settle the question debated for centuries whether the Virgin Mother had or had not any taint of original sin. It seemed, too, that this new consciousness of power might be accompanied by a real sympathy with the social ideals of the rising populations. In France Lamenais sought a union of Catholicism and socialism under the cry 'God and Freedom'. Pius was not himself unmoved by the possibility, but his political ideals were stiffened when the rising nationalism of Italy and the establishment of a kingdom under Victor Emmanuel by the agency of Garibaldi in 1861 led to the loss of the papal states. After 1871 the Pope, while retaining the privileges of a sovereign, was allowed to preserve of his territories only the Vatican, the Lateran, and the Castel Gandolpho, and consequently declared himself a prisoner. In 1864 a *Syllabus of Errors* was published which denounced all such results of liberalism as the separation of Church and State, non-sectarian education, and the toleration of varieties in religion. The process of standardisation was completed in 1870 by the holding of the Vatican Council, which affirmed the doctrine of Papal Infallibility, a doctrine the precise meaning of which has been so debated both by its friends and its foes that it had better be stated in the following words of the decree: 'The Roman Pontiff, when he speaks *ex cathedra*, that is, when in the discharge of the office of pastor and doctor of all Christians, by virtue of his supreme apostolic authority, he defines a doctrine regarding faith or morals to be held by the universal Church; by the divine assistance promised to him in blessed Peter, is possessed of that infallibility with which the divine Redeemer willed that His Church should be endowed.'

This decree was not passed without much opposition, though only two votes were cast against it in the Council. The most notable opponent was Döllinger of Munich, the great ecclesiastical historian. He was excommunicated, but many who sympathised with him formed themselves into a separate Church, called the Old Catholics, which still possesses a number of adherents in Germany and Switzerland. They have continued their episcopal succession, deriving their orders from the Jansenist Church of Utrecht, which itself developed in 1723 as the result of the papal condemnation in 1713 of the *Moral Reflections on the New Testament*, by Pasquier Quesnel, a leading Jansenist. The future of the Old Catholics is somewhat doubtful. They are dwindling in numbers and do not seem to have much vitality, but in the eyes of many they remain as a valuable witness to a non-papal Catholicity. The succeeding Pope, Leo XIII, although a man of wide sympathies and statesmanlike abilities, was powerless to heal the schism. Nor was he more fortunate in his relations with the secular government of Italy, owing to his intransigence in the matter of the papal states. Nevertheless he healed the breach between the Papacy and the German Government, and taught the French clergy to show themselves more sympathetic towards the Republic. He earned the suspicion of some of his own people because of his scholarly leanings, opening the Vatican library to students and fixing upon the teaching of Thomas Aquinas as the norm for the papal Church. But although he was willing to seek possibilities of reunion with the Orthodox Church, he showed himself less open towards the English Church, and in 1896 definitely pronounced Anglican Orders invalid.

In Germany the result of the Declaration of Infallibility was at first to draw out the pronounced opposition of Bismarck, who banished the Jesuits and passed the Falk Laws against the Catholics in 1873. This he did in the belief that the bishops had become mere 'functionaries of a foreign sovereign who, by virtue of his infallibility, is the most absolute monarch on the globe'. Later, however, he changed his tactics, and, seeing in the Papacy an ally against socialism, repealed the Falk Laws. The result has been to make Catholicism a permanent element in German political life, and to create a definite Catholic Party in the Reichstag. In France the course of change has taken the opposite direction. At one time the Jesuit interest in education and democracy seemed to carry all before it, and there was a widespread revival of religion in France after 1870. But the Government was not persuaded of the good intentions of the clergy towards the public. In 1901 religious orders were excluded from sharing in the work of education. Some refused to conform to the law, and in 1903 many of their houses were suppressed and their property confiscated by the State. Under Pius X the breach widened, and when he unwisely protested against a visit paid by the President of the Republic to the King of Italy, France broke off diplomatic relations with the Papacy. This was followed in 1905 by the *Loi de la Séparation*, which declared all ecclesiastical property to be the possession of the State and decreed that religious bodies who desired to claim the use of it must henceforth form themselves into recognised associations for the purpose. In spite of the fact that all State aid was withdrawn from Catholics and Protestants alike, Pius forbade his clergy to enter into such *associations cultuelles*. In point of fact, while the bulk of the Churches have continued in the use of their property the Church has been relieved of the necessity for the upkeep of some great buildings which even the State finds a white elephant. The necessity of relying entirely upon voluntary contributions has reduced the clergy to a severe degree of poverty, but it has quickened the spiritual sense of the Catholic half of the nation. It was that half which provided much of the moral strength of the French people during the Great War.

CHAPTER XVII

THE OXFORD MOVEMENT

AT the beginning of the nineteenth century the Church of England was in a bad way. The effect of Methodism had been to reduce very considerably the number of its adherents. It has been calculated that whereas a hundred years earlier not a twentieth of the nation refrained from attendance at its services, by this time a quarter of the people were acknowledged Dissenters. The emotional appeal of evangelicalism had died down and its Calvinism had become largely formal. Its exponents had congregated mostly in fashionable watering-places, where, since they denied themselves the gaieties of life, little was left them but the listening to sermons, with which they combined meditations upon death. They had no corporate sense and tended to neglect both the fabric of the churches and the observance of sacred seasons. These were better guarded by the remnant of the old High-Church party, which had been reinforced in 1789 by the return to communion of the Scotch bishops and most of the non-jurors. But they had settled down to an almost completely static view of churchmanship, combining Church and State in one entity, after the manner of Hooker, while glorying in a profound admiration for the 'incomparable liturgy' of the Book of Common Prayer.

Yet there were not wanting signs of a continuance of devout spirituality combined with a due sense of the importance of the visible Church and its sacraments. This was well illustrated in the life of the great layman, Dr. Johnson, who had said that he would willingly stand before a battery of cannon to restore the powers of Convocation. The well-known fact that at S. Paul's Cathedral on Easter Day, 1800, there were only six communicants was balanced by the fact that in the Lincoln diocese a sixth of the total number of communicants received the Sacrament. In contrast to the evangelical group at Clapham, there was a group of High-Churchmen at Clapton who were instrumental in founding the National Society in 1811 and the Additional Curates Society in 1837. Another society for which they were responsible, the Church Building Society, is witness to their recognition of the need for coping with the tremendous increase of the industrial population. In the year 1818 Parliament passed an Act granting a million pounds for church building, and it has been estimated that between that year and 1833 no less than six millions were spent on that object alone. In the realm of thought churchly ideals were strongly maintained by Alexander Knox, who was born in Limerick in 1757 and died in Dublin in 1831. He derived his views from the early High Churchmanship of Wesley, but carried them much farther, disliking the name Protestant and holding that the Vincentian Canon was best expressed at that time in 'the genuine central essence of our own reformed Episcopal Church'. These views he taught to John Jebb, Bishop of Limerick, who developed them in an appendix to a volume of sermons published in 1815. In Cambridge much the same type of view was taught by Hugh James Rose, who, as 'Christian Advocate' in the university, did much by his preaching to lay a satisfactory basis for apologetic, and by his founding of the *British Magazine* in 1832 provided a medium by which similar views might reach a larger public.

But outside purely ecclesiastical circles there were influences that were making for the development of a fresh spirit of piety. Newman himself later distinguished three of these in the works of Scott, Coleridge, and Wordsworth. The importance of Sir Walter Scott was that he helped to stir up a vivid and popular interest in the Middle Ages. Not that he really understood the period any more than the architects of the new churches understood the Gothic that they set themselves so assiduously to imitate. But the light and colour, the music and the vestments, all the gay pageantry of the Middle Ages were introduced by him to a generation wilting away in the blight of a dull and drab monotony. If Newman read him, Keble wrote on him, and found in his conversion from Presbyterianism to Anglicanism a proof that he saw in the English Church the fairest reproduction of all that he had praised in the Middle Ages. While Scott found a new world in the old, Wordsworth found an equally new and romantic world in the beauties of nature. To him the 'primrose by the river's brim' was a key to unlock the mysteries of the infinite. Nothing could be richer or more surprising to a generation that had been brought up to worship business solidity and success. The fact that this nature-mysticism was linked with the growing veneration for the English Church expressed in the *Ecclesiastical Sonnets* was enough to make him the peculiar possession of men who looked for a Church revival. Coleridge is joined to the Lake School even on its religious side by his *Ancient Mariner*.

> He prayeth best who loveth best
> All things both great and small,
> For the dear God who loveth us
> He made and loveth all.

But on his philosophical side he paved the way for two schools. By his *Aids to Reflection* he opened the path to liberalism. Nevertheless five years after its publication he issued, in 1830, his *Constitution of Church and State*, in which he drew a sharp distinction between the national Church and the universal Church, and so freed the minds of Englishmen from that insularity which had long been their bane in ecclesiastical matters. Of the spiritual romanticism engendered by these influences, Church-loving as well as nature-loving, the most notable example appeared in 1827 when Keble published his *Christian Year*. His modesty was such that he would not have published the poems at all had it not been for the earnest entreaties of his aged father, and even when he yielded he did not append his signature. But the ground had been better prepared than anyone knew, and their pellucid piety, fresh and clean as the flowers of which they sang, found so universal a welcome that the book ran through no fewer than ninety-five editions during its author's life. It is obvious that the time for revival had come.

It often happens that a new spirit will grow without

becoming fully conscious of itself until contrasting forces appear and compel it to realise itself in opposition. The reviving churchly spirit of the early nineteenth century might have spread until it mildly pervaded the whole of ecclesiastical society had it not found itself definitely opposed to certain tendencies and certain acts, which served to make it more clearly articulate, and, while narrowing its channel, gave it fullness and strength. The Oriel Common Room of that period was the home of the finest intellects in the University of Oxford. From that college had proceeded the scheme for Honours Examinations in the University, and it had thrown open its own fellowships to competitive examination. By making its fellowships the most coveted intellectual prize of the day, it had succeeded in collecting together the best men. At that time it was dominated by the group of thinkers known as the Noetics. They were not historians and they knew little of the philosophical movements of the Continent, but they had been strongly affected by the French Revolution and disregarded the arbitrament of authority in matters of the mind, treating every question as an open question and endeavouring to settle it by reference to fundamental principles. Under its Provosts, first Copleston and then Hawkins (whom Newman helped to elect in preference to Keble), the group discussed the difficulties confronting the Church. Hawkins was himself a High Churchman of the old type, believing in tradition and apostolic succession without its concomitant theory of grace. Blanco White, who had once been a Spanish priest, contributed both a knowledge of Roman Catholicism from within and also an essentially sceptical outlook. Whately was a severe logician without historical sense who wished to invite disestablishment without disendowment. But most noteworthy was Thomas Arnold, who became Headmaster of Rugby in the year of the publication of Keble's *Christian Year*. His was an essentially religious mind, which would rather have seen the establishment of paganism than the existence of a State without an official religion. He was convinced that nothing could save the Church of England as then constituted, and proposed to go back to Hooker's view of Church and State as two sides of the same thing. But inasmuch as it was clearly impossible

THE OXFORD MOVEMENT

to unite all religious people on the basis of historic Christianity, he proposed to substitute for it a wider confession, which would unite all except Quakers, Roman Catholics, and the extremer type of Unitarian. It was against the background of this Noetic temper that the spirit of a new churchly group of Oriel men was to see itself clearly expressed.

But certain practical matters made the distinction all the clearer. The Church had failed dismally to cope with the rise of the new industrial population, and it was in this class of society that the tremendous increase of dissent, already noticed, had chiefly taken place. Politically, such men suffered under a ridiculous system of representation which practically disenfranchised them. A modest measure of relief was offered in the Reform Bill of 1831. Ecclesiastically this would have the effect of giving them a voice in the affairs of the Church, and it would be difficult after this to regard Parliament as a sort of lay synod, the members of which were faithful to the Church on whose affairs they legislated. The clergy took alarm and the new corporate spirit set itself against a reform which was welcomed by all men of liberal views, and indeed was necessary in order to avoid a revolution. But further, the Whig Ministers were suspected of actual designs upon the Church and its property. Lord Grey had uttered an ambiguous warning to the bishops to 'set their house in order', and an earnest of what might come was seen in the proposals about the Church of Ireland. That Church was certainly in an anomalous position. The bulk of the Irish people had never accepted the Reformation settlement, the language difficulty making it impossible for them to appreciate the Book of Common Prayer. It had therefore been easy for the Roman Catholics, when they set up their own hierarchy in 1614, to undertake the spiritual guidance of the greater part of the nation. The Irish Church was no longer the Church of the people. Out of a population of eight millions it could not muster more than 850,000 adherents, and yet it was the established Church drawing the tithes. As an instance of the absurdities that might occur we may quote the example of the incumbent who drew a thousand pounds a year, without having a single person to minister to or a church to minister in. The peasantry rose against the tithe and refused to pay it, and Parliament compensated the clergy. But in 1833 a Bill was introduced to bring about a certain measure of disendowment and to suppress two of the four archbishoprics and eight out of the eighteen bishoprics. It seemed intolerable to enthusiastic churchmen that Parliament should thus interfere with God's heritage, and their resistance was enough to defeat the Government. These events stirred the Church to its depths, and the movement that now began in Oxford seemed the expression of all that was felt by those who were at all affected by these dangers to religion.

To understand the course of events as they now occurred we must turn back to the Oriel Common Room and make a fuller acquaintance with some of its other occupants. Of these the most attractive was Keble. He had had already a brilliant university career. After being taught at home he had won a scholarship at Corpus, taken a double First, been elected Fellow of Oriel, and won the English and Latin Essay Prizes, all before he was twenty-one. He had later been made Tutor of the college, but resigned that office and refused the offer of a colonial archdeaconry in order to help his father in his country cure. Naturally his appearances at Oxford were not frequent, but in 1831 he had further reason for multiplying them when he was made Professor of Poetry, and his influence was greatly increased after the publication of the *Christian Year*. Of these poems, Arnold, to whose son Matthew he was godfather, said: 'Nothing equal to them exists in our language.' He had imbibed catholic doctrine from his father, and there is little evidence of any advance or change of view in his teaching, but he handed it on to several pupils whom he taught in the country, and they developed it. Of these the most brilliant was Richard Hurrell Froude, who, after a less successful course in the schools, was elected Fellow of Oriel in 1826. He was a handsome and gallant figure, courting danger on horseback and at sea. This recklessness came out in his conversation and in his theological views. He loved the Caroline divines and the non-jurors, but hated the reformers. This dislike was extended to the Roman Catholics, whom, after personal acquaintance with them abroad, he dubbed the 'wretched Tridentines'. He was, however, condemned by phthisis to an early death and his influence on the course of events was exercised mainly through his greatest friend, John Henry Newman. Newman was the son of a London banker, and had been brought up under strong Calvinist teaching. At the age of fifteen he had had an experience of conversion of which he never doubted the genuineness. He was not distinguished in the schools at Oxford, but retrieved his credit by obtaining an Oriel Fellowship in 1822. Here he went through a period of mild liberalism, coming chiefly under the influence of Hawkins and Whately. It was probably his intense personal friendship for Froude that emancipated him from this. Keble he reverenced from a distance until Froude brought the two to understand and love each other, an act which Froude regarded as the one great deed of his life. In 1828 his college appointed Newman Vicar of S. Mary's, a post which gave him an adequate platform for his teaching in later years. More learned than any of these was Edward Bouverie Pusey. He was the grandson of the first Lord Folkestone, and was educated at Eton and Christ Church, showing equal skill as sportsman and scholar. In 1822 he secured his First in spite of much hunting, and the next year was elected Fellow of Oriel. He went to Germany for a course of study and spent fifteen hours a day at Semitic languages. On his return he published a volume in defence of German scholarship, which had been attacked on the score of rationalism by Hugh James Rose, but afterwards his admiration for the German divines weakened and he withdrew the book from circulation. In 1828 he was ordained deacon, and while still in the diaconate was appointed Regius Professor of Hebrew, an appointment which carried with it a canonry at Christ Church. At first he occupied a position of some detachment from the views of the other three friends, and it was only gradually and by force of circumstances that he came to be regarded as leader of the new movement.

Such were the members of the group that was aroused to action by the attack which they believed was threatened against the Church. At least it was certain that ecclesiastical matters were being made the subject of legislation by the State, and the Church was not being consulted. The immediate effect was to throw into strong relief the existence of the Church as a distinct entity, and to raise the question, What was the proper organ of its authority? In the absence of an effective Convocation the only answer possible was the episcopate. Hence to these men the bishops assumed a greater importance than they had ever occupied in the history of the English Church. As in the days of early Christianity, when Gnosticism was the danger, Irenaeus had called upon the faithful to rally round the bishops, so it was now. The bishops' own guarantee was seen now as then to rest in the Apostolic Succession. But in the absence of a sufficiently critical view of history this succession was regarded as being conveyed in a mechanical manner by the invariable laying-on of hands. Yet it would be a gross mistake to think that the conception was completely wooden. Behind the episcopate so conceived lay the awful authority of God Himself, and obedience to that authority was necessary for the attainment of holiness of life. It was their passionate recognition of holiness as the fundamental note of the Church and of the true Christian life that raised these men to the summit of religious leadership. They were profoundly dissatisfied with the slackness and indifference that they saw around them. They desired to see the Church to which they belonged producing saints as in the days of old, and they set themselves with a passionate zeal to cultivate holiness in themselves and to make it possible for their contemporaries. Newman with his Calvinism had always been a creature apart, but Keble with his flowers and his choir boys at cricket, Pusey with his horse and gun, Froude with his sailing-boat at sea, had plenty of contact with the normal interests of healthy men. Yet all alike were austere in their conduct, and found the best road to the preservation of purity of life in the services and sacraments, the round of fast and festival that formed the daily routine of the Church. If there is any contrast between a society that is founded on holiness and one that is founded on an authoritative ministry, they, at least, were unaware of the conflict.

The sense of a vocation to action was strongest in Newman. In 1832 he accompanied Froude who had been ordered to Italy for his health. While in Sicily he himself fell sick of a fever, but he felt that he could not die: 'I have a work to do', he said, and on the way home he composed the poem, 'Lead, kindly Light, amid the encircling gloom.' A few days after their return Keble was in Oxford preaching the Assize Sermon at S. Mary's. He took for his text 1 Samuel xii. 23, 'Moreover, as for me, God forbid that I should sin against the Lord in ceasing to pray for you: but I will teach you the good and the right way.' His theme was National Apostasy, and he charged the State with infringing apostolic rights and of thus being guilty of a direct disavowal of the sovereignty of God. From this date, July 14, 1833, the Oxford Movement may be said to begin. The first step was a meeting at Hadleigh Rectory under the charge of Hugh James Rose. Keble and Newman were absent, and no definite steps were decided upon except to fight for Apostolic Succession and the integrity of the Prayer Book. But the same year an Association of Friends of the Church was founded, and the next year an address to William Howley, the Archbishop of Canterbury, professing adherence to the 'apostolical doctrine and polity of the Church of England' was signed by 7,000 clergy and 230,000 heads of families. And in 1833 Newman had already begun the *Tracts for the Times*.

Tracts were no more highly favoured as a means of propaganda then than they are to-day. In the eyes of many they had been brought into disrepute by their evangelical associations. But these tracts had an immediate and immense success, not only through the persistence with which the Oxford friends rode round distributing them among the country parsonages, but also through the brilliant clarity of their style. The first three were by Newman himself, and had all the urgency of a trumpet call: 'Fellow-labourers, I am but one of yourselves, a Presbyter; and therefore I conceal my name. . . . Yet speak I must; for the times are very evil, yet no one speaks against them'. All are urged to stand up in support of the bishops, for whom martyrdom would be a blessed termination of their course. The clergy are to rely, not on birth or popularity, but on their apostolic descent, and the Church is to recognise that the State has not created it and cannot destroy it. Other writers joined in, and by the end of the year twenty tracts had been published. The next year Pusey entered the lists with a tract on fasting, and when he had contributed his treatise on baptism the character of the tracts definitely changed from their popular to a more scholarly type. Pusey's accession gave the Tractarians 'a position and a name', and enabled them to bring forward the heavy artillery that was to prove a match for liberalism. For a time the writers carried everything before them, and it looked as if the whole English Church might be won to their view. Especially did Newman's doctrine of the *Via Media* become popular. He had turned his attention to the Roman controversy in 1836. While the fashionable view was to regard Rome as Antichrist, he could find in the Roman Breviary the 'Substance of the Devotional Services of the Church Catholic'. Nevertheless he wrote three tracts definitely against Romanism and its exclusive claims. What, then, was to be said to those who saw in Rome the true exponent of his own ideals? The answer was to distinguish between Catholicism and Roman Catholicism, and to place the English Church side by side with the Eastern Orthodox and Rome as part of the one universal Church. Indeed, as retaining all the original deposit of Church order without accretions of unjustifiable doctrine and practice, the English Church was in a better position than either of the others. This view had already been enunciated by Alexander Knox, but it was Newman who gave it the name of *Via Media*, and it seemed absurd enough to some in days when the Anglican Church was small and struggling, and in ecclesiastical colour largely Calvinist.

But now there began to appear signs of a gathering storm. In this year yet another Fellow of Oriel came into prominence, when R. D. Hampden was appointed Regius Professor of Divinity. Hampden's orthodoxy had been brought in question four years before, when, in his Bampton Lectures, which were thought to be inspired by Blanco White, he had seemed to doubt the doctrines of the Trinity and the Atonement. He had followed up this sensation in 1834 with a pamphlet urging the admission of dissenters to the University. Pusey and Newman led an opposition to his appointment as professor, which was joined by Mr. Gladstone, but they were unsuccessful, the Prime

Minister, Lord Melbourne, refusing to let Hampden withdraw. But they were successful in getting a statute passed which prevented the new professor sitting on the board for nominating select preachers. The attack on Hampden moved Arnold to defend his old Noetic friend in the *Edinburgh Review*, heading his article with the title 'The Oxford Malignants', and characterising Newman's colleagues as 'the Judaising party'. The lines of cleavage were thus clearly drawn. In 1837 suspicion of the good faith of the Tractarians was aroused by the publication of Isaac Williams's tract *On Reserve in communicating Religious Knowledge*. The charge of Jesuitism that this occasioned was quite unjust, but a more reasonable storm of anger burst forth on the publication of Froude's *Remains* the next year. It is amazing that his friends should have thought this the favourable opportunity to publish the brilliant indiscretions of the departed hater of the Reformation; their own principle of reserve might here have been applied with benefit. Bagot, Bishop of Oxford, now censured some phrases in the tracts, and although, when Newman offered to stop the series, he was unwilling to press the matter so far, he certainly made Newman feel that his relations with the bishops upon whom he had pinned his faith were not very secure. His own theological foundations were also beginning to crumble. In working on the history of the Monophysite controversy he seemed to find a parallel between the position of Eutyches and the present position of the Anglican Church; and his discomfort was increased when he read an article by Wiseman, one of the papal vicars-apostolic and later cardinal, in the *Dublin Review*, where the same parallel was drawn between Anglicanism and Donatism. The magic of the phrase, '*Securus judicat orbis terrarum*' shed a glamour over the Roman claims which would not fade. The climax came when he published Tract XC. He had tried for some time to draw a distinction between authoritative and popular Roman teaching. Now he tried to show that Anglicanism was quite consonant with the true Romanism and was only opposed to ignorant corruptions. This he does by attempting to prove that the Thirty-nine Articles ought to be interpreted in accordance with the general background of Catholic doctrine. He does

216 HISTORY OF THE MODERN CHURCH

not believe that they can be directed against the Tridentine Decrees, which in fact were not published till two years after the Articles were compiled, and he does believe that they were expressed with a vagueness that purposely left the bounds of comprehension as wide as possible. He concludes that they can be directed only against popular superstitions which have no place in official Romanism, and in order to prove this he exercises such dialectical skill in squaring the Articles with the Decrees that he seems in some cases to make the Articles say what they expressly deny. It was this that aroused against him so great a storm as to turn the success of his movement into contempt. Questions were asked in Parliament, a letter from four tutors appeared in *The Times*, the heads of houses protested, and on the bishop's intervention Newman discontinued the series of tracts. A further shock for Newman in this year of crisis was the foundation of an Anglo-Prussian bishopric in Jerusalem. The bishop was to unite all Protestants in the Holy Land, get his Orders from England, and subscribe to the Augsburg Confession. Newman declared that if the proposal went through it would cut his ground clean from under him, but he was powerless to stop it. He retired to Littlemore, where he had built some cottages with the intention of helping men to live a community life, and there began the long-drawn agony that was to end in his severance from the English Church.

Everything, indeed, seemed against him. In 1843 Pusey was suspended from preaching before the University for two years because of a sermon he had delivered on the subject of the Eucharist. The next year a definitely Romanising tendency in the Movement made itself vocal in the publication by W. G. Ward, of Balliol, of his *Ideal of a Christian Church*, in which he claimed the right to hold all Roman Catholic doctrine and yet remain in the Church of England. For this effort Ward was deprived by the University of his degrees, but an effort to censure Newman was stopped by the veto of the Proctors and was not renewed. Newman had so relied on authority in the Church that it was impossible for him to remain when that authority turned against him. In 1843 he had already retracted the hard things said by him in former years against the Roman Church. Later in

THE OXFORD MOVEMENT 217

that year he resigned his living, and began to live as a layman. For the next two years he occupied himself with the *Essay on the Development of Doctrine*, in which he tried to find as solid a ground for Romanism as he had once found for the *Via Media*. And then he followed Ward and Faber into the fold of the Roman Church. The Tractarian party was thus broken in pieces. For the moment it seemed as if the whole Oxford Movement must come to an end. But Pusey had become its leader in 1841, and Newman's retirement had given time to such men as Isaac Williams, J. B. Mozley, and R. W. Church, to establish their own position of influence in the van of the movement. Also, Cambridge had developed a strong party in favour of it. The Camden Society had been founded in 1839 to apply its principles to such practical matters as the services and the churches, and there was a strong body of supporters at Trinity College. The result was that the movement broadened out and affected the life of the Church at every point. One sign of the unfailing determination of the men who were left was the foundation of the *Guardian* newspaper in 1846 by Church, Mozley, and others as a weekly organ of Church principles.

It was in the pastoral life that the movement produced its most marked effect. John Mason Neale became Warden of the almshouse known as Sackville College in 1846, and made himself famous as a hymn-writer, a historian, and a novelist, but he came under condemnation because he used crosses, lights, and frontals in his chapel. Here we see the influence of the Camden Society and of the logic that impels men to express their belief in outward ceremony. As soon as the belief in the Real Presence had been recognised as part of the Church's Catholic heritage, many of the medieval accompaniments of divine worship were restored, and the restoration fitted in well with the romanticism of the time. But it aroused vigorous opposition among men who were accustomed to the barest churches and associated everything 'histrionic' with Romanism. The ambiguity of the Prayer Book rubrics left plenty of room for difference of opinion about the legality of the changes made, and the rest of the century is largely occupied with wearisome litigation on the subject. Often the mob took matters into their own hands and expressed their disapproval by rioting in the churches. Such opposition was shown against Neale himself on many occasions. The London church of S. George's-in-the-East became notorious in this same respect. In 1859 there was serious rioting there which ended in the resignation of the rector, but Charles Lowder, one of the assistant clergy, hung on to his task and won in the end a deserved and widespread popularity. G. R. Prynne, of S. Peter's, Plymouth, who during a cholera epidemic had been the first to restore the daily Eucharist, was attacked on another score, that of reviving the sacrament of penance. In order to protect the exponents of the Catholic views the English Church Union was founded in 1860, and in direct opposition to it there was founded five years later the Church Association. One of the earliest objects of the Association's attack was A. H. Mackonochie of S. Alban's, Holborn, who was first driven to exchange his living and then deprived, returning to S. Alban's to work as assistant. For the better management of these affairs the Public Worship Regulation Act was passed in 1874 with the avowed intention of 'putting down Ritualism'. Its penalties were not harsh, but their intention was defeated by the accused persons whose consciences would not allow them to obey their judges, and this frequently led to imprisonment for contempt of court. In 1888 the Association reached the climax of its labours in an attack upon the best-loved prelate in the country, Bishop King of Lincoln. His case was tried by the Archbishop of Canterbury, Dr. Benson, in person, and no one had a greater claim to respect as ecclesiastical historian and liturgiologist. His judgment was favourable to the ritualists, but by dissociating ritual from doctrine he established a platform upon which all, if they had been animated by good will, might have found a possibility of agreement.

More strictly doctrinal matters also agitated public opinion. The Tractarians were roused to anger in 1847 when Lord John Russell actually appointed R. D. Hampden, who had already made himself so notorious, to the bishopric of Hereford. Evangelicals as well as Tractarians joined in an unavailing protest. The same year saw the famous Gorham Case. The Bishop of Exeter, Dr. Philpotts, had refused to institute Gorham to a living because he found him heretical on the subject of baptismal regeneration, asserting that such regeneration was dependent upon worthy reception. The case came before the Privy Council, who assumed that Gorham meant that regeneration does not invariably take place in baptism, and then declared that this was not an unlawful view. The decision created a great stir and led to a fresh batch of secessions to Rome. The most noteworthy of the new converts was Archdeacon Manning, who had been one of the tract-writers. This was in 1850, and the Papacy recognised its opportunity by establishing a Roman Catholic diocesan episcopate in England. Manning, who became an ardent ultramontane, secured the favour of Pius IX and became Archbishop of Westminster in 1865, and Cardinal ten years later. Newman, who was his rival and the most eminent of the Roman Catholics, but by no means ultramontane, did not get his cardinalate until 1879. Many have seen another instance of Roman Catholic triumph in the disestablishment of the Church of Ireland in 1869; but when the scant numbers of that Church in proportion to the total population are remembered, the measure must seem but an overdue act of justice. And in any case its consequence has been to redouble the spiritual effectiveness of that Church. In England, in spite of much opposition, the life of the Church was quickened in all directions by the Oxford Movement. It would be manifestly absurd to claim for the Movement all the tremendous growth and development of the past century. Nevertheless there can be no doubt that it was the Tractarians more than any others who fostered that new impulse which has renewed the strength of the whole Church in this country. And for one departure, the restoration of the monastic life, they were entirely responsible.

The first effort at such a restoration came as early as 1841, when Marian Rebecca Hughes was dedicated to a religious life under vows at S. Mary's, Oxford, by Pusey. Three years later, with the help of Gladstone, a house was founded for Sisters of Mercy as a memorial to the poet Southey. Several of its members went out to help Florence Nightingale in the Crimea, and it was afterwards absorbed in the Community of the Holy Trinity, Devonport. In 1847

220 HISTORY OF THE MODERN CHURCH

the Community of S. Thomas the Martyr was founded at Oxford, and the next year the Wantage Sisters. In 1849, under Marian Rebecca Hughes already mentioned, was founded the Society of the Holy and Undivided Trinity. In 1852 the Community of All Saints was begun in connexion with the church of that name in Margaret Street, London, and in 1851 the Clewer Sisters were started, while in 1854 John Mason Neale was responsible for the Community of S. Margaret at East Grinstead. It would be tedious to enter upon a longer enumeration, but it must suffice to say that the number of professed nuns of the Anglican Church to-day is reckoned as twice the number of those in the country at the Reformation. For men the same opportunities were opened by R. M. Benson's foundation of the Cowley Fathers (Society of S. John the Evangelist, 1866). Father Kelly founded the Society of the Sacred Mission at Kelham in 1891, and Bishop Gore founded the Community of the Resurrection, Mirfield, in 1892, both of which institutions do an invaluable work in the training of ordinands. Fr. Adderley's Society of the Divine Compassion (1894), and the Benedictines, whose rule was revived at Pershore in 1898, are further developments of the monastic ideal in the Anglican Church. All these Orders have done much, not only at home by conducting missions and retreats, but also abroad by their extensive activities in the mission-field, to build up that higher type of spiritual life in the Church which inspired the most ardent longing of the original Tractarians.

CHAPTER XVIII

EDUCATIONAL AND SOCIAL MOVEMENTS

WE have seen how on one occasion Pusey defended the theologians of Germany and afterwards repented. We must now consider the type of thought that was then in question. We shall find that whereas the Oxford Movement rejected some elements of Reformation thought, German theological science rejected others. In Germany the whole static view of revelation had disappeared as the result of the Enlightenment, and scholars began to apply ever more accurate historical tests to the records of religion and particularly of Christianity. Hegel's philosophy found an echo in the reconstruction of the early history of the Church as attempted by F. C. Baur. Essential Christianity was a Messianic Judaism which had been fulfilled in Jesus and was taught by Peter. This was the thesis. The antithesis was to be found in the teaching of Paul, who made Jesus into a God. The conflict between the two is the keynote of all the history of the first two centuries, but by the end of that time a synthesis was being found which is represented by the creeds of the early Catholic Church. Of course, such a reconstruction meant the redating of many of the documents, but Baur, with the key in his hand, felt no doubt about his ability to do this with success. He rejected all the Pauline epistles except Romans, Galatians, and Corinthians, which alone show signs of the supposed conflict, and he made Matthew the oldest gospel, because it is Judaising, and put Mark late, because it attempts to hide the conflict. D. F. Strauss pushed investigation farther into the sources for the life of Christ. He took it for granted that Jesus lived, but regarded His life as purely human. At the time when He was born the Jews were looking for a wonder-working Messiah. All their expectations of a divine deliverance of humanity they poured into the mould of the Christ idea and attached ultimately to Jesus; thus the Christ of the New Testament is really the creation of a myth. It was this theory that gave rise to the popular, artistic, and insincere *Life of Jesus*, by the Frenchman, Ernest Renan, which appeared in 1863. A more moderate type of Christology was to be found in the historical works of Neander and the doctrinal works of Dorner, but the real difficulty that had to be faced was the question whether in the last resort it was easier to regard the Church as the source of Christ or Christ as the source of the Church. This was felt by Albert Schweitzer, who went back to the hint given by Reimarus and resuscitated the idea of an eschatological Christ. But, inadequate as that solution may be, that it does not involve surrender to a dry and wooden rationalism can be judged from the noble self-sacrifice of Schweitzer, who abandoned a great career in Europe to work among the natives of the west coast of Africa as a medical missionary.

In the meantime much work was being done on the Old Testament. The French scholars, Simon and Astruc, had already pointed to the possibility of different writers being at work where duplicate narratives of the same event are found. Eichorn carried the distinction farther in 1780, relying chiefly, but not wholly, upon the use of different divine names. Hupfeld in 1853 was the first to point to a distinction of authorship even where the one name Elohim is used. Vater, in the meantime, had shown in 1805 that the problem concerned, not merely Genesis, but the whole Pentateuch, and Ewald in 1823 proved that the different fragments belonged to documents that had once been distinct, but were now pieced together to form a unity. The complete theory which now holds the field was invented by Eduard Reuss in 1834 and published by his pupil K. H. Graf in 1865, whence it is often called the 'Grafian hypothesis'. It was some time before these views had much influence in England, although H. H. Milman, afterwards Dean of S. Paul's and author of the famous *History of Latin Christianity*, may be said to have adopted a generally critical attitude in his *History of the Jews*;

and such views were very acceptable to the Broad Churchmen who succeeded to the influence of the Oriel Noetics. Of these one of the best known was F. W. Robertson, of Brighton, whose sermons were read by thousands not privileged to hear them. Two who were more prominent in the councils of the Church were A. P. Stanley, who became Dean of Westminster, and F. W. Farrar, who became Dean of Canterbury; and perhaps the best-known layman was Lord Tennyson, whose *In Memoriam*, published in 1850, put the religious philosophy of the group into unforgettable words. A new element was brought into the discussion in 1859 when Darwin published his *Origin of Species*, which made the theory of evolution a living issue for every religious teacher. The next year seven friends, mostly of Oxford, and including Benjamin Jowett, the Master of Balliol, and Frederick Temple, the future Archbishop of Canterbury, joined together in producing a volume of *Essays and Reviews* in order to protest against the stiff orthodoxy which now had the upper hand, especially at Oxford, and had become a 'system of terrorism, which prevents the statement of the plainest facts, and makes true theology or theological education impossible'. Unfortunately the writers had never even read over each other's compositions, and so all had to bear the blame for the audacity and flippancy of some. Among the more striking views expressed was that of Wilson that there should no longer be required any subscription to formularies on the part even of the clergy, and with that may be compared the pregnant injunction of Jowett to 'interpret the Scripture like any other book'. But a still greater stir was made in 1862 by the case of Bishop Colenso, who after nine years' hard work in his diocese of Natal put out the first part of a book entitled *The Pentateuch and Book of Joshua Critically Examined*. Along with many theories that are now generally accepted, he asserted that the historical existence of Moses is doubtful and that Joshua is certainly a mythical character. The real difficulty lay, not in the opinions themselves, but in the fact that entirely unheard-of theories touching the sacred text should be published so light-heartedly by a responsible bishop. He was excommunicated by his Metropolitan, the Bishop of

Cape Town. But he refused to give up the temporalities of his see, and was upheld in his refusal by the Judicial Committee of the Privy Council, to whom he appealed. Another bishop was consecrated and a schism was thus created. But on the death of Colenso an opportunity was sought for putting an end to the very undesirable state of things. The other bishop resigned in 1891, and both parties agreed to accept the Archbishop of Canterbury's nominee. Archbishop Benson nominated his own chaplain, Arthur Hamilton Baynes, and the quarrel became insignificant.

In spite of this contretemps, interest in Biblical research was still maintained and was strong enough to secure a revised version of the Bible. This was begun in 1870 on the initiative of the Canterbury Convocation alone, York not thinking the time favourable. Two companies were appointed, one for the revision of the Old Testament and one for the New; they had power to invite distinguished scholars to co-operate and worked in harmony with two similar companies in America. The Revised New Testament was published in 1881 and the Old in 1885, and the Apocrypha in 1896. For beauty of diction the Revised Version cannot compare with the Authorised, but in accuracy of text and translation it is immeasurably superior. In Oxford studies on the Old Testament were carried on in the most painstaking and accurate manner by S. R. Driver, whose work was parallel to that done for New Testament studies by the great Cambridge scholars, Lightfoot, Westcott, and Hort. In Scotland Robertson Smith introduced the comparative method for the elucidation of the history of Hebrew religion. The epoch-making nature of his discoveries was only limited by the fact that the religion of South Arabia provided the only Semitic cult that was then well enough known to satisfy the needs of comparison. His boldness in speculation cost him the Professorship of Hebrew, which he had held at Aberdeen since 1870. It was clear that a place must be found for evolution in the history of revelation. Without it the Old Testament was becoming an inexplicable enigma, but with it the science of historical criticism was able to fit things into their place. An attempt to think out the old faith in the light of the new conceptions was made by a group of

EDUCATIONAL AND SOCIAL MOVEMENTS

friends who belonged to the school of the Oxford Movement and found their common meeting-place in the house that had been erected in honour of Pusey. In a volume of essays entitled *Lux Mundi* they succeeded in welding together evolutionary and Catholic ideas. It seemed strange to many that such men should be found incorporating into their own traditionalist system ideas that might more properly belong to the Broad Churchmen. And, indeed, when Liddon, now the inheritor of Pusey's leadership, saw Charles Gore's contribution on the Holy Spirit and Inspiration he was exceedingly shocked. Nevertheless the authors of *Lux Mundi* have set the tone for their own school in the universities ever since, as the latest similar volume, *Essays Catholic and Critical*, clearly shows. To this school 'the real development of theology is . . . the process by which the Church, standing firm in her old truths, enters into the apprehension of the new social and intellectual movements of each age . . . and is able to assimilate all new material'.

This assimilation of new thought has not been found so easy in the Roman Church. Even Leo XIII, towards the end of his life, showed considerable alarm at the growth of disquieting tendencies in the interpretation of the Scriptures. It was the state of things in France that had chiefly stirred that alarm. There the Catholic Institute of Paris had been founded in 1878, and among its early teachers were Louis Duchesne and Alfred Loisy. The former's boldness in criticising ecclesiastical legends was paralleled by the latter's courage in the sphere of Biblical criticism. In 1885 Duchesne was suspended for a year, and in 1893 Loisy was compelled to resign his professorship. In the latter year Leo issued the encyclical *Providentissimus Deus* condemning the new methods of Biblical study. But Modernism, as it was called, had already spread into many seminaries. A distinction was drawn between the truths of faith and those of history, and it was held possible to accept the whole Catholic system while doubting the historicity of the facts upon which it was based. Nevertheless Leo refused to condemn explicitly even Loisy's book *L'Evangile et L'Église*, which, published in 1902, created a world-wide sensation. Pius X had no such scruple.

In the year of his accession, 1903, five of Loisy's books were placed on the Index. But outside France many Roman Catholic writers defended his general position. The Italian Fogazzaro published his novel *Il Santo* in 1906; in Germany Franz Kraus and Hermann Scell maintained a succession of 'Modernist' writings; and in England the Jesuit, George Tyrrell, and the Baron Friedrich von Hügel were recognised leaders of liberal theology. Tyrrell was expelled from the Society of Jesus in 1906, but von Hügel, who in his *Mystical Element of Religion* (1908) gave an epoch-making book to the world, escaped actual censure. A definite condemnation of the whole Modernist system was made in the encyclical *Pascendi* in 1907. In this document the Pope sought to show that all modernist errors sprang from a particular philosophy, which he had little difficulty in claiming to be false. But the Modernists replied in *The Programme of Modernism* that whatever philosophy one adopts the progress of historical criticism has made some new apologetic imperatively necessary. The leaders of the movement remained faithful to the Roman Catholic Church and resolved to inaugurate no schism. To this resolution they adhered, although Tyrrell was excommunicated in 1907, and Loisy in the following year and others later. Since these measures proved ineffective to stop a flood of anonymous modernist literature, Pius issued an injunction by which he imposed an oath on all professors of Roman Catholic universities and on all ordinands, to the effect that they adhered to all the condemnations and prescriptions contained in the encyclical *Pascendi*. Many took the oath under constraint and without admitting that it was binding on their consciences. This meant the end of Modernism as an open movement in the Roman Church, though how far it continues underground it is impossible to say.

One effect of the repression of Modernism was to put a stop for the time to the efforts made in certain Roman Catholic circles to make terms with the social movements of the day. In England, on the other hand, strenuous attempts were made later in the nineteenth century, and still continue, to establish a real sympathy with the working classes and to acquire an understanding of their aspirations.

EDUCATIONAL AND SOCIAL MOVEMENTS 227

The chief glory of the evangelical 'Clapham Sect' had been the support they gave to the proposal for the abolition of the slave-trade. They did not themselves start the agitation, but it was not until Wilberforce brought his tremendous energy to bear on the question that the abolitionists had any chance of success, and it was he who by his fervour carried Pitt into action on the matter. They fought the case in Parliament from 1787, and in 1792 they succeeded in passing a motion for gradual abolition. The Act for total abolition was passed in 1807 and the Act for the emancipation of the slaves in 1833.

The party's neglect of the industrial movement was to some extent redeemed by Shaftesbury's splendid work in the Factory Acts. It was the Church that led the way in the education of the poor. We have already spoken of the Charity Schools at the beginning of the eighteenth century. Sunday-schools were in existence here and there soon after the middle of that century, but the great impulse to their spread came from the newspaper proprietor, Robert Raikes, who established and supported four such schools in Gloucester in 1780. The movement on behalf of them spread widely and rapidly. Hannah More established many in and around Cheddar, and the Methodists took up the scheme with great zeal. It was in these schools that many poor children received the whole of their education. Wherever possible experiments were made in week-day-schools, and a new epoch was started when Dr. Bell, in 1799, introduced into elementary education the monitorial system that he had learned when a chaplain in Madras. By this system, as originally practised, the pupils taught each other, and the difficulties with regard to finance and staff were greatly reduced. It was used independently and with great success by Joseph Lancaster, a Quaker lad of sixteen, who founded a day-school at Southwark, which numbered a thousand scholars. But his teaching was undenominational while that of Bell was definitely Anglican. It was in order to preserve Church teaching that the National Society was founded in 1811, while the British and Foreign School Society, in support of unsectarian teaching, came into existence in 1814. The conflict between the rival theories was so sharp that it was found impossible to frame a unified scheme of national education, yet neither side was willing to accept the alternative of completely secular instruction. Government at first contented itself with assisting the voluntary organisations, but the societies soon found themselves unable to meet the ever-growing demand for new schools and more elaborate equipment, and Board Schools were provided under public, as distinct from denominational, control. Forster's Education Act of 1870 sought to fill up the gaps left by the voluntary system, and, by the Cowper-Temple Clause, secured that in the Board Schools there should be given a 'simple Bible teaching' without creed or catechism. This dual system has continued ever since in spite of many efforts to break it down, but the continually increasing cost of maintaining education at a level required by the growing sensitiveness of succeeding generations makes central control more possible and the voluntary principle ever harder to retain.

In the sphere of higher education a somewhat similar difficulty was created by the requirement of subscription to the Thirty-nine Articles before matriculation to the universities. A petition against such subscription was presented on behalf of Dissenters to Parliament as early as 1772, but relief was not obtained until the test was abolished in 1871. In the meantime a proposal for a non-sectarian college came to maturity in 1827 when University College, London, was founded, and a charter was granted for the University of London in 1836. To meet the needs of Church students in London, King's College was founded in 1829 and was incorporated in the University when the charter was granted. Since that time a number of new universities have been started in the provinces, and strenuous efforts have been made on voluntary lines for the adequate expression in them of Church principles. Durham (1832) has several Church of England colleges as constituent parts of its university. Manchester (1881) has three such Halls and most of the modern universities have Church hostels attached to them.

The nineteenth century saw great changes in the method of preparing candidates for ordination. It had come to be thought that the ordinary education of a gentleman was

EDUCATIONAL AND SOCIAL MOVEMENTS

sufficient for anyone who desired to take Holy Orders, but the higher ideal of clerical life fostered by the Oxford Movement soon made a more specialised training necessary, and therefore devotional, theological, and practical studies were added to the requirements of the arts degree. Consequently this became the great era of theological colleges, no fewer than twenty-one being founded in England alone during the nineteenth century. The earliest was founded at S. Bees, in 1816, and Lampeter was founded for Wales in 1822. The movement was thus already on foot before the Tractarians had begun their special teaching, but when the effect of that teaching was felt the colleges multiplied rapidly. Chichester was founded in 1839, Wells in 1840, S. Aidan's, Birkenhead, in 1846, Cuddesdon in 1854, Lichfield in 1857, Salisbury in 1860. Nor was the zeal for clerical education confined to one particular school of thought. Wycliffe Hall, Oxford (1877), and Ridley Hall, Cambridge (1879), witness to the anxiety of evangelicals not to be left behind. The special needs of the mission-field were not forgotten. Mr. Beresford Hope, a member of the Cambridge Camden Society, one of whose objects was the restoration of ruined ecclesiastical buildings, bought the old abbey of S. Augustine at Canterbury, and there a missionary college was opened in 1848. S. Boniface College, Warminster, followed in 1860, and other colleges for the same purpose were started at Burgh and Dorchester in 1878. Many of these colleges stand partly within and partly without the diocesan organisation, and it cannot be said that they have yet been satisfactorily welded into the general system of the Church as a whole. It is the inalienable right of the individual bishop to decide on the fitness of any candidate he ordains to the ministry. For long this meant the recognition of standards that varied considerably between the various dioceses. After many efforts to produce a common level an approach to uniformity was effected by the establishment of the General Ordination Examination, which is managed by a Central Advisory Council of Training for the Ministry. This degree of centralisation has involved a general inspection of the theological colleges and may lead to a more adequate representation of them in the councils of the Church. The emergence of this great zeal for specialised colleges does not mean that the Church has lost its interest in the work of the older universities. Two foundations, at least, witness to the contrary. At Oxford, the memory of the founder of the Oxford Movement was perpetuated by Keble College, which was incorporated in 1870, and at Cambridge the somewhat similar institution of Selwyn College, in memory of a former bishop of New Zealand and Lichfield, was incorporated in 1882.

It has already been pointed out how much the Church of England lost by its failure to take an adequate interest in social matters during the period of the Industrial Revolution. The first person to rouse it to a sense of its duty in this matter as a general principle was Frederick Denison Maurice, who had come over to the Church from Unitarianism and was ordained in 1834. He laid the foundations of a liberal Catholicism in his book *The Kingdom of Christ*, which was a defence of the Church as the Kingdom of Christ on earth against the non-sacramentalist conception of the Quakers. This gained him the two professorships of English Literature and Theology at King's College. He took advantage of the disappointment of the working classes over the results of the Reform Bill to start a Christian Social movement very like that of Lamenais in France. He denounced the common belief in unrestricted competition as the folly of expecting 'universal selfishness to do the work of universal love'. This political liberalism brought suspicion upon him, and the publication of his theologically liberal views on eternal life and death gave the Council of the College an opportunity to dismiss him from both his professorial chairs. But in the reaction that followed a Working Men's College was founded in 1854, and he was made its principal. He was later engaged in controversy with Mansel, the Dean of S. Paul's, who held in his Bampton Lectures of 1858 that all revelation is contained in the Bible and that we must judge what is right from what is there told us of God's actions, while Maurice held that we must judge God's actions, as there described, from what our universally derived knowledge tells us is right. He became Professor of Moral Philosophy at Cambridge in 1866, and had a profound influence on a rising school of thinkers and writers of whom the most notable was Charles Kingsley.

With Kingsley was inaugurated the era of 'muscular Christianity' with its emphasis upon the need of a concurrent development of spiritual and physical powers. In the *Saint's Tragedy* he declaimed against a false asceticism, and in *Yeast* and *Alton Locke* against degrading social conditions in country and town which made difficult any cleanliness whether of soul or body. At this time he was still under thirty years of age, and he imparted a youthful optimism to the Christian social movement which lasted long after he himself had settled down to middle-aged views and the dignity of the Chair of Modern History at Cambridge in 1860. The interest thus aroused in the welfare of the poor resulted in the foundation of the Christian Social Union in 1887 by Brooke Foss Westcott, and others. Westcott was the great Cambridge textual scholar who became Bishop of Durham and used his social knowledge with marked effect in the settlement of the Durham coal strike in 1892. His combination of theological learning and social science has been almost converted into a tradition in the person of Charles Gore, Bishop successively of Worcester, Birmingham, and Oxford. It has widened out so as to affect profoundly all Christian denominations, and many efforts have been made to promote concerted action with regard to social questions on the part of the different Christian bodies. Very elaborate preparations were made for a Conference on Christian Politics, Economics, and Citizenship, which was held at Birmingham in 1924, and continuation committees still carry on the work of study and education in these matters. Copec, as it has come to be called, was itself but the British preparation for the Universal Conference on Life and Work which was held at Stockholm in 1925, and has succeeded in linking up the national Christian social movement with similar movements throughout the world.

CHAPTER XIX

THE EASTERN CHURCH IN RECENT TIMES

WE find ourselves in a totally different atmosphere when we turn to the East. During the nineteenth century the Church of Russia remained the predominant partner among the Orthodox Churches. With its membership of ninety millions and its sixty thousand clergy outside the monasteries it possessed a capital importance from weight of numbers alone. We have seen how Peter the Great put an end to the Patriarchate. From his time the Church was governed by the Holy Synod, which was in effect no synod at all, but an ecclesiastical committee under the supervision of a Procurator appointed by the Tsar. This Synod was recognised as a 'brother' by the Patriarchs of Constantinople and Antioch, but in point of fact the successive monarchs were all-powerful in its affairs. This was shown even in the case of a woman ruler like Catherine II, who had a political rather than a religious interest in the Church. She improved on Peter's method of administering the monastic property by seizing practically the whole of it for governmental purposes. She had herself been brought up as a Lutheran, and although she had accepted Orthodoxy without a qualm, she sat loose to its profession and was able to display an independent attitude towards other varieties of religion, so long, at least, as they gave no political trouble. Thus she checked the persecution of Old Believers and allowed mosques to be built in Kazan, and sheltered the Jesuits when they were officially suppressed in 1773. She was an admirer of French institutions and founded the Smolny Institute for the education of the daughters of nobles, which she modelled upon the Institute founded at S. Cyr by Madame de Maintenon. She also introduced a scheme for providing schools throughout the country at the rate of one for every two hundred families, but as there were neither buildings, books, nor teachers the task was difficult, and she sought help from abroad. Consequently the instruction given in her schools followed the purely secular ideals of the Encyclopedists and earned much distrust on the part of the clergy, who became the enemies of popular education for many years.

Much the same attitude was adopted towards the sectaries and the Jesuits by her son and successor Paul, but he did one good service to the secular clergy by attaching a portion of glebe to the parish churches, and so relieving them of a little of their appalling poverty. Alexander I carried on this tradition of open-mindedness towards foreign religions in the early part of his reign, and actually gave permission in 1812 for the foundation of a Russian branch of the Bible Society. This, however, produced a fondness on the part of the Bible readers for holding meetings other than the regular church services, and showed up the inability of the half-educated clergy to answer the questions that they raised. The after-effects of the French Revolution and the campaigns of Napoleon added to the growing distrust of foreign religion, and a period of intolerance began. In 1815 this revealed itself against the Jesuits, who in that year were banished from S. Petersburg and in 1819 from the whole of Russia. It was charged against them that they had mismanaged their estates, drawn converts from Orthodoxy, and intrigued in favour of Napoleon. Alexander's own religion was of a devout and mystical type. In 1815 he proposed the Holy Alliance, which was to unite the Governments of Europe in an endeavour to live in Christian amity with each other and to make the law of Christ effective in their internal administration. But the Governments concerned confounded Christianity with the divine right of kings, and the effort was ruined by their determination at all costs to maintain their own autocracy.

Under Nicholas I the struggle between the Crown and the people entered upon a definite phase. As the result of the December Revolution, which heralded his accession in 1826, he instituted the secret police, who were to watch for any approach to disloyalty, and succeeded so well as to reinforce the nation's growing hatred of bureaucratic oppression. Disloyalty in religion as well as in politics must be punished, and heretics had a hard time. Among those specially attacked were the Doukhobors, or 'spirit-wrestlers', so-called because they resorted to no other force than that of the Spirit. They had come into existence about 1740 as the result of the teaching of a Prussian non-commissioned officer, who is believed to have been a Quaker. Alexander I had allowed them to form a settlement at Milky Waters, near the Sea of Azov, where they began to practise Communism. Their leader, Kapoustin, began to teach that Christ was incarnated in himself and would be born again in his successors. They forbade war, and when Nicholas tried enlisting them in the army they refused to carry arms, although they would perform any tasks of a peaceful nature. Torture failed to reduce them to obedience, and in 1841 he had them removed from Milky Waters to the Wet Mountains of Georgia. There their wild neighbours were much impressed by their refusal to resist violence, and soon allowed them to remain in quiet, so that they prospered and multiplied. Abroad, Nicholas showed the same zeal for Orthodoxy. When the Turks harassed the Greeks he formed an alliance with England and France and the Turkish fleet was destroyed at Navarino. Poland invited his interference by proclaiming a republic in 1831. He not only crushed the movement with great ferocity, but treated the Uniate Church of the country with such cruelty as to bring about its petition to be received back into the Orthodox fold. His desire to be regarded as the protector of Orthodox believers in Turkish lands and of Orthodox rights in the holy places of Jerusalem brought about the Crimean War in 1853. England and France, believing that the religious claims covered territorial ambitions, ranged themselves on the side of Turkey. Nicholas's own energy could not atone for the complete incompetence of his officials, and the consequent disasters embittered the nation still further against the autocracy. During this reign the Metropolitan of Moscow was the saintly and scholarly Philaret. He had been a pupil of his predecessor, Platon, who had himself written the first scientific *History of the Russian Church* in 1805, and drawn up a Shorter and Longer Catechism. At the request of the Holy Synod, Philaret revised these Catechisms, but he was suspected of sympathy with the views of Cyril Lucar and got himself dismissed to his diocese. There he carried on a scheme for the translation of the Scriptures with such energy that a complete vernacular Bible was ready for publication at the time of his death in 1867. By this time Alexander II was on the the throne, and Philaret is best remembered as being responsible for the drafting of the edict by which, in 1861, that Tsar emancipated nearly twenty-three million serfs. But the emancipation was not complete, many of the serfs finding themselves worse off in liberty than they had been in servitude. Out of the consequent disappointment Nihilism came into being, with its determination to destroy all existing institutions in order that a new society free from restraints might be built up. Alexander tried to remedy some of the most trying abuses by making the universities autonomous, opening secondary schools, and arranging for the foundation of elementary schools by the local Zemstvos. But by a curious irony little that was of value to Church and State came from this improved education. The intelligentsia were incurably irreligious; Bakunin, in particular, who had been a disciple of Hegel, proclaimed that the servant of God becomes the slave both of Church and State. The clergy were entirely incapable of seizing their opportunities. Even the bishops had too little learning to combat atheistic arguments, while the black clergy lived the life of peasants in their monasteries, and the white clergy were sunk in direst poverty amid the routine of their parishes. In 1873 the Government became alarmed at the spread of revolutionary ideas among the youth studying abroad and ordered their return, thereby spreading the seeds of revolt in every city of Russia. But the common people remained staunch in their adherence to the 'Little Father' and the Church, and it was not among them that the many attempts to assassinate the Tsar originated. In 1877 the Russians were so moved by the stories of Moslem atrocities in the Balkans, and particularly of the massacres of Bulgarian Christians which had taken place the previous year, that they declared war on the Turks. After its victorious conclusion they aimed at protection of other Christians under Turkish rule, and encouraged the Armenians to work for the establishment of an independent state. These aims were cut short by the murder of Alexander II in 1881.

There ensued a period of reaction under Alexander III. This was led by Pobiedonostseff, the Procurator of the Holy Synod. The universities were deprived of their self-government, and an abortive attempt was made to transfer the control of the elementary schools from the Zemstvos to the clergy, while secondary education was confined to the aristocracy. All dissentients from Orthodoxy were persecuted and the Jews were driven to the side of the revolutionaries by efforts to exterminate them. Of the sects the Stundists were the special objects of attack. They had come into existence about 1865 in the south-west, and derived their name from the *stunden*, or hours of devotion, conducted by a German pastor and attended by many of the Russian peasantry. About 1870 a revival was initiated by some Baptists from Prussia, and manifested itself especially in an attack on the image-worship of the national Church. When arguments failed to reduce them, fines and imprisonments were imposed, and many of the Stundists were separated from their wives and children and despatched to remote exile. The clergy vigorously supported this harsh procedure and so alienated still further the sympathies of the more lively spiritual forces in the nation. This was the more to be regretted since the rise of industrialism in Russia at that time was drawing many of the peasants into the cities and turning them into a proletariat. The Russian Church showed itself even less capable of coping with the new situation than the English Church had done at the beginning of the century. The close identification of the Church with the autocracy rendered this a matter of the deepest gravity.

The result of all this was seen in the reign of Nicholas II, the last of the Tsars. War broke out with Japan in 1904, and the disasters of that year were followed in the next by the massacre of 3,500 workmen who had marched to the Winter Palace with a pathetic faith in the power of the Tsar to remedy their ills. The promise of constitutional government was falsified by the repeated dismissal of the

Duma, until it was so packed as to be a mere part of the bureaucratic machine. Some of the clergy were at last roused to a feeling of fellowship with the oppressed classes, and, after an article signed by thirty-two priests had appeared in the Moscow Press in 1905, demanding ecclesiastical reform, a more liberal spirit was shown in the Holy Synod; but it was prevented from coming to fruition by Pobiedonostseff, who was still the evil genius of the Government. His reactionary policy had driven 7,300 of the Doukhobors to emigrate to Canada in 1899, but he was powerless to prevent relief being granted to the Old Believers in 1905, when they were at last permitted the free exercise of their religion. A relative at Court and a European reputation protected Count Leo Tolstoy, whose reduction of Christianity to the gospel of non-resistance had much in common with the teaching of the Doukhobors, and whose rejection of the sacraments robbed excommunication of its terrors. The Church pursued him with petty spite and had no part in the world-wide expressions of sorrow that greeted the news of his death in 1910. An embarrassing associate of religion was Rasputin, who from being a jail-bird became a kind of peripatetic saint, and acquired complete ascendancy over the Tsaritsa after a lucky prophecy that she should have a son. By persuading her that his own safety was linked up with that of the sickly boy, he confirmed himself in a position from which he was able to dominate much of the policy of Church and State while still maintaining his disreputable manner of life, and it was not until the disturbances of the Great War that his enemies were able to bring about his assassination in 1916. That act was the prelude to the downfall of the autocracy. Nicholas was compelled to abdicate in 1917, and he with all the Imperial family was butchered in cold blood on the night of July 16, 1918.

The Bolshevists who emerged as masters from the revolution were led by Lenin, a Russian, and Trotsky, a Jew. They were entirely materialist in their outlook, and regarded the very existence of the Church as a danger to their enterprise. It was of no advantage to them that the long-heralded National Assembly was at that time actually sitting at Moscow and working out a scheme of Church reform. Unfortunately the elections to it had taken place while the fortunes of the revolution were still undecided, and it was long before it was generally realised that the *de facto* Government had come to stay. Consequently the Assembly allowed itself a freedom of speech about Bolshevist actions that were regarded as treasonable by the new rulers and prevented any possibility of a *rapprochement*. The most important act of the Assembly was the restoration of the Patriarchate, which had been in abeyance since the time of Peter the Great. Three candidates were chosen by ballot, but the final decision between these three was by lot. The lot fell upon Tikhon, who, without being a man of outstanding ability, was saintly, lovable, and courageous. He had need of all these qualities, for in the very month of December 1917, in which he was enthroned, the Bolshevists had shown the line they were determined to take with the Church. They confiscated all ecclesiastical landed properties, withdrew all schools from ecclesiastical control, and instituted civil marriage. Then in January 1918 they withdrew all Government subsidies for the support of the Church. This was followed in that year and the next by a ruthless persecution of the clergy, in which twenty-eight bishops and 1,215 priests were done to death. The monasteries were attacked and 686 of them dissolved before the end of 1922. A few of the older monks were allowed to remain as watchmen or workers for the new institutions that entered into possession of the buildings, but it is said that as many as 5,000 of the less fortunate inmates were killed. The complete disestablishment of the Church was followed by an effort to root out religion from the universities, and professors who clung to their faith were dismissed. Government control of the libraries and of the Press steadily militated against the publication of Orthodox literature. The greater part of the peasantry soon absorbed the Communist ideas, but many were unwilling to surrender their religion. In order to undermine the faith of the latter, exhibitions were made of the relics around which much of Orthodox piety had gathered, and they were displayed as specious frauds. From 1922 began a campaign to substitute a militant atheism for religion in the training of the young, especially those in the Government children's

THE EASTERN ORTHODOX CHURCH

homes, and the adolescents were appealed to by public travesties of the Christian festivals. Tikhon made himself a marked man by his outspoken proclamations against these outrages upon religion. In 1922, when a number of priests were executed for anti-revolutionary conspiracy, he was himself placed in confinement. Bolshevism stopped short of the full example set by the French Revolution in making all priests outlaws, but adopted a clever expedient in encouraging schism within the national Church. Soon after Tikhon was imprisoned he was persuaded to hand over the administration of Church affairs during his absence to a board of progressive priests. This was assumed to imply his abdication, and it was announced that a General Assembly would be called to decide the future of the ecclesiastical constitution. During the famine of 1922 there was a demand for the surrender of the Church treasures for the purposes of relief. Tikhon had been willing to contribute such objects as were not essential for the cult, but objected to the forced surrender of all valuables. The progressive priests thereupon announced the formation of the 'Living Church', and asserted that they had taken over Tikhon's transferred authority. Many of the clergy who refused compliance with the order to hand over their treasures were shot, and the Government did all in its power to enforce the recognition of the new Church administration. The Sobor, or General Assembly of this Renovated Church, met in 1923 and 1925, and was marked by a determination to remain on good terms with the Government, a wish to reform the liturgy, and a decided preference for the white or parochial clergy against the black monks. In 1923 Tikhon regained his liberty on signing a letter that repudiated monarchist intrigues, and promised loyalty to the Soviet Government. He died in 1925 after doing much to re-establish the prestige of his own section of the national Church. In 1927 the Tikhon parishes numbered 35,000, while those of the Renovated Church numbered 17,000. No Patriarch has succeeded Tikhon, but in the summer of 1927 the Metropolitan Sergius, the *locum tenens*, managed to secure Government recognition of a Central Synod for the Tikhon Church, and this may mean a concordat between the old Church and the Soviet Government, with a new era of freedom for religious development. It is time that something should be done, for the period of confusion has almost emptied the village churches, although the peasants still cling to the observances of religion in marriage and baptism. In the cities, however, there seems to have been a revival of religion among the intelligentsia, and Orthodoxy is well represented among them, while the poorer classes are more affected by Baptist revivalists. Within the Church, the revolution has decreased the power of the bishops and strengthened that of the laity, who now exercise considerable rights, not only over the fabrics of churches, but in the selection of their parochial clergy. There has taken place a simplification and beautifying of the liturgy, which has had a marked effect on the worship-loving Russians, and a strong 'Eucharistic movement', which is dated from the preaching of Father John of Kronstadt, has filled the services with a new meaning. Spiritual direction is greatly increasing, and the ascetic ideal is finding new forms in lay communities which keep vows while still living in the world.

The story of other parts of the Orthodox Church is largely that of their emancipation from Turkish rule and its consequences. Serbia was put under a Russian protectorate in 1826, and after the Russo-Turkish War of 1828-29 it had its own ruling prince. In 1830 its Church was emancipated from the control of the Phanar and began to regard the Metropolitan of Belgrade as its head, its autonomy being recognised by the Oecumenical Patriarch in 1879. During the Great War most of its theological students were educated in Oxford and were ready at its close to take their part in seizing the opportunity presented by the expansion of Serbia into Jugo-Slavia. In 1921 Belgrade was promoted to the rank of a Patriarchate, thus succeeding to the medieval Serbian patriarchate of Pec. It now has four metropolitans and twenty-two bishops under its jurisdiction.

Greece was rescued from the Turk and declared an independent monarchy as the result of the Battle of Navarino (1827). It had the misfortune in 1920 to find itself opposing its old enemy without support at Smyrna. Its troops were ignominiously driven into the sea and its resources ruined. Nevertheless the century had been one of considerable expansion and progress. The Church shared in this growth of independence. In 1833 it declared itself free of exterior control and placed its government in the hands of a Holy Synod, its independence being recognised by the Oecumenical Patriarchate in 1850. The monasteries, which have always been a strong feature of ecclesiastical organisation in Greece, proved themselves somewhat difficult to deal with. In 1833 there were as many as 593, but the following year 412 of these were suppressed by the Government as containing less than six monks apiece. A movement towards a more representative form of self-rule has recently led to a reform of the Synod. Hitherto that had been a small ecclesiastical committee, but now it has been widened to include all the bishops of the kingdom, and there is a possibility of the addition of houses of clergy and laity. Together with this improvement in machinery there has gone on a quickening of spiritual life. A movement that includes intellectual, social, and devotional endeavour is receiving many adherents, while its organ, the newspaper *Zoe*, has attained an amazingly wide circulation.

The Church in Rumania declared itself independent of any foreign bishop in 1864, and its independence was actually recognised by the Oecumenical Patriarch in 1885. It has paid for this privilege by a complete subservience to the State, which sequestrated its monasteries, secularised much of its possessions, and placed it under the Ministry of Education. Consequently the clergy are hopelessly underpaid, and the peasantry, although deeply attached to their religion, are prone to superstition. In Bulgaria the way was prepared for ecclesiastical independence by an intellectual revival during the first half of the nineteenth century. The movement was strongly supported by Russia, who was afraid of a wholesale defection of the Bulgarians to Rome. In 1860 the rule of the Oecumenical Patriarch was repudiated, and after ten years of struggle the Sultan was induced to make the Bulgarian Church independent under an Exarch of its own. The Patriarch condemned this demand of a national Church for its own Government as **the heresy of** Phyletism **and excommunicated its exponents.**

EASTERN CHURCH IN RECENT TIMES

Nevertheless the Bulgarian Church persisted in its independence, and so paved the way for the State to demand civil autonomy. As an independent State, Bulgaria participated in the two Balkan Wars, the second of which threw her into the arms of Germany and so led to her losses in the Great War. Her Church still remains autonomous and out of communion with the Oecumenical Patriarchate, although recognised by the rest of the Orthodox Church.

Of the separated Eastern Churches, the most important are the Armenian, the Jacobite, and the Coptic, which are all Monophysite, and the Assyrian, which is Nestorian. The Armenian, which was the first Christian national Church to be brought into existence, has had a most tragic history in modern times. Towards the end of the nineteenth century the Turks suspected it of revolutionary designs and submitted it to terrible persecution. Under Abdul Hamid II, between 1894 and 1896 a hundred thousand Armenians were massacred, and many thousands have since perished under the Young Turks and even under Kemal. The consequence is that, of the three million Armenians still remaining, less than three hundred thousand continue under the rule of the Turk, the rest having sought refuge elsewhere. The Jacobites, named after the sixth-century leader, James Baradaeus, are the Monophysites of Syria. They number less than two hundred thousand and own the Patriarch of Antioch as their chief. They are closely connected with the Christians of S. Thomas in Malabar, of whom mention has already been made. The Copts are the Monophysites of Egypt. They obtained freedom to practise their religion when the British occupied the country after the Battle of Tel-el-Kebir in 1882. They number well under a million, but they maintain a number of monasteries and are organised in eighteen dioceses. The neighbouring Church of Abyssinia has close relations with the Copts, accepting the same interpretation of Christology. It has, however, peculiar features of its own, for it preserves more than any other Christian Church the primitive traces of its Jewish ancestry, practising circumcision as a preliminary to baptism and allowing Nazarite vows. The Assyrians, or Church of the East, represent the ancient Nestorian Church of Persia. After the conquests of Tamerlane, these Christians found refuge from the ravages of Islam in the mountainous country of Kurdistan. They maintained a precarious existence and were divided by a schism, but since 1885 many of them have been cared for and educated by a mission sent out by the Archbishop of Canterbury. They returned this kindness by fighting as allies of the English in the Great War, and were consequently well-nigh exterminated by the Turks after the war was over The remnant, to the number of about forty thousand, have been settled under British protection in Irak.

Most of these Eastern Churches have suffered losses at the hands of Roman Catholic missionaries. Considerable sections have thus been detached and have become Uniate Churches, which, while accepting the Roman authority, are allowed to keep their own Eastern rites. The largest of them is the Ruthenian Church, numbering three and a half million members, mostly in Poland, and there is also a strong Uniate Church in Rumania. The most influential of the Uniates are the Catholic Armenians, who have missions all round the Levant. The Maronites are unlike the rest of the Uniates in that they were not detached from another Church, but trace their ancestry back to the Monothelites of the fifth century. They derive their name from John Maro, a religious leader of that period who had a following in the monasteries of the Lebanon. They were united with Rome in the twelfth century and have remained faithful to that allegiance ever since.

CHAPTER XX

AMERICAN CHRISTIANITY

THE religious history of the United States is in many respects a reflection of that of Europe, although it has some distinctive features. There exists now a complete religious liberty, and no favour is shown to one creed above another, but it has not always been so. Almost every part of the country has had in the past an Established Church, and has passed through the experience of disestablishment. In the beginning each colony had its own Church and each religious party demanded its own parcel of territory for its own religion. The *cujus regio* principle has never had a more adequate opportunity of self-expression, but by almost general agreement it gave way to the method of universal toleration. The Church of England was fully established with a parochial system in Virginia, Maryland, and the Carolinas; but disestablishment came as the natural result of the War of Independence in 1776. Congregationalism was established in Massachusetts and the neighbouring colonies, and the Puritans' dislike of toleration was shown by the hanging of four Quakers in Boston. Inasmuch as New England Puritanism had no ties with the English Government, its establishment was not destroyed by the revolution, but died a lingering death, not being extinct in Massachusetts till 1834. However, an Act for Establishing Religious Freedom had been passed in 1785 under President Jefferson. It provided that henceforth no man was to be compelled to attend or support any religious body, and that all should be free to maintain any religious view or profession they pleased. This Act was intended by its promoters as something of an attack upon religion, but it has since been universally welcomed by the nation. Nevertheless untrammelled freedom has revealed one undoubted evil in the tendency to split up into sects on the slightest provocation, and the fissiparous character of American sectarianism has become the amazement of the nations.

The 'Great Awakening' was a period of religious enthusiasm corresponding to the evangelical revival in England. It had been prepared for by the preaching of Frelinghuysen in New Jersey and Jonathan Edwards in Massachusetts, and was brought to its consummation by the tour of George Whitefield through the English colonies in 1740. But it was itself the cause of division. Among the Congregationalists those who welcomed the revivalist methods were known as New Lights, while those who objected to them were the Old Lights. A similar schism on the same ground appeared among the Presbyterians, dividing them into New Side and Old Side. The division spread into university life, Harvard and Yale remaining Old Light in sympathy, while Princeton was founded in 1746 by the sympathisers with the New Light school. The revival, which had produced effects likely to be permanent in American religion, was itself extinguished by the people's absorption in the conquest of Canada (1755-63), the War of Independence (1775-83), and the framing of the new constitution (1789). In the consequent serious depression of religious zeal there was given to several inherent difficulties an opportunity to make themselves felt.

The Episcopal Church had shared little in the enthusiasm generated by the revival, but the practice of its own more sober type of religion had been rendered difficult by the absence of any local bishop. An Episcopal Church without a bishop was a sufficient anomaly, but many efforts were made on both sides of the Atlantic to keep it in that position. Between 1766 and 1775 the Presbyterians and Congregationalists of Philadelphia and Connecticut patched up their own quarrels to unite against the urgent petition of the Episcopalians to be allowed to invite the appointment of bishops under the Church of England. The objections alleged were mostly against the costliness and pomp of the bishops—in short, against a prelatic episcopacy. The same objections were felt by many in the Home Country, although

AMERICAN CHRISTIANITY

Queen Anne, Archbishop Tenison, and Bishop Sherlock had all supported the project. It was not until the War of Independence was over that American churchmen elected Dr. Seabury and sent him across the sea to seek consecration He arrived in 1783, but political complications prevented the English bishops from consecrating him, and he was forced to have recourse to the non-juring bishops of Scotland, by three of whom he was consecrated in Aberdeen on November 14, 1784. Immediately upon his return he set about the task of filling up the depleted ranks of the ministry. Some doubts, however, were cast upon the validity of his ordinations, and before long it was decided to send other candidates for consecration to England. As the result of this, Dr. White, of Pennsylvania, and Dr. Provoost, of New York, were consecrated by the Archbishops of Canterbury and York with others at Lambeth in 1787. Disputes about validity were ended when both lines joined together in the first episcopal consecration that ever took place in America in 1792.

In the meantime, owing largely to the lack of episcopal supervision, a serious difficulty had arisen in New England over the Creed. The oldest Anglican Church in those parts, King's Chapel, Boston, had lost its rector in the migration of Tory families after the war. The layman who thereupon took over the task of conducting the services found that he had scruples about the references to the Blessed Trinity in the Prayer Book. The congregation in 1785 agreed to excise all mention of a Trinity from the services, and thus 'the first Episcopal Church in New England became the first Unitarian Church in America'. The congregation after this had the boldness to ask, first Seabury and then Provoost to ordain the layman who had initiated these changes, and on meeting with a refusal made him pastor without ordination. Thus Unitarianism became possessed of a distinct organisation. The bishops were able to check any further progress towards Unitarianism in the churches under their care, but there was a great slide among the Congregationalists. No fewer than a hundred and twenty-six of their churches rejected Trinitarian doctrine. The University of Harvard also went over to the Unitarian side in 1805; but while almost the whole of Boston and its immediate neighbourhood adopted these views they had few followers outside that area.

Close akin to the Unitarians and coeval with them in origin are the Universalists, who believe in the ultimate salvation of all mankind. They were formed out of the junction of two very different streams of thought, one Calvinist, the other Arminian. The leader of the former school was John Murray, who believed that Christ died for all, and that therefore blessedness must be conferred on all at the Judgment. The leader of the other school was Elhanan Winchester, who taught that ultimate blessedness is the reward of free submission to God: to such submission all would be brought, those who delayed it being led to it by punishment here or hereafter, although punishment could not, in the nature of the case, be eternal. A fresh turn was given to such speculations by Hosea Ballou, who was an Arian with a Socinian view of the Atonement: the purpose of Christ's death was to show forth the love of God, and that love would win all men to itself. Under his leadership the Universalists accepted a Unitarian view of God.

The combined effect of the war and the reduced Christology was to bring religion in America to a lower state than it had yet reached. The closing years of the eighteenth century represent the low-water mark, but immediately afterwards the capacity for quick recovery, which is a marked feature of American religion, showed itself in a second Awakening. The revival began in Kentucky and Tennessee, where in July 1800 many of the families drove their teams to the woods of Logan County and encamped for several days in order to engage in common worship and preaching. This was the first of the camp-meetings that form so strange a phenomenon in the religious life of the times. 'A population *perfervido ingenio*, of a temper peculiarly susceptible of intense excitement, transplanted into a wild country, under little control either of conventionality or law, deeply engrained from many generations with the religious sentiment, but broken loose from the control of it and living consciously in reckless disregard of the law of God, is suddenly aroused to a sense of its apostasy and

AMERICAN CHRISTIANITY 249

wickedness.' Hence came the hysterical phenomena for which these camp-meetings are famous. The heterogeneous mass of men, women, and children living together without the wholesome distraction of the ordinary pursuits of everyday life gave themselves up to religious exercises that proved a severe strain upon the nervous temperament. Even spectators who had no religious interest in the scene would often find themselves manifesting the same physical convulsions as were sometimes the accompaniment of genuine conversion. But, in spite of all that can be said in criticism, these meetings led to a revival whose effects were certainly more profound than those of the Great Awakening in 1740, although they also seem to have set the precedent for that alternation between extreme zeal and dull apathy which seems a somewhat marked feature of American religion. One evil result of the second Awakening, as of the first, was the impetus it gave to the rise of sects who split off from their parent Churches because of their attitude towards the revival and its methods. The coldness of the Presbyterian body was particularly resented by many of the members, and they took advantage of an acute difference over the educational qualifications to be demanded of candidates for the ministry to cut themselves off and found the new sect of the Cumberland Presbyterians.

A better result of the new Awakening was the entry upon a great task in the founding of theological colleges. The Sulpicians had had their seminary at Baltimore since 1791, but non-Roman students had learnt their theology either in the secular colleges or in the parsonage of some scholarly pastor. But after Harvard had gone over to Unitarianism an Orthodox Protestant Seminary was founded at Andover in 1808. This set a great example. In twenty years no less than seventeen theological colleges were started, including the General Seminary for the Episcopalians in 1819, and the number has been increased manifold since then.

The colleges were a great help in organising Christian opinion against some of the evils that threatened the social life of the nation. One of the worst of these was the practice of duelling, which was so prevalent as to make it possible for challenges to be threatened in Congress itself. The death of the widely respected Alexander Hamilton in a duel in 1804 roused public indignation and gave point to the anti-duellist teaching of Lyman Beecher, which was largely instrumental in procuring a law for the disenfranchisement of persons found guilty of this offence. Another scandal of the times was the treatment of the native Indians. Among those who had benefited most from Christian teaching and civilisation were the Cherokees, who occupied a fully guaranteed reserve in the beautiful country adjacent to the State of Georgia. The greed of the whites for farm land led them to break their treaties and take possession of this Naboth's vineyard. The missionaries suffered heavily in their efforts to thwart the project, but the leaders of Christian opinion, such as Theodore Frelinghuysen, set up so gallant a fight on behalf of the natives when the matter came before Congress that they were only beaten by one vote. Drunkenness was another vice against which the various denominations made a heroic struggle. The Society for the Promotion of Temperance was founded in 1826, and effected a considerable change in the social habits of the time without recourse to legislation. This, however, had one bad effect in paving the way for the establishment of special houses for excessive drinking, and the American 'saloon' soon became a notorious scandal. More drastic reform seemed to be needed, and about 1850 the Prohibition agitation began which has achieved its triumph in our own day.

More serious in its national consequences than any of these efforts was the campaign made against slavery. In the early years of the nineteenth century the whole of Christian opinion, both in North and South, was united in condemnation of this practice. But about the year 1833 a decided change began to make itself evident in the South, where many ministers suddenly found themselves able to prove the justice of slave-holding from the Scriptures. This difference led to division in the Churches. There is no doubt that it lay behind the great schism of 1837 in the Presbyterian Church between New and Old School, although other points of doctrine and organisation were the alleged causes. Similarly, it was responsible for the deliberate division in 1844 of the Methodist Episcopal Church between North and South.

In the Episcopal Church these differences were not so acutely felt. When the Civil War broke out in 1861, relations between the divided areas became impossible; but in the General Convention, held in New York in 1862, the fiction was continued of calling the names of the southern dioceses, and seats were assigned to their representatives, though none was present. The Bishop of Louisiana, indeed, took combatant rank as a major-general in the Confederate Army, but he died of wounds, and when peace was declared in 1865 some of the southern bishops sat in the General Convention of that year, and the Church thus led the way in the welding together of the separated states. This it was the better able to do because it had now awakened out of the state of apathy that had characterised it in the first decade of the century. 'No fact', says a somewhat unsympathetic historian, 'in the external history of the American Church at this period is more imposing than this growth of the Episcopal Church from nothing to a really commanding stature.' The increase of numbers was due, not to immigration, as was the case with the Roman Catholics, but to the conversion of many members of other denominations who were attracted to it by the beauty of its worship and by its preference for steady growth in Christian culture instead of a violent and fluctuating emotionalism.

These features of the life of the Episcopal Church were emphasised as a result of the spread to America of the influence of the Oxford Movement. Under that influence was founded an interesting experiment in seminary life at Nashotah. In 1842 several men, who had been undergraduates together at the General Theological Seminary, established a centre there from which they endeavoured both to reach the ill-educated people of the neighbourhood and to train young men for ordination. They lived a common life of poverty, worship, and self-support, without monastic vows, but in such a manner as to earn for their institution the title of 'the Clugny of the American Church'. A less pleasing result of the Oxford influence was that it actually produced a small schism. This was in 1873, when a dispute on the subject of baptismal regeneration came to a head, and Dr. Cummins, the assistant Bishop of Kentucky, objecting to the prevalence of Catholic teaching, founded the 'Reformed Episcopal Church'.

The Roman Catholic Church in America, as elsewhere, suffered considerable vicissitudes before the outbreak of the Civil War. Great difficulty in its administration was occasioned through the independence of spirit engendered among its lay folk by life in a new republic. This led to trusteeism' or the determination of the laity to manage the property acquired by their own contributions, a tendency that was not overcome until more than one important Church had been put under an interdict. Mutual jealousies among the various orders of monks and the different nationalities composing the body of adherents furnished other difficulties. More important was the dislike stirred up among the bulk of the American people by what was felt to be the foreign character of Roman Catholicism. This sometimes took entirely unjustifiable forms, as in the case of the riots provoked by the scandalous stories of Maria Monk, who claimed to have been a nun in Montreal, and in 1836 persuaded the credulous to accept her account of secret horrors in the convent. On the other hand there was neither Liberalism nor Gallicanism among the Roman Catholics of America, and as there was no tradition of the semi-independence of a national Church, the faithful could be bound more closely to the Papacy than was possible in most other countries. The testing-time of efficiency came during the Great Immigration that took place in the first half of the nineteenth century, when the population increased from five to twenty-three millions. The majority of the immigrants came from Ireland and other Roman Catholic countries, and as they were mostly poor the strain on the existing organisation was severe. The clergy were compelled to give their attention to the towns, and in the subsequent movements of population towards the west it was the various Protestant bodies who were always first in the field. The consequence was seen in very great losses to Roman Catholicism. How great those losses were will never be known, but in 1893, when the total population had mounted to seventy millions and the Roman communion numbered only nine millions, one of their own members asserted that on a conservative estimate his Church had lost no fewer than twenty million adherents.

To the period before the Civil War belongs also the origin of two types of American religion that have caused no small stir in other countries. The first is that of the Mormons or Latter Day Saints. The most charitable view of Joseph Smith, the founder of this body, is that he was an epileptic. Symptoms of this disease mingled with the phenomena of his conversion, which took place in 1829. Three years later a vision disclosed to him the hiding-place of the *Book of Mormon*, wherein, engraved on gold plates, was an account of the way in which America had been colonised by the lost Ten Tribes of Israel, the modern Red Indians, to whom our Lord had appeared after His resurrection, but failed to prevent them becoming so sinful that they had to be cut off from the rest of the world for many generations. Later visions explained how the Kingdom of God was to be built up in these latter days. The most obvious outcome of the revelations was a series of unsound business enterprises in the City of Missouri, which was declared to be the New Zion. So many converts joined the band of 'saints' that they were able to defy the Government, but popular fury was aroused to such an extent that Smith and his brother were murdered in 1844, while lying in prison under a promise of protection from the governor. Brigham Young succeeded to the leadership of the body, and under him they made the great trek to Salt Lake Valley, where they founded a new Zion in 1847. He maintained his prestige by murder and assassination, but escaped the due reward of his deeds because President Lincoln had his hands full with the Civil War. The gravest cause of offence was the practice of polygamy, which they justified both on the ground that it was comparable with that 'celestial' marriage that would give a widower who had remarried the possession of both wives in heaven, and also on the ground that since souls were pre-existent it was right for a man to provide as many bodies as possible for those souls to inhabit. Under Young's successor, Wilfrid Woodruff, the 'saints' made terms with the Federal Government, and were given the privileges of a state on condition of abandoning polygamy.

The other type is that of the Adventists, who believe in an immediate second coming of Christ. This, indeed, is a view that has appeared at intervals from the very beginning of Christianity. The current phase of it dated from the teaching of William Miller, a farmer of Vermont, who on the basis of calculations from Daniel and the Apocalypse, fixed the date of the Parousia for April 23, 1843. Some of the conditions of the early Church were reproduced in the excitement of this expectation, many giving up their business to await the end of the world, and some contributing of their goods in a kind of voluntary Communism for the support of their poorer brethren. In spite of the natural disappointment when the prescribed date had passed, numbers still clung to the essential hope of an early millennium, some combining with it a determination to observe no other day as holy than the seventh in each week. The growth of modern criticism and a better understanding of apocalyptic literature have not even yet succeeded in making 'adventism' impossible.

After the close of the Civil War immigration began again on an immense scale, and the energies of the United States were engrossed in the endeavour to make one nation out of many races. The Roman Catholics were tempted both to oppose on religious grounds the 'common school' system of American education and also to organise some, at least, of their churches on a racial basis. The papal legate, Monsignor Satolli, refused, however, to countenance the project to divide his Church into different languages each with its own hierarchy. Since Pius X in 1908 granted to the members of his communion in America the same degree of autonomy as is allowed in European lands, they have become less alien and more definitely American, and form, at the present time, the most numerous Christian body in that country. It would have been well if American Christianity as a whole could have shown some equally strong tendency to unity. But the successful unifying of the diverse peoples on the political side is in sharp contrast with the religious divisions which still number over 150 sects. Nevertheless the most marked movement in the present century has been in the direction of Christian unity. Evolutionary methods of studying Church history have contributed largely to this movement, although the deposition of Professor C. A. Briggs by the Presbyterian Assembly in 1893 and the outbreak of 'Fundamentalism' in Dayton, Ohio, in 1925, show that the old methods have not surrendered without a struggle. Recognition of the social implications of religion have also contributed towards unity. The Young Men's Christian Association, founded in London by George Williams in 1844, has spread very widely in the States and has brought many denominations together. Missionary necessities have furthered the same cause. The Student Volunteer Missionary Movement, started in 1886, has, together with the Student Christian Movement, brought together educated people of differing religious views at the most impressionable period of their lives and prepared the way for more definite efforts after unity. Of these the most imposing was the formation of the Federal Council of the Churches of Christ in America in 1908. It includes thirty denominations in the endeavour to make a combined Christian witness in the affairs of national life. A movement that may prove still more important in its world-wide effects was inaugurated by the Episcopal Church in 1910, when it set on foot its proposal for a Conference on Faith and Order which should comprise representatives from the whole of Christendom. Thus the complete absence of State aid and control, which has left American Christianity free to indulge a tendency to indefinite subdivision, has left it free also to inaugurate a return towards the original Christian unity. In this movement the Episcopal Church, whose influence is far greater than might be gathered from its numbers, has taken an important and increasing share.

CHAPTER XXI

REUNION MOVEMENTS

ACTIVE effort for the reunion of Christendom has been the most remarkable phenomenon of recent Christian history. If America, with its many sects all on a position of equality in the eyes of the State, has proved a particularly fruitful soil for such growth, the general tendency has nevertheless been universal. For this there are many reasons. Historically, most people have become convinced that the foundation of one visible Church was inherent in the very beginning of Christianity. Doctrinally, it has become more and more difficult to justify the existence of warring sects. Practically, the claims of the mission-field have made such divisions seem wasteful and extravagant, and the claims of the work at home have made it necessary to show a united front against the social evils of the day. In face of the great tasks that loom before the new generation, the barriers that were raised by old controversies seem crumbling to decay. And the Great War, both by throwing together many nations and many schools of thought, and also by holding before men the hope of a new world of unity and peace, has quickened the efforts and energies of all who look forward to an ultimate reuniting of the Church on earth. As we study the record of these movements we find that behind the struggles of to-day stretches a long line of past endeavour. No sooner had the Reformation achieved the break-up of Christendom than tentative efforts began to be made to piece it together again. Until recent times those attempts have been abortive; it is the significant feature of the present day that at last some definite steps have been taken towards retrieving this failure.

1. ROMAN CATHOLICISM

Even before the Reformation Rome had had her experience of schism and learnt how difficult a wound it was to heal. Twice, at least, at Lyons and Florence, it seemed that she was on the point of healing the breach between herself and the Orthodox Church of the East, but on both occasions the hope proved premature. In the sixteenth century the tide of Mohammedan invasion divided sharply between East and West, and there was less prospect than ever of unity. It is true that the influence of Roman theology was felt at the Council of Jerusalem in 1672, but in general the relations between the two communions grew more and more bitter. In default of union on a large scale, a few small branches of the Orthodox have, as we have seen, made their submission to Rome and been allowed to retain their own rites while accepting papal government, but the existence of these Uniate Churches has not improved the general relations.

After the Reformation the Papacy was regarded with the most virulent hatred in Protestant countries, and the Pope was generally believed to be Antichrist. In England the rise of specific Anglicanism made a juster view possible, and Andrewes, at least, found himself able to pray for reunion both with East and West. Under Laud writers on both sides explored avenues of approach. In 1633, the year when Laud became Archbishop of Canterbury, one of the Queen's chaplains, a Franciscan, Christopher Davenport, defended the validity of English ordinations and sought to explain the Articles in a manner satisfactory to Rome. A short time afterwards, Montagu, Bishop of Chichester, was suggesting to Panzani, a papal envoy, a conference in France where the differences could be discussed, and he seems also to have been ready to acknowledge a purely spiritual supremacy of the Pope. But the Civil War showed how impossible were such ideas in that period. Under Charles II it looked to some spectators as if the English Church might reunite itself to the Roman by submission, and in 1663 terms were drawn up, probably with the connivance of the King, but certainly without the knowledge of the clergy, for turning the Anglican communion into a

Uniate Church. This project was effectively stopped by the outcry that arose over the 'Popish Plot' in 1678, and although a few pamphlets on reunion were written during James II's reign there was no discussion of the subject on the grand scale until 1717. By that time Wake was Archbishop of Canterbury, and he, having lived some time in Paris, was deeply interested in the affairs of the French Church, whose Gallicanism showed many points in common with Anglicanism In such circumstances it was natural that the possibility of an understanding should be explored. Cardinal de Noailles, Archbishop of Paris, was in sympathy with the proposal, and the historian Dupin started a correspondence with Wake. Dupin found suitable explanations of the Articles, and Wake defended Anglican Orders; but the Jesuits worked upon the Government and nothing further was done. One French priest, Courayer, was strong enough to brave Jesuit displeasure and publish a defence of Anglican Orders in 1723, but his enemies drove him from the country and he was compelled to take refuge in England, where he remained till his death.

After this there was nothing noteworthy until the Oxford Movement and the fresh hopes it aroused of a better mutual understanding. Such hopes were wrecked upon the intransigence of the English ultramontanes, and the efforts that were made to get the case reasonably considered at the Vatican Council in 1870 came to nothing. Nevertheless the Tractarians had a profound influence on the question in two directions: they put an end to the old unreasoning fear and hatred of Rome as of something unclean, and they established the right of Anglicans to interpret their Articles and liturgy in a Catholic sense. The next step was to arouse a better feeling on the other side. This was attempted by Lord Halifax in 1894 when, through his friendship with the Abbé Portal, he was able to get the question of Anglican Orders discussed to such purpose that the Pope, Leo XIII, was constrained to appoint a Commission to go into the whole matter. Three, at least, of the Commission were convinced that the Orders were valid, but a further commission of Cardinals had to adjudicate upon the question, and here the influence of Cardinal Vaughan, who like most English Roman Catholics was heartily opposed to any

REUNION MOVEMENTS 259

yielding on the point, triumphed. The Pope, acting upon their decision, issued the Bull *Apostolicae Curae* in 1896, which refused to recede from the uncompromising attitude that Rome had already taken up. Fortunately the Pope not only issued his condemnation, but gave his reasons, and these were dealt with *seriatim* by the English archbishops in a 'Response' of the following year. This affirms the Catholic position of the English Church in regard to the priesthood, the Real Presence, and the sacrifice in the Holy Communion, and is as remarkable for the purity of its Latinity as for the precision of its historical scholarship.

Not daunted by this defeat, Lord Halifax and the Abbé Portal started a new series of conversations in 1921 at Malines, under the Archbishop Cardinal Mercier, the subject of discussion being the Primacy of the Roman see. The few theologians of the two Churches who took part in the first two conversations in this series found their numbers increased and a slightly more official character given to their deliberations at the third meeting in 1923. The death of Cardinal Mercier was not allowed to stay the progress of the discussions, for his place was taken by his successor at Malines, Monsignor Van Roey, who had already taken part in them, and they were resumed in 1926. However, Pius XI the Pope tired of the negotiations in 1928 and issued an encyclical, in which he, in effect, disowned any scheme of union that was not based on complete submission to the Holy See, and drew a sharp distinction between the Orthodox Churches, which have valid orders, and the Anglican Church, which has not. This was, no doubt, done with a view to the *rapprochement* that had recently taken place between the Orthodox and Anglican Churches; but it had also the effect of limiting the scope of a promising new movement in Belgium, where at Amay-sur-Meuse had been founded the Benedictine Order of the Monks of the Union of the Churches, with the object of working for the reunion of Christendom. Their work was done on the best lines, and their monthly magazine, *Irénikon*, was devoted to the study of the subject, especially as it affected the English and the Eastern Churches. Since the papal encyclical the monks of Amay, like the rest of the Roman world, have been compelled to concentrate their attention on the East.

2. Orthodoxy

The Eastern Churches, as we have seen, are divided into the Orthodox, the Separated, and the Uniates. The Uniates have already made their terms with Rome. The Separated are divided from one another and from the rest of the East by age-long national rivalries with theological niceties to furnish an excuse. There remain the Orthodox. We have already discussed the mutual relations between them and the Papacy. Their relations with the rest of Western Christendom have never been close until our own day, although they have never been without points of contact. As early as 1559 Melanchthon was corresponding with the Patriarch Joseph II to bring about a union between Lutherans and Orthodox. The theologians of Tübingen, towards the end of the sixteenth century, tried to accomplish an approximation of doctrine, and the tragic Patriarch, Cyril Lucar, who was murdered in 1637, had first ruined his influence on account of his Calvinistic leanings.

This Cyril was the first Greek of importance to have relations with the English Church after the Reformation. In 1611 he was visited by George Sandys, son of the Archbishop of York, to whom he made very light of the differences between the English and the Greeks. He not only maintained a courteous correspondence with James I, Charles I, and Laud, but also sent one of his priests to be educated at Balliol. This custom lasted after his death, for a future Bishop of Smyrna not only studied at Balliol, but served as a chaplain at Christ Church until he was expelled by the Puritans in 1647. In 1677 a church was actually built in London for the Greeks through the influence of Bishop Compton, and it was served by the Metropolitan of Samos, who was then resident in the city. As a result of his work a scheme was promoted to bring twenty Greek students, five from each Patriarchate, to Oxford for study. A number of the students settled down at Gloucester Hall, now Worcester College, but they did not take kindly to the life of the place and the scheme was presently abandoned. Several Orthodox prelates were entertained in this country during the succeeding period. The visit of Arsenius, Archbishop of the Thebaid, in 1714 led to an important attempt

REUNION MOVEMENTS

on the part of the Non-jurors to establish union between themselves and the Eastern Church. Although Arsenius's own colleagues in the East would not deviate by a hair's-breadth from their position in order to conciliate the Non-jurors, he had in the meantime carried the proposals to Russia, where, under the influence of Peter the Great, they might have come to fruition had it not been for that monarch's death in 1725, just as a conference was being prepared.

These negotiations of the Non-jurors are important, not only in themselves, but also because they brought the great Archbishop Wake into the question. It was impossible for him to stand by and watch a schismatic body usurp the place that rightfully belonged to the official Church of the country. He therefore took the opportunity in 1725 of writing to the Patriarch of Jerusalem and explaining to him the exact position of affairs between the Non-jurors and the Church of England. At the same time he expressed the deepest regard for the Church of the East. 'Meanwhile we, the true Bishops and Clergy of the Church of England, as, in every fundamental article, we profess the same faith with you, shall not cease in spirit and effect (since otherwise, owing to our distance from you, we cannot) to hold communion with you and to pray for your peace and happiness.' As in the case of English relations with the Roman Church, this is the last occasion on which there is anything important to record until we come to the Oxford Movement.

The immediate result of that Movement was to send William Palmer, a Fellow of Magdalen College, Oxford, to Russia in order to explain Anglicanism to the bishops there and to seek communion with them. In the latter effort he was not successful, although a *Harmony of Anglican Doctrine with the Doctrine of the Eastern Church*, published by him in 1846 and translated into Greek five years later, did much to promote a better understanding. The Jerusalem bishopric, on the other hand, might easily have widened the breach, particularly when the second bishop, John Gobat, a Swiss, began to proselytise from the Eastern Churches; but the energetic protests of many English churchmen and the conciliatory efforts of George

Williams, Fellow of King's College, Cambridge, who went out as the first bishop's chaplain, turned it into an opportunity of securing a fuller appreciation of the Anglican claims. After the Crimean War had checked progress for a time, a committee was appointed by Convocation in 1863 to confer with a committee of the American Church on the possibility of intercommunion, first with the Russo-Greek Church and later with the other Eastern Patriarchates. In 1874-75 conferences were held at Bonn between representatives of the Eastern, Anglican, and Old Catholic Churches; in 1897 the bishops assembled at the Lambeth Conference despatched the Bishop of Salisbury to communicate to the Eastern Patriarchs the resolutions on Unity passed by that Conference; and the next Lambeth Conference in 1907 set up a permanent committee on relations with the Eastern Patriarchs. In the meantime the greatest honour had been shown by the respective Churches to each other's delegates on various official visits, and a society, originally founded in 1864 and now known as the 'Anglican and Eastern Churches Association', continued to join people of both sides in mutual intercourse.

The Great War served to draw closer the bonds between the two communions. It was English arms that were responsible for the deliverance of Jerusalem and the holy places from Turkish dominance in 1917, and it was Anglicans who were responsible for the maintenance and education of Serbian students for the ministry during the period of the war. In 1920 a delegation from Constantinople visited the Lambeth Conference, and the result was seen two years later when the Patriarch of Constantinople communicated to the Archbishop of Canterbury the conclusion of his Synod that 'the ordination of the Anglican Episcopal confession of bishops, priests, and deacons possesses the same validity as those of the Roman, Old Catholic, and Armenian Churches possess, inasmuch as all essentials are found in them which are held indispensable from the Orthodox point of view for the recognition of the *Charisma* of the priesthood derived from Apostolic succession'. In 1923 the synods of Jerusalem and Cyprus concurred in this recognition of the validity of Anglican Orders. The revival of Anglican pilgrimages to the Holy

REUNION MOVEMENTS

Land in 1924 did much to strengthen this growing friendship, and in 1925, in commemoration of the Council of Nicea (325), the Patriarchs of Alexandria and Jerusalem and official representatives of all but one of the Orthodox Churches joined with the Archbishop of Canterbury and other Anglican bishops in an official liturgy at Westminster Abbey, and with the Archbishop of Wales and Welsh bishops at S. David's. This does not yet mean complete intercommunion, but the first and most important step towards it has been taken. When it is remembered that the Orthodox Churches of the East number, perhaps, 120 millions of adherents, it will be realised that the Anglican communion has at last been lifted out of that somewhat isolated position with regard to the rest of Christendom which it had occupied since the Reformation.

3. Protestantism

In no sphere are the centripetal forces of the present time more evident than among the various bodies that owe their origin to the Continental Reformation. That in itself represents a complete reversal of policy. The weakness of Protestantism was always its tendency to division and subdivision. The conciliatory efforts of Melanchthon and the various efforts after a Pan-Protestant league, made by such leaders as Gustavus Adolphus and Cromwell, proved powerless against this fatal tendency, and sects multiplied themselves in indescribable confusion. But once men began to view the Bible critically and revelation historically, they became less insistent upon the niceties of doctrine and administration that had seemed so important in bygone controversy. It is perhaps natural that the divisions most easily made should be the ones most easily mended.

It was in Germany that harmonising influences first made themselves felt. The evangelical Churches of that country were divided for the most part into Lutheran and Reformed. Over these the great philosophical movements of the eighteenth and nineteenth centuries swept, affecting the members profoundly, but not producing any great disruption. As a result, the contrast between Lutheran and Reformed became less sharply defined, and in Prussia they were united in 1817 to become one ecclesiastical organisation. Credal traditions were in this case left untouched, the Reformed parishes retaining the Heidelberg Catechism while the others clung to Luther's Small Catechism. A similar variety in liturgical use was also allowed, and on this basis was constructed the largest of German territorial Churches, 'the Evangelical Church of the Old Prussian Union'. There are twenty-seven other territorial Churches in the German states, thirteen of which call themselves Lutheran, twelve Evangelical, and two Reformed. When the German Empire attained its unity in 1871 it might have been thought that the Churches would have followed suit, but it needed the events of the Great War to bring that about, and it was not until 1922 that the 'German Evangelical Church Federation' was formed. Even this does not imply the formation of one united Church. It is rather a federal association for common work and witness, the faith of the constituent Churches being left untouched.

Scotch Protestantism shows the same alternation between division and union. The ultimate cause of division has generally been the exercise of patronage, by which it was possible for ministers to be forced on unwilling congregations. The first trouble of the kind produced the Secession Church when Erskine, of Stirling, in 1733 proclaimed the right of the congregation to choose its own minister. The second occurred in 1761, when Gillespie, of Carnock, refused to countenance the installation of a minister over an unwilling congregation and led out a number of followers to form the Relief Church. To have two separate Churches making the same witness was soon seen to be absurd, and in 1847 the two schisms joined together to form the United Presbyterian Church. But in the meantime a much more serious schism from the State Church had occurred. Warmed by evangelical piety and disgusted by the coldness of contemporary ecclesiastics, Thomas Chalmers led an energetic protest against the foisting of 'moderate' ministers upon devout congregations. No redress was procurable either from the General Assembly or from Parliament, and so he and his followers, including 474 ministers, abandoned the Establishment in 1843 and founded the Free Church of

Scotland. History repeated itself and there was found no reason why the Free Church and the United Presbyterian Church should remain separate. They were consequently joined together in 1900 into the United Free Church of Scotland. Unfortunately a small minority of the original Free Church, consisting of sixty-three congregations, could not agree to this union, and they, remaining separate under the popular designation of the 'Wee Frees', provided a celebrated case in ecclesiastical law; for they laid claim to the whole property of the original Free Church on the ground that they alone maintained the first purity of its doctrine, and they were successful in their plea. The absurd situation resulting from this decision of the courts was only relieved by the intervention of Parliament, which divided the property on an equitable basis between the claimants. Since that time the differences between the new United Free Church and the Established Church have become less and less important, and negotiations have been successfully carried on to merge the two bodies into one. The consummation of this design was effected on October 2nd 1929, by which act the most important step towards the consolidation of Presbyterianism in Scotland has been successfully taken.

The tendency towards reunion has marked Presbyterianism in other lands. Canada which received that faith, with its divisions, mainly from Scotland, united all its Presbyterian Churches into one body in 1875, and then led the way to a wider union of non-episcopal communions in the United Church of Canada in 1925. The needs of the mission-field have accelerated such movements elsewhere. In South India there is a remarkable instance of this. There the Presbyterian and Congregationalists have joined together to form the South India United Church, and that United Church is now negotiating for a possible union with the Anglican communion in those parts.

In England the cause of Protestant reunion has not progressed so rapidly. The Methodists have made many efforts to unite their various separated bodies, but financial difficulties, especially those connected with the payment of the ministers, stood in the way. In default of complete reunion one group formed the United Methodists in 1907.

A Free Church National Council, in imitation of the Anglican 'Church Congress', began to meet in 1892. This binds together for mutual intercourse the various Nonconformist bodies, and as its membership is made up on a territorial basis it ignores sectarian divisions. It has been successful in producing a catechism which expresses the fundamental beliefs accepted by the constituent bodies, and on more than one occasion it has succeeded in impressing Nonconformist views upon the political opinions of the country. Local Free Church Councils extend its work throughout the parishes and provide a common platform for those who do not accept the episcopalian form of Church government. In 1917 this National Council, which had a merely voluntary membership, was transformed into a Federal Council composed of official representatives of the associated bodies. One result of this closer co-operation has been to assist in breaking down the final barriers between the Methodists. In 1929 an Act was at last passed through Parliament, the object of which is to enable the Wesleyan Methodists, the Primitive Methodists, and the United Methodists in Great Britain to unite together in one Church in the year 1931, provided that they decide by a majority of 75 per cent. so to do. An illustration is here afforded of the immense value of co-operation and federation as preliminary steps towards corporate reunion.

4. ANGLICANISM

The greatest work for reunion has been done by the Church of England and its daughter communions. Holding to the historic polity, and being at the same time peculiarly sensitive to every new movement of thought, the Anglican communion is especially adapted to perform the functions of a 'bridge Church' between the representatives of Catholicism and Evangelicalism. Of this position it has been conscious from the very beginning of the Reformation. On more than one occasion Henry VIII entered into negotiations with the Lutheran princes and divines, but withdrew from them when it became obvious that he would be expected to abandon too much of the old faith. The Elizabethan settlement, as we have seen, is best understood

REUNION MOVEMENTS 267

as an effort to combine the truth of both elements. As such, it commended itself to more than one Continental scholar, notably Saravia and Casaubon. In 1618 four Anglican divines attended the Synod of Dort, and protested vigorously against that Synod's questioning of episcopacy. In 1704 an interesting move was made by Frederick, the first King of Prussia, who, wishing to unite Calvinists and Lutherans and to gain for his bishops the Apostolic Succession, had the Book of Common Prayer translated into German as a first step in that direction. But the early death of the King prevented his schemes from coming to maturity. Archbishop Wake, who showed himself so interested in the prospect of reunion with the Roman and Orthodox Churches, also engaged in abortive negotiations with the Lutheran Church of Sweden. A further project of his for a complete understanding with the Moravians who had settled in England was only wrecked because of the legal difficulties that compelled them to register as Dissenters.

This was the end of reunion schemes for upwards of a century, and then came the ill-fated Jerusalem bishopric affair. This, at least, showed the necessity of working through the Church's official channels, and successive Lambeth Conferences took up the task in earnest. The Moravian question was considered as far back as 1888, but nothing of importance was done until 1897, when a committee was asked to consider the historical and doctrinal points at issue. The committee reported in 1907 that the way to intercommunion was at present barred by the great uncertainty whether the Moravians possessed the historic episcopate. Steps were then proposed by which the Anglican Church might assist the province of the *Unitas Fratrum* in the British Isles to enter upon the privileges of the Apostolic Succession, but in spite of the greatest willingness upon both sides various difficulties, such as the proper method of administering the sacraments of Confirmation and Holy Communion, have so far prevented this desirable consummation.

More satisfactory progress was made in respect of reunion with the Lutheran Church of Sweden. In 1888 the Lambeth Conference resolved that efforts should be made to establish friendly relations. In 1897 a committee was appointed to go into the question of Swedish Orders. In 1908 a Swedish bishop attended the Conference, and the following year a Commission appointed by the Archbishop of Canterbury visited Sweden. In 1911 John Wordsworth, Bishop of Salisbury, published his Hale lectures on the *National Church of Sweden*, and in accord with the position taken up in that work the Commission reported that 'the succession of bishops has been maintained unbroken by the Church of Sweden . . . and that the office of priest . . . has been in intention handed on throughout the whole history' of that Church. The way was thus laid open for definite steps of intercommunion. With the Old Catholics, friendly relations were established in the reunion conferences at Bonn already mentioned. The Lambeth Conference of 1888 desired to maintain those relations, and in 1897 an offer of communion was made. In 1908 the expressions of friendship were repeated, although in that year an unfortunate incident occurred in the consecration of the Rev. A. H. Mathew by the Old Catholic bishops for work in England. This, however, was due to a misapprehension, and when a protest was made the Old Catholics undertook in future 'not to make trouble by encroaching on the order of a friendly Church'. In 1925 they recognised the validity of Anglican orders, and since then the two churches have shared in consecrations to the episcopate.

Such is the history of efforts after reunion with the foreign reformed Churches. The efforts after what is called 'home reunion' go back equally far. There was organised dissent in England from the time of the Elizabethan settlement, although the first dissenting chapels were not actually built until the reign of James II. The erection of these buildings was due to the failure to find any means of incorporating the definitely Puritan bodies in the national Church at the Restoration. The Presbyterians, in particular, had expected to be rewarded for their services in helping to bring back Charles II, but the Savoy Conference defeated their hopes. Another attempt at comprehension was made, as we have seen, at the Revolution, but the proposals were regarded as an attempt to presbyterianise the Church, and were never even put to the Lower House of Convocation.

REUNION MOVEMENTS

Following upon this the Presbyterians tended more and more towards Unitarianism, and it is noteworthy that Archbishop Wake, who was so ready to seek union with Christian bodies outside England, made no such offers to Dissenters at home. The other dissenting bodies, the Independents, Baptists, and Quakers, had no wish to be comprehended in a State Church. The Evangelical Revival, which produced such close relations between the 'enthusiastic' clergy and the Dissenters, brought no scheme for actual union, but in the end added the Methodists to the separated bodies. So large a proportion of the nation was now outside the ministrations of the Church that in 1832 Thomas Arnold, of Rugby, produced his scheme for widening the national Church, so as to include all Christian bodies. This was met by a storm of disapproval, and the development of the Oxford Movement led to the formulation of a definite basis upon which alone reunion could be satisfactorily sought. The form was laid down by the Lambeth Conference of 1888 in the terms of what is known as the Quadrilateral. It comprises the Holy Scriptures as the rule of faith, the Apostles' and Nicene Creeds, the sacraments of Baptism and Holy Communion, and the historic episcopate. Progress on these lines was necessarily slow, and some impatience was manifested in the mission-field. This came to a head in 1913 at Kikuyu in East Africa, where it was proposed to inaugurate a federation of Protestant missions in which Anglicans would be involved on a basis of intercommunion without waiting for the adjustment of questions relating to the ministry. Dr. Weston, Bishop of Zanzibar, challenged the lawfulness of this proceeding, and two years later the Archbishop of Canterbury issued a statement in which he deprecated any partial and local attempts at solving such grave questions, and, while recognising the rights of the bishops to admit non-Anglicans to the Holy Communion, forbade Anglicans to receive the Sacrament from ministers not episcopally ordained. The Kikuyu proposals were modified, and a less ambitious Alliance of Missionary Societies in that area was completed in 1918.

Thus far had the proposals for home and foreign reunion gone when the Lambeth Conference met in 1920. It was attended by 252 bishops, and gave the greater part of its attention to this subject. As a result it sent out an appeal to all Christian Churches in which it took the unprecedented step of proposing to solve the vexed question of the ministry by the mode of deference to one another's conscience. 'To this end, we who send forth this appeal would say that if the authorities of other communions should so desire, we are persuaded that, terms of union having been otherwise satisfactorily adjusted, bishops and clergy of our Communion would willingly accept from these authorities a form of commission or recognition which would commend our ministry to their congregations, as having its place in the one family life.' Much consideration was given to this appeal throughout Christendom in the succeeding years. In regard to home reunion a report signed by the two Archbishops and the Moderator of the Free Church Council was issued in 1922, which accepted one visible Church as the ideal, affirmed episcopacy as the right form of government for the United Church of the future, and recognised the Free Church ministries of the present as real ministries of Christ's Word and Sacraments. The Federal Council of the Free Churches welcomed this view of their ministries, but regretted that the Anglican Church still insisted on episcopal ordination, and in 1925 dismissed the committee which had been considering the question on the ground that for the moment no further progress was possible. Matters have gone much farther than this in regard to foreign reunion. In 1922 intercommunion was established with the Church of Sweden, and two English bishops have taken part in the consecration of two Swedish bishops in Upsala Cathedral. In 1922 three synods of the Eastern Orthodox Church, as we have seen, affirmed the validity of Anglican Orders. The daughter Churches of the Anglican communion have also been busy forwarding the cause of reunion. In Scotland the Primus, with the Archbishop of Canterbury, expounded the Appeal to the General Assemblies. In Canada negotiations were opened up with the United Church. In Australia conferences were held with Congregationalists, Methodists, and Presbyterians. In India there is a fair promise of satisfactory terms of union being arranged with the South India United Church. The American Church successfully carried through its gigantic plans for a World

Conference on Faith and Order. The Conference was held at Lausanne in 1927, and was attended by five hundred delegates representing eighty-seven communions, including the Eastern Orthodox. Reports were drawn up and transmitted to the Churches, and a Continuation Committee was formed whose duty it is to receive the replies of the various bodies concerned, and, if they are favourable, to arrange for a further conference.

CHAPTER XXII

MODERN MISSIONS

THERE is no more glorious chapter in the modern history of Christianity than that which tells the story of its work in the mission-field. The bulk of that work has been built up in the last century, which has been the great age of the missionary societies. Government interest in missions died down after the seventeenth century, the missionary no longer being regarded as a necessary agent in colonisation. On the contrary, the effort to introduce Christianity seemed more likely to bring, not peace, but a sword; and so we find the Honourable East India Company charging itself with the upkeep of heathen temples while it refused the first English missionary to India a passage in a British ship and would not allow him to land on British territory. The deistic flavour of religion during the eighteenth century made the Churches only too ready to acquiesce in this neglect of the heathen, and if it had not been for the Roman Catholic Church the work of evangelisation would have almost died out. In 1784 there were, apart from the Roman missions, not more than six missionary societies and two hundred missionaries in the world, and of the latter at least half were Moravians. By the end of the century, when the population of the world was about 960 millions, the number of the Christians was not greater than 174 millions, and the vast majority of them were, of course, in Europe.

It was the growth of pietism in Germany and the Evangelical Revival in England that began to beat back the forces of indifference. With the former are connected the Moravian missions. It is said that one out of sixty of the Moravians goes to the mission-field, and it is to them that is due the credit for the awakening of Christendom to this essential requirement of the faith, for during the twenty years from 1732 to 1752 they did actually found more missions than the rest of Protestant Christendom had done since the Reformation. Their influence upon England was direct and immediate. It was seen in the birth of many missionary societies of an evangelical character. The Baptists founded theirs in 1792 and the interdenominational London Missionary Society came into being three years later. In 1799 was founded the largest of all, the Church Missionary Society, and the Religious Tract Society came into existence in the same year. In 1804 the British and Foreign Bible Society began the great work, which now enables it to circulate the Scriptures in five hundred different languages. A host of other societies followed in the early years of the nineteenth century, and the zeal thus engendered stirred the Roman Catholics to still greater efforts, for France, now relieved of war, founded the Society of the Propagation of the Faith at Lyons in 1822.

It was well that these organisations were in the field thus early in the nineteenth century, for great as were their opportunities when the century opened, still vaster possibilities were to be presented when it had run half its course. The year 1858 marks an epoch in missionary work. In that year the interior of China was opened to Europeans by the Treaty of Tientsin, and Japan was thrown open by the Treaty of Yedo. In the same year the East India Company and its anti-missionary policy came to an end together, and toleration for the missionaries came in with the rule of the Crown. And in that year also Livingstone opened up Africa by his second great journey, and the Universities' Mission to Central Africa was founded. We must briefly sketch the history of missions in these and other areas.

1. INDIA

Modern missionary work in India may be said to begin with Christian Schwartz, who landed there in 1750 and laboured there till his death in 1798. He was a Lutheran, but was supported by the S.P.C.K. He had an amazing career, and won such general admiration that he was actually made Regent of Tanjore. The first Englishman, apart from Company chaplains, to engage in the work was William Carey, a cobbler, who was sent out by the Baptist Society in 1792. He established himself at Serampore in Danish territory and translated the New Testament into Bengali, thereby affecting all subsequent Bengali literature. A college, intended to train Indians for missionary work among their own people, was a less successful venture, but it set the right ideal for future work. Henry Martyn, a Cambridge senior-wrangler and an Anglican chaplain, landed at Calcutta in 1806, and translated the New Testament and Book of Common Prayer into Hindustani before moving on to Persia. The pathos of his apparent failure (he made only one convert) and of his early death at the age of thirty-one did more to bring other workers into the field than any spectacular triumph could have done. A new charter granted to the East India Company in 1813 ordered the appointment of a bishop for the oversight of work among Europeans. To Bishop Middleton, consecrated in accordance with this provision, is due the founding of Bishops' College, Calcutta, for the training of Indians as missionaries. To Calcutta in 1830 came Alexander Duff, the first missionary to be sent out by the Established Church of Scotland. He struck out a new line by starting the first of many schools for the education of the higher castes through the medium of the English language, and by so doing he had a profound influence on the educational policy of the Government. The loyalty of the Indian Christians was demonstrated in the Mutiny of 1857, and in the following year the Crown took over the administration from the Company with a greatly enhanced belief in the value of missionary work. This has resulted in a close collaboration between Government and the societies in the work of education. It was only the missionaries who could supply trained teachers even for elementary schools, and without the missionaries it would have been impossible to build up a system of higher education. Combined efforts have now resulted in the foundation of about forty colleges, of which half grant degrees, in addition to eleven Roman Catholic colleges and twenty-three seminaries. Even among the Indians educated in these colleges the work of conversion is slow. When it is accomplished a difficult question arises out of the caste system. Lutherans have agreed for the most part with Roman Catholics in the preservation of the system within Christianity, but Anglicans have led the way in the repudiation of caste, and consequently have lost many thousands of their converts to the Roman Catholics. But outside the system there are fifty million outcastes. Among them great mass movements towards Christianity began about 1870. This has been particularly noticeable in South India, where in the Diocese of Dornakal, Bishop Azariah, the first Indian Bishop of the Church of England, presides over 85,000 Christian outcastes. So great has been the change wrought in the condition of these people that the nationalist leader, Mahatma Gandhi, has struggled to induce the Hindus themselves to imitate the Christians in breaking through the system and coming to the relief of these unfortunates. In some respects the greatest obstacle to education throughout India is the position of the women, who in their seclusion have not yet learned to wish for enlightenment. The consequence is that there is much tuberculosis among the girls, and that in some parts the death-rate among infants of less than one year of age is 660 per thousand. Nevertheless the gradual industrialisation of the country, in spite of all its attendant evils, is opening doors more and more widely to the missionaries, and the societies are perfecting their machinery to meet the opportunity. The progress towards unity in South India has already been mentioned. It has a certain parallel in the formation of a National Christian Council for all India (1913), in which Indians take a leading share. The Anglican Church in India has been freed from its legal connexion with the Church of England, and so is now able to control its own customs and adapt itself to Indian habits, since the dioceses in India, Burma and Ceylon became a self-governing Province in 1930.

2. AFRICA

Modern missions in Africa date from the collection of liberated slaves on the west coast. By 1846 fifty thousand had been gathered in Sierra Leone. In 1852 an Anglican bishopric had been established, but the death-rate among the workers was appalling, and the low standard of morals attained by the converts was an added disappointment. Nevertheless the efforts made in that region were not without a certain success, for some freed slaves who had learned Christianity there took its teaching to the Yoruba country, and in response to their appeal the C.M.S. set up a thriving mission among the Yorubas and especially at Lagos, which has produced several African bishops. So successful has the work been that the Churches in Lagos and district are no longer connected with any society, but support their own missions. One of the African bishops was Samuel Crowther, who had been a slave and was then educated in the C.M.S. College at Fourah Bay. He was consecrated at Canterbury in 1864, and sent to organise a mission on the Niger, where, before the discovery of the cause of malarial fever, white men could not live. He was himself of too saintly a character to believe the reports, only too justifiable, that came to him of the immorality of some of his staff, and the consequence was that the work of future missionaries was made doubly difficult. However, the ideal of the Christian character was ultimately re-established, and it was possible in 1890 to extend the work to the fine tribe of the Hausas in Northern Nigeria. This was of peculiar importance both because the Hausa language will carry one through North Africa to the Sudan and also because the majority of the tribe are nominal Mohammedans. Any considerable conversion of the Hausas would serve as a check to the missions of Islam, which threaten to extend southwards to Central Africa. One of the most striking evidences of the advance of West Africans under European influence in recent years has been the growing need of educational work. In 1925 S. Augustine's Theological College was opened at Coomassie in the Anglican diocese of Accra, and Government itself has started a native university at Achimota in the same diocese, which it has placed under a well-known missionary, the Rev. A. G. Fraser.

In Central Africa Livingstone's call was answered by the establishment of the Universities' Mission in 1858. The work was begun on the Shiré River and extended eastwards to the shore of the continent and to the island of Zanzibar, dividing itself ultimately into four dioceses. In 1873 a cathedral was erected on the site of the old slave-market at Zanzibar. Projects have recently been set on foot to link this work with that which has been done by the C.M.S. on the east coast. Their mission was begun in response to a call from Stanley in 1875. He had formed a very high opinion of the character and promise of the Baganda, but the tribe proved treacherous to the Christians. In 1885 three Christian boys were executed, and the same year Bishop Hannington was murdered, and at least two hundred native Christians lost their lives in the persecution. The mission struggled on successfully against many adverse circumstances until Uganda was made a British protectorate in 1894, by which time it already had six of the Baganda ordained as deacons. Since then it has increased and consolidated itself into a self-governing Church with a rapidity and thoroughness to which there is no parallel in the history of the Church since the ninth century.

In South Africa the modern story begins with the arrival of the Moravian missionary, George Schmidt, at Cape Town in 1737. He was soon driven out by the jealousy of the Dutch ministers, who themselves did nothing for the natives, but attended solely upon their own people. The colony was annexed by England in 1806, but little of importance was done for missions until Robert Moffat, who had been an under-gardener in Scotland, was sent out by the London Missionary Society in 1816. In half a century of active work he established a strong mission among the Bechuanas and translated the whole Bible into Sechuana. His son-in-law, the ex-factory boy, David Livingstone, sent out by the same Society, spent eleven years as a missionary and twenty-one as an explorer. The change in his life was determined by the action of the Boers who attacked his mission and carried off two hundred of the children as slaves. Henceforth his unique strength was spent in the effort to find trade-routes and outlets to the sea which would make slavery unnecessary. To Bechuanaland belongs the story of the Christian chief Khama, who having won his kingdom by force of arms, banished heathen customs from it and governed efficiently in accordance with Christian principles. The first Anglican bishop was

Dr. Gray, who ruled at Cape Town from 1847 to 1872, and saw South Africa covered with a net-work of dioceses. He had, as we have seen, grave disciplinary difficulties with Dr. Colenso, the first Bishop of Natal, but in spite of that South Africa has become one of the finest fields of Anglican missionary enterprise. This is fortunate, since it is here that some of the most difficult questions arising out of the contact of white and coloured races call for solution. The Colour Bar Bill and the Segregation Bill are recent Government efforts to meet the occasion, but since the blacks vastly outnumber the whites these measures might lead to ugly situations were the temper of the natives once aroused. It is well in these circumstances that nine-tenths of native education is in the hands of the missionaries.

3. The Far East

It was the London Missionary Society that started modern work in China by sending Robert Morrison to Macao in 1807. Since it was a capital offence to be found teaching Chinese to a foreigner, Morrison was compelled to live in complete retirement while he learned the language, but that he did with such success that he was able to publish a Chinese dictionary, and also, before the end of his twenty-seven years' work, to translate nearly the whole of the Bible into Chinese. Many societies took advantage of his work, sending their agents to the ports and then farther inland as the country was opened up, the Americans being particularly prominent in this field. The first English Bishop was Dr. George Smith, who arrived in 1850 and carried on his work in the midst of the Taiping Rebellion. The American Church had had a bishop at work in Shanghai since 1844. There was considerable expansion until the Boxer Rising of 1900, in which several missionaries were killed, provided a momentary check, but after that progress was renewed until no fewer than eleven dioceses were in being. These were supplied from England, America, and Canada, but in 1912 they were united into an independent Holy Catholic Church of China, thus setting a valuable example of the results of co-operative work by various Churches of one communion. Another example of co-operation is furnished by the China Inland Mission (1865), though not on quite the same lines, since its missionaries belong to different denominations, the members of each denomination being grouped together. The most remarkable accession this mission received to its staff of workers was that of 'the Cambridge Seven', a body of graduates who included among their number the captain of the cricket eleven and the stroke of the University boat. Special attention has been paid in this field to medical work, about five hundred doctors being employed by the various agencies. Educational work, both elementary and advanced, has also been of first-rate importance. This has had a curious effect upon the rising nationalism of China. On the one hand, in the early part of the Taiping Rebellion a concerted attack was made against heathenism, and on the other the Boxer Rising was directed partly against the missions. In the recent revolutionary fighting one, at least, of the competing generals, Feng Yu Shiang, was a Christian. The Roman Catholic missions have had a chequered history. In 1815–16 they lost many martyrs, one of whom, Bishop Boric, was tied to a stake and slowly cut to pieces. In the middle of the nineteenth century they began to revive, and their bishops helped to bring on the Boxer Rising by claiming the rank and dignity of mandarins. Nevertheless the heroism of the priests has had its effect, and their converts number a million and a half.

Japan was thrown open in 1858, and the Roman Catholic missionaries discovered descendants of their old converts to the number at least of twenty thousand who still observed the Christian festivals in secret and practised the rite of baptism. America was the first country to take advantage of the new opportunity, two of the missionaries of the Episcopal Church actually arriving before the treaty came into force. Japanese Christians were still persecuted till 1873. The first English missionary to arrive was the Rev. George Ensor, of the C.M.S., who began his work by converting the man who had come to assassinate him. Great progress was made when Japan began to be interested in Western ideas. Indeed, there was at one time a danger that Japan would adopt a kind of syncretistic Christianity as a new national religion. In 1887 it was found possible, as later in China, to unite the Anglican missions from America and England into the Nippon Sei Kokwai, or Holy Catholic Church of Japan. By 1912 this independent Church was strong enough to provide its own theological college for training Japanese students for the ministry, and by 1923 it was ready to form two new self-supporting dioceses, under the superintendence of two Japanese bishops.

4. Islands of the Pacific

The special feature of missionary work in this region has been the effort to teach a low and degraded type of humanity to understand the arts of civilisation. This was apparent in the first mission to New Zealand, which was undertaken by the Rev. Samuel Marsden, the Anglican chaplain at Sydney, accompanied by a schoolmaster, a carpenter, and a shoemaker sent out by the C.M.S. The party arrived in 1814, having had to wait two years before they could get transport on account of the evil reputation of the Maoris for cannibalism. By 1835 the work was so flourishing as to win the unstinted admiration of Charles Darwin. A check occurred in 1860 when the second Maori War began. At that time the Hau Hau fanaticism, a religion compounded of some of the worst of the old tribal customs and certain perversions of Christianity with the outward sign of barking like a dog (Hau Hau), swept the country and impelled two-thirds of the Maori Christians to apostatise. The greatest name among the missionaries of the period and locality is that of George Augustus Selwyn, who had been consecrated first Bishop of New Zealand in 1841, and who, when he retired to England in 1867, had divided his one diocese into seven, and had built up an autonomous Church. In 1903 that Church completed the task of making itself independent of outside help for its own mission work, and in 1926 was able to constitute the Maoris as a distinct diocese under its own bishop.

In Polynesia the London Missionary Society tried the experiment of sending out artisans and mechanics to teach the natives trades, as it was felt that they could not become Christians until they had been to some extent civilised.

MODERN MISSIONS

It was found, in point of fact, that results are much better when the teaching of Christianity precedes the teaching of industrial methods. The effects subsequently achieved in the raising of the whole standard of life in these islands have been little short of miraculous. In Melanesia, Bishop Selwyn laid down a method which has ever since been followed. He collected a number of native boys and took them to New Zealand to be trained for evangelistic work among their own people. This method was taken up by John Coleridge Patteson, a Fellow of Merton College, Oxford, who was consecrated Bishop of Melanesia in 1861, and presently established the school at Norfolk Island. Patteson, who had a marvellous gift for picking up their many dialects, was beloved by the islanders, but in the end he suffered tragically for others' misdeeds. A 'labour ship' had visited one of the islands and forcibly carried off five of the inhabitants. The Bishop was the next white man to visit the place, and the islanders murdered him in revenge for the loss of their companions. Since this date, 1871, fourteen others in this mission have given their lives for the faith. Other societies have been well represented, one of the noblest missionary lives being that of the Rev. J. G. Paton, of the United Presbyterian Mission, who served long enough to see at least one island completely evangelised. The Rev. James Chalmers was a member of the London Missionary Society, who had already done ten years' work at Raratonga when he went to join the mission in New Guinea in 1877. For twenty-four years more he did invaluable work, showing an extraordinary power of dominating the fiercest tribes. At the end of that period he went with a colleague and twelve students to break new ground on the Aird River, when the whole party was set upon, slaughtered, and eaten by the inhabitants. The heroism of the native Christians has at least equalled that shown by the Europeans. During the first twenty years of the mission in New Guinea no fewer than 120 Polynesian teachers who had volunteered for the work either died of fever or were murdered. But that it has all been well worth while is known, not only on the evidence of Charles Darwin, but also on that of R. L. Stevenson and of many Government agents.

282 HISTORY OF THE MODERN CHURCH

5. THE MOHAMMEDAN WORLD

It is estimated that there are two hundred millions of Mohammedans in existence, of whom the bulk are in Asia, while forty-two millions are in Africa, and a small proportion is to be found in almost every country. For them practically nothing was done by the Christian Church between the time of Raymund Lull in the thirteenth century and that of Henry Martyn at the beginning of the nineteenth. The effort to repair the omission was dogged by the fatality of early deaths. We have already referred to the way in which Henry Martyn's efforts in Persia were cut short. In 1887 Ian Keith-Falconer, the Reader in Arabic at Cambridge, established a mission on behalf of the United Free Church of Scotland at Aden, but he died at the end of four months' toil. In 1891 another great scholar, Bishop French, left Lahore in order to initiate work among the Arabs at Muscat, but he also died after four months' residence. Nevertheless, in spite of these initial difficulties, the work has been continued in these places, and the sacrifices made have not been in vain. Perhaps the best strategic point for missions to Moslems is the great Mohammedan university of El Azhar in Cairo. Here work was begun on behalf of the C.M.S. by the Rev. Douglas Thornton, who died in 1907, and was continued by the Rev. W. H. T. Gairdner, who died in 1928. Here is seen a witness of the change that is coming over the spirit of Islam, for whereas a generation ago no Christian would have been allowed to enter the building it is now possible for Christian teachers to meet there the Moslem students from many lands, and the Gospels have actually been distributed there. This change is in keeping with the altered political situation of the Mohammedan world. Where Moslem rulers have not lost independent power, they have been subject to revolution. The Turkish Empire has abandoned its religious character, the Caliph has been deposed, and an intellectual 'modernism' pervades Islam wherever it has been in contact with Western thought. Thus a great opportunity has been opened to Christians to seize this Eastern Renaissance and turn it to good use. A conference of workers among

Moslems was held in 1924, and arrangements were made to take full advantage of the situation.

Such, then, in brief outline and with many gaps is the story of the work done by the Churches in modern days in the mission-field. For the most part it is the missionary societies that have borne the greater part of the burden. But it has become obvious that the societies are no longer capable of meeting the need. The Great War broke down the barriers between races, and modern invention has improved the means of transport and communication to such an extent that the world has become one in a closeness of unity that it has never experienced before. Different types of civilisation affect each other, not in trickling streams, but with the consolidated force of their whole impact. In such circumstances it has been necessary to make the whole Church rather than a mere society the unit of missionary agency. This has long been understood by the Moravian Church, of which it could be said that it is its own missionary society. In the Anglican Church that has proved difficult both because of the native strength of the societies and because of the different types of thought that they in some cases represent. Nevertheless steps have been taken in that direction, and unprecedented efforts have been made to arouse the whole Church to a proper sense of its missionary vocation. Representative committees first met to consider the needs of respective parts of the mission-field. Their reports were presented as the 'World Call' to the Church in 1925. Carefully graduated 'schools' were held in which the reports were studied by the dioceses and parishes, and the co-operation of university undergraduates was enlisted to make their contents known to the general public in a series of Missionary Campaigns. The result has been a great increase in contributions of money and in offers of service. The careful organisation of this World Call was possible because there had been formed a Missionary Council for the whole Church of England, which, while leaving the societies free to do their own work, definitely set itself the task of stirring up zeal and interest in circles that had not been reached by the societies, and of inducing the official organisations of the Church to make themselves responsible for the vital work that had hitherto been allowed to depend upon the enthusiasm of the few. Behind the whole scheme lay the unique knowledge and statesmanlike ability of the Chairman of the Council, Dr. Donaldson, sometime Archbishop of Brisbane and afterwards Bishop of Salisbury.

CHAPTER XXIII

CONCLUSION

IF the desire for reunion and zeal for missions are two of the marked tendencies of recent years, another may be taken to be the desire to free the Church from excessive interference on the part of the State. Sometimes the State itself takes the initiative and rids itself of a burdensome connexion. This occurred in Ireland, where the disestablishment of the Irish Church in 1869 put an end to the anomaly by which a minority Church alone received official recognition. It occurred also in Wales. An Act for the disestablishment of the Welsh Church was passed in 1912, but its operation was delayed by the outbreak of the Great War, and the Church was not actually disestablished until 1920. Since then it has been organised as a separate province under its own archbishop and governing body. The opportunity of refashioning its organisation has brought with it a considerable improvement in its financial position, in spite of some temporary hardship; and its increased efficiency may be judged both from the fact that it has provided itself with two new dioceses and that its number of communicants shows an annual increase.

In England the endeavour was made to secure some of the advantages of disestablishment without its corresponding disadvantages by framing a comprehensive scheme of legislative machinery, which should have the double effect of building up the internal government of the Church on a representative basis and of expediting the passage of ecclesiastical measures through Parliament. This began with the Church membership; constituted councils for the parish, the rural-deanery, and the diocese; set up a new National Assembly for the whole Church of England; and culminated in a committee of both Houses which relieved Parliament of the necessity for amending ecclesiastical legislation presented to it by the Assembly and left it only a power of veto. The Act bringing this machinery into existence was passed in 1919, since when it has facilitated the despatch of a vast amount of ecclesiastical business which in the old days would have been postponed indefinitely because of the congestion of the parliamentary agenda. At the same time it left all standing rights, including those of Convocation, intact, and the resulting duplication is cumbersome in the extreme. Also the Convocations have shown themselves on occasion exceedingly jealous, lest they should be in appearance or in fact swallowed by the Church Assembly. It was felt, moreover, that the kind of business with which Convocation was most competent to deal—namely, that relating to faith and worship—would be just that which would be most easily passed through Parliament by means of the new machinery. But in the one important instance in which this belief was put to the test the opposite result was seen. This was the case of the Revised Prayer Book.

As early as 1904 a Royal Commission had been appointed to inquire into alleged breaches of the law relating to the conduct of Divine Service, and had reported that letters of business ought to be issued to the Convocations with instructions to consider the preparation of a new rubric touching the ornaments of the minister and such modifications in the law relating to the conduct of Divine Service as would secure 'the greater elasticity which a reasonable recognition of the comprehensiveness of the Church of England and of its present needs seems to demand'. Letters of Business to this effect were issued in 1906, and in response to them the Convocations spent fourteen years in a careful revision of the Book of Common Prayer. By the time their proposals were ready the new legislative machinery had come into operation and it was necessary for the suggested changes to be approved by the National Assembly. The Revised Table of Lessons went through without difficulty, but the official proposals with regard to the rest of the book met with a much more anxious scrutiny. Six more years of discussion in the Assembly and the Convocations followed, and finally an alternative book to be used side by side

CONCLUSION

with the existing book was agreed upon by overwhelming majorities in both bodies in 1927. The measure to which the alternative book was annexed was then brought before Parliament. It was passed by the Lords, but thrown out by a majority of thirty-three in the Commons. Stunned by this result, but willing to believe that the rejection was due to some misapprehension, the Bishops decided to ask the Church to insert some explanatory modifications in the measure in order to make it more palatable to Parliament, and then to present it again. The Convocations and the Assembly once more revised their work and the measure was brought before the Commons in June 1928, only to be rejected by a majority of forty-six. This final rejection created a very difficult situation between the Church and the State. On the one hand the bishops could not wish to flout the authority of Parliament, but on the other they could not very easily condemn any congregation if it took advantage of forms that had been accepted by every legislative body of the Church. Consequently in September 1928 they issued a statement that in the exercise of their legal or administrative discretion they would be guided by the proposals approved in 1928 by the Houses of Convocation and the Church Assembly. When this resting-place had been reached the aged Randall Davidson laid down the office of Archbishop of Canterbury and was succeeded by Cosmo Gordon Lang, who, as Archbishop of York, had been his colleague throughout these trying negotiations.

Of the reason for Parliament's rejection of the proposed Prayer Book there can be no doubt. It was the fear lest by the use of the new liturgical forms there should occur some falling away from the principles of the Reformation and lest the Church should take on a more 'catholic' colour than had characterised it in the past. In this fear the House of Commons showed itself sensitive to a notable characteristic of recent ecclesiastical history. Whatever may be true of Parliament, it is certainly the fact that in religious circles, both in England and abroad, there has been a much more intelligent appreciation of the historic character of Christianity. The willingness of many Nonconformist divines to emphasise in reunion discussions the ideal of one visible Church with its historic episcopate is a sign of this. More definite signs are to be found in the Free Catholic movement associated with the name of Dr. Orchard, and in that Catholic school among the Presbyterians of Scotland which was led by the late Principal Cooper. Again, there is the High-Church Movement among the German Lutherans, of which the most notable leader is Dr. Heiler, a former priest of the Roman Church. Indeed, in Germany and Holland the drift of theological thought in a catholic direction is very marked. On the whole this has told to the advantage of Roman Catholicism. In some countries, indeed, as for instance in Mexico, where there has been a serious quarrel with the State, and in Czechoslovakia, where there has been a schism and the formation of a national Church, Roman Catholicism has experienced grave difficulties, but in most it has issued stronger and more numerous from the throes of the Great War. In England, however, the sympathy with the historic aspect of Christianity has been coupled with an almost universal acceptance of the critical method which is incompatible with the Roman interpretation of Catholicism. The method that was widely condemned as 'modernist' when it was applied in the volume of essays published in 1912 under the title of *Foundations*, reappeared in *Essays Catholic and Critical* in 1926, and was applied extensively in the Anglo-Catholic commentary on the Bible in 1928. If Catholicism has come into its own since the Oxford Movement it is a Catholicism that has a very different intellectual background from that of the Council of Trent.

The second quarter of the twentieth century saw rapid development of the world revolution, which had already got well under way during the preceding period. A second world war still further hastened the process. The balance of power was affected. Russia and the United States emerged as the two major rival forces with other nations ranging themselves on either side until there occurred a sharp division between east and west. This division deepened into acute opposition, and it has been with the greatest difficulty that the United Nations, an international organisation which succeeded the League of Nations,

CONCLUSION

prevented the antagonism from degenerating into open war.

Financially the two wars told very heavily upon the British Empire. It was no longer able to maintain the great navy which had for so long policed the seas and preserved the peace of the world. Constitutionally, too, great changes took place in its organisation. India, Pakistan and Ceylon shared with Canada, Australia, South Africa and New Zealand the honour of a dominion status which implied all but complete independence within one Commonwealth and Empire. Eire regarded herself as altogether outside the Empire and did not share in the second war. Britain herself, in spite of economic stringency, developed into a Welfare State in which the Government regarded itself as responsible for the total well-being of every citizen. This means that the State has taken over many of the functions formerly performed by charitable societies and particularly by the Church. The State with its larger financial resources can perform some at least of these functions more adequately than the independent societies were ever able to do. At the same time the State cannot supply many of the personal and spiritual influences without which the help given will be only partially effective. One of the greatest necessities of the day is a more careful delineation of the part to be played by voluntary societies both religious and secular within the Welfare State.

In the religious sphere the world situation has been most closely reflected in the Oecumenical Movement. This is the most significant factor in the ecclesiastical history of the twentieth century. It is an effort on the part of practically all Christian bodies except the Roman Catholics to overcome the disabilities caused by their divisions and to find some basis of co-operation and mutual aid. Its origins can be traced to a meeting called by Archbishop Temple at Bishopsthorpe in 1933 of ten officers of various religious bodies and to a gathering of twenty-five Church leaders at Westfield College, Hampstead, in 1937. These meetings changed the focus of interest from discussions *about* the Churches to discussions *of* the Churches. Almost inevitably they led to a resolution to create some sort of common organisation, which while encouraging the theological work undertaken by 'Faith and Order', could emphasise the importance of common tasks such as had hitherto been dealt with by 'Life and Work'. These suggestions were considered at a World Conference on Church, Community and State held at Oxford in 1937, at the second World Conference on Faith and Order held at Edinburgh in the same year, and at a World Meeting of the International Missionary Council held at Tambaram, in India, in 1938. These meetings paved the way for a great conference at Amsterdam in 1948, at which a World Council of Churches was formally constituted. No fewer than 160 Churches from nearly fifty nations are represented on this Council. It is in no sense a super-Church nor can it legislate for the constituent Churches. It provides a common meeting-ground for discussion, and an instrument for common action and for the expression of a common mind in face of world needs. In Britain its business is transacted through the British Council of Churches, inaugurated in 1942, on which eighteen different denominations are represented. The success achieved at Amsterdam was repeated at Evanston (Chicago) in 1954 when the second Conference of the World Council of Churches was held. Indeed the success was almost too great. There was an embarrassingly large attendance which made difficult the adequate transaction of business and raised extravagantly high hopes, particularly in U.S.A., of an immediate reunited World Church. The extravagance led to some inevitable reaction, but disappointment will no doubt give way in its turn to a realisation that the wounds of the Church cannot be lightly healed and to a determination nevertheless to press on with a necessary task. It was the latter mood that was reflected in the third Conference held in New Delhi (1961).

From this movement the Roman Catholic Church has stood aloof. The period, however, has not been without happenings of great moment for that body. In countries under Communist Governments it has suffered varying degrees of persecution and many of its hierarchy have lost life or liberty. In its homeland it has enjoyed some restoration of its temporal power. Ever since 1879, when the Papal States were incorporated into the Italian Kingdom, the Pope had refused to leave the Vatican or to accept any of the money offered by the State in compensation for his loss of territory. In 1929 an agreement was reached with Mussolini by which the full and independent sovereignty of the Holy See was recognised in the city of the Vatican, an area of 109 acres with a population of 940. At the same time a financial arrangement was made in compensation for the losses of the See through the earlier alienation of its territory, and a concordat was completed for the regulation of Church and religion in Italy. Not the least important element in the temporal power is that it enables the Papal court to receive ambassadors from other governments and to demand diplomatic privileges for its own emissaries to other countries. If the Papacy has thus consolidated its position in the material sphere it has done so also in the sphere of doctrine. At the climax of the jubilee year 1950 Pope Pius XII announced a new dogma, that of the bodily assumption of the Blessed Virgin Mary. This had long been a pious opinion among Roman Catholics, but it now became for the first time a necessary article of faith. In 1958 Pius was succeeded by John XXIII who signalised his accession by announcing that he would hold an Oecumenical Council in 1962. It was soon learnt that, whatever the wishes of the Pope himself might be, this council would not admit as members representatives of churches that did not acknowledge the papal obedience. Nevertheless the new pope showed his own oecumenical spirit by receiving in audience Geoffrey Fisher, Archbishop of Canterbury. It was the first time that an Anglican primate had paid such a visit to a reigning pope since the Reformation.

The Orthodox Churches have suffered a chequered career in the second quarter of the twentieth century. In Russia persecution died down during the second world war, when it was necessary to enlist the goodwill of every citizen. Many of the churches are now open for public worship and are said to be crowded. But if the right to worship has been conceded there appears to be no liberty of propaganda; and in the schools children are subjected to a steady atheistic pressure. In the satellite countries also the clergy are closely watched and many of them have suffered on charges of treasonable activities. The effect has been to weaken the authority, however tenuous, of the Oecumenical Patriarch in these countries and to promote division among the Orthodox Churches. Such differences are inevitably reflected among adherents who live in western countries. Nevertheless the dispersion of the orthodox has led to their doctrine and liturgy becoming more widely known than ever before. Their Churches not under Soviet influence have taken an active part in the Oecumenical Movement, where their witness to the special values of historic Christianity has been of first-rate importance. At the last Conference of the World Council of Churches (New Delhi 1961) even the Russians applied for admission to membership of the Council.

Christian missions have been diversely affected by the second world war. The splendid conduct of converted Papuans has drawn an almost embarrassing amount of attention to New Guinea, where the desire of Australians and Americans to repay a gladly acknowledged debt needs careful guidance. In Africa progress continues to be maintained, although in South Africa there were grave difficulties over the colour bar, culminating in the secession of that country from the Commonwealth. Indeed almost the whole of Africa was in a ferment during this period owing to the upsurge of nationalism and racialism. Among the Kikuyu many atrocities were committed by the Mau Mau, a body of religio-political terrorists. Belgian missions in the Congo and Portuguese in Angola suffered in the peoples' struggle for independent nationhood. Much the same kind of story is true of Asia. In Japan missionaries are apparently given a warm and sincere welcome. China, on the other hand, has expelled foreign missionaries and the native Church is doing its best to hold on without them in the face of an unsympathetic Government. Rising nationalism has also made the work difficult in Persia and Irak. But in India and Pakistan, now that the British Raj no longer prevails, missions are recognised for what they are and not as the instruments of a 'foreign imperialist power'. The main difficulty in most places is to compete with rising costs. Charities always suffer during inflationary periods; it takes a long time for the income of the societies to rise in proportion to the falling value of money. That involves inevitable economies in plant and man-power. But it throws greater responsibilities on the younger churches themselves. By such means the Kingdom of God is advanced.

One noteworthy incident in the mission field which caused considerable comment was the inauguration of the Church of South India (see p. 265). It was built out of a combination of Anglican with Methodist, Congregationalist and Presbyterian Missions. For the first time elements of Anglicanism formed a complete union with elements of non-episcopal Churches. The basis of the scheme was episcopal, but misgivings were caused in Anglican circles by the deliberate decision to welcome the ministrations of officers from the home bodies who had not sought episcopal ordination. In the end the Anglicans on the spot determined to cement the union without waiting for a formal decision from Lambeth. As the new Church would be leaving for a time at least the actual membership of the Anglican Communion such decisions seemed to them unnecessary. But they did obtain their freedom to effect the union from the General Council of the Church of India, Burma and Ceylon. Consequently the four Anglican dioceses of Madras, Travancore, Tinnevelly and Dornakal united in September 1947 with the Methodist and South India United Church to form the Church of South India. The step was certainly a courageous one, for not only must the relations of the new Church with the Church of England remain undecided for some years but, because of that very fact, monies which were held in trust for Churches within the Anglican Communion could no longer be sent out to the four ex-Anglican dioceses. In spite of these disadvantages a pressing need was felt to cement similar unions in other parts of India. Both North India and Ceylon devised schemes for the purpose, and found means by which it was hoped to avoid the difficulties raised for the Church of South India.

During the period now under review three Lambeth Conferences have been held. In 1930 the assembled bishops gave a good deal of attention to questions of marriage and sexual relations. They recommended careful education in these subjects, advised against the celebration of marriage according to the rites of the Church in the case of a divorced person whose former partner was still living, and, while emphasising the duties of parenthood and condemning the practice of conception control from motives of selfishness, luxury or mere convenience, allowed that other means than complete abstinence might be used under the guidance of Christian principles. The last point caused a division and was finally carried by 193 votes to 67. The Conference of 1948 consisted of 325 members, the largest number of Anglican bishops ever to assemble. The subject considered was the Christian doctrine of man. Inevitably it was discussed against the background formed by the recent war and by the rapidly developing movement towards Christian co-operation. The bishops, while reassuring that 'war as a method of settling international disputes is incompatible with the teaching and example of our Lord Jesus Christ' recognised that 'there are occasions when both nations and individuals are obliged to resort to war as the lesser of two evils'. They urged at the same time 'that the use of atomic energy be brought under such effective international inspection and control, as to prevent its use as a weapon of war'. They distinguished between Marxian and Christian Communism, condemning the former as contrary to Christian faith and practice. They urged the study of Communism, so that it might be possible to judge which elements in it are incompatible with the Christian view of man and which are a true judgement on the existing social and economic order. A large part of the report was devoted to the relations between the Anglican and other communions, and a motion emanating from China that women should be submitted to the priesthood was decisively rejected. The Conference of 1958 was equally useful if less spectacular. The way for it had been prepared by a Pan-Anglican Congress at Minneapolis, U.S.A., in 1954. This meant that by the time they met at Lambeth most of the bishops were already personal friends as well as official partners in a great enterprise. Their report contained nothing startling. They reaffirmed their position on moral problems by accepting the principle of 'family planning', as it was now called. They also carried on the work of the last conference in providing some kind of central organisation for the Anglican Communion. The Conference of 1948 had supported the opening of St. Augustine's Canterbury as a

CONCLUSION

central college for the clergy of the whole communion. The Conference of 1958 arranged for the appointment of an Executive Officer for the Anglican Communion. In the event an American bishop, Stephen Bayne, was appointed with an office at Lambeth.

In Britain the teaching of religion was greatly strengthened by the Education Acts of 1944 and 1945. Every child now receives instruction in doctrine and worship unless his parents deliberately withdraw him. At the same time the standard of school buildings was pitched so high that it was feared the Church of England might lose 99 per cent of its schools. Actually, although the more rural dioceses were so engrossed in the endeavour to raise the stipends of their clergy, restore their Church buildings and train both teachers and ordinands that they could not find the money needed to take full advantage of the Acts, the position of the schools in other dioceses has been vastly improved.

A welcome measure of domestic reform was carried through in 1948 when Queen Anne's Bounty and the Ecclesiastical Commissioners were united to form a single body under the title of the Church Commissioners. Both the earlier bodies were concerned with various aspects of the payment, housing and relief of the clergy. It is now a matter of considerable convenience to the beneficiaries to deal with one office instead of two, and the economies effected by the amalgamation add to the financial help they receive.

In the sphere of theology the centre of interest has shifted. The debate on eschatology still continues. Schweitzer's apocalyptic interpretation of Christ has been countered by Dodd's theory of a 'realised' eschatology, and a combination of the two views has appeared in Cullmann's *Christ and Time*. The main interest, however, has lain in Karl Barth's return to a Calvinistic dualism with its tremendous emphasis on the 'otherness' of God and the uniqueness of revelation. This 'theology of crisis' appeared specially suited to an age of cataclysm, and though to many it seemed exaggerated it has served a good purpose in stressing those things that are specifically Christian and in weaning us away from a tendency to reduce religion to the status of a philosophy. From this development has sprung a new concentration of thought upon the nature of the Church. There has been revealed an unexpectedly wide range of agreement among scholars of different confessions which has not been without effect on the course of the Oecumenical Movement. Parallel with this has come a fresh concern with the Christian interpretation of history. The devastating effect of two world wars has thrown into strong relief the incapacity of merely human thought to offer any satisfactory rationale of existence. Not only professional theologians but also men and women of letters such as, in this country, Charles Williams, T. S. Eliot, Dorothy Sayers, C. S. Lewis, Christopher Fry and many others found in the Christian revelation the only adequate clue to the riddle of the times.

There were indeed many defections from Christianity, especially among the satellite states of Russia where Governments strove to realise the ideas of Marxian Communism. In eastern lands there were still only small Christian minorities, 2 per cent in India, 1 per cent in China and half 1 per cent in Japan. Yet these minorities were signs of progress. 'For the first time in its history', says Latourette, 'Christianity was becoming really world wide and not a colonial or imperial extension, ecclesiastically speaking, of an Occidental faith.' He further notes that the general trend has been away from the idea of a Christendom as an area in which everybody was baptised as a matter of convention to that of a *corpus Christi* into which individuals were admitted of their own volition and in which they found themselves part of a self-conscious minority in an alien world. Nevertheless he sums up his monumental seven-volume *History of the Expansion of Christianity* by asserting that the faith of Christ is a stronger influence in the world to-day than it has ever been.

The ecclesiastical history of the period from the Reformation to the present day includes the story of many movements from all of which the Church has had something to learn. If the Christian thought of to-day has found it necessary also to go back behind the sixteenth century and to include within its scope the whole course of development, it is able to offer a better hope of a complete synthesis than has ever been possible since the earthly life of its Divine Founder. Attempts have been made to remedy the disunion that was so marked a feature of the modern age. The claims of reason that came so prominently to the front in the Enlightenment have been compared and balanced with the old authoritarianism of Bible and Church. The missionary enthusiasm of the evangelical revival has stirred a wider circle in our own day. The claims of history, although not universally accepted, have never been more clearly understood than in recent years. Of all this wealth of Christian experience the English Church is in a peculiar sense the guardian: it touches life at so many points, and has none of the marks of a sect. It is in the great tradition, and yet is open to every breath of new thought. Whether it can continue to hold together within its own polity and worship those two characteristics of Catholicism and Evangelicalism which were impressed upon it in the sixteenth century has been questioned by some who have watched most anxiously its recent history. If it cannot do so, Christendom will be left in the position of the Reformation period, but if it can do so it will bridge the gulf between many, if not all, of those Churches which belong predominantly to one or the other of those traditions. For that high end its position in the British Empire, as the mother of great independent daughter Churches, comprising many races in many lands, especially fits it. As the Empire is gradually transformed into a vast commonwealth of free and independent peoples, so the Church may lead the way to a corporate union of free and autonomous societies in one Catholic and Apostolic Church.

SELECT BOOK LIST

GENERAL

Cambridge Modern History.
Catholic Encyclopedia.
Encyclopedia Britannica.
Encyclopedia of Religion and Ethics.
The Faiths, Varieties of Christian Expression, ed. Jacks, L. P. 1926 ff.
The Church Universal. 8 vols. ed. Hutton, W. H. 1906 ff.
History of the Christian Church. Walker, Williston. 1959.
Religion Since the Reformation. Pullan, L. 1923.
Outlines of Church History. Sohm, R. 1904.
Lectures on Modern History. Acton, Lord. 1906.
Outline of Church History. Schubert, H. von. 1907.
History of the Expansion of Christianity. 7 vols. Latourette, K. S. 1945.

REFORMATION

BEARD, C. *The Reformation* (Hibbert Lectures, 1883), new ed. 1927.
DAWLEY, P. M. *John Whitgift and the Reformation.* 1955.
GAIRDNER, J. *Lollardy and the Reformation in England.* 4 vols. 1908–13.
HUNT, E. W. *Dean Colet and His Theology.* 1956.
JACKSON, S. M. (editor) *Heroes of the Reformation.* 1898 ff.
KIDD, B. J. *Documents Illustrative of the Continental Reformation.* 1911.
LINDSAY. T. M. *History of the Reformation.* 2 vols. 1906–7.
MACKINNON, J. *Luther and the Reformation.* 4 vols. 1925–30.
MARITAIN, J. *Three Reformers: Luther—Descartes—Rousseau.* 1928.
POLLARD, A. F. *Henry VIII.* New edition. 1951.

SELECT BOOK LIST

REYNOLDS, E. E. *St. Thomas More.* 1953.
RIDLEY, J. G. *Nicholas Ridley.* 1957.
SMITH, P. *The Age of the Reformation.* 1920.
TILLICH, PAUL. *The Protestant Era.* 1951.
WILLIAMS, CHARLES. *James I.* 1934.

ENGLAND

ABBEY and OVERTON. *The English Church in the Eighteenth Century.* 2 vols. 1887.
ADY, C. M. *The English Church.* 1940.
ANSON, P. F. *The Call of the Cloister.* 1956.
BALLEINE, G. B. *History of The Evangelical Party.* 1951.
BRILIOTH, Y. *The Anglican Revival.* 1925.
BROOK, V. J. K. *Whitgift and the English Church.* 1957.
BROOK, V. J. K. *Archbishop Parker.* 1962.
BROWN, C. K. F. *History of the English Clergy.* 1800–1900. 1953.
CHURCH, R. *The Oxford Movement.* 1891.
CLARK, H. W. *History of English Non-Conformity.* 2 vols. 1911–12.
COCKSHUT, A. O. J. *Anglican Attitudes.* 1959.
DARK, S. (editor), *Great English Churchmen Series.* 1937 ff.
DIXON. *History of the Church of England from the Abolition of the Roman Jurisdiction.* 5 vols. 1878–92.
ELLIOTT-BINNS, L. E. *The Early Evangelicals.* 1953.
EMMOT, E. B. *The Story of Quakerism.* 1929.
GEE and HARDY. *Documents Illustrative of English Church History.* 1896.
GWATKIN, H. M. *Church and State in England to the Death of Queen Anne.* 1917.
HODGKIN, T. *George Fox.* 1896.
LLOYD, ROGER. *Church of England in Twentieth Century.* 2 vols. 1950.
LUNN, A. *John Wesley.* 1920.
MALDEN, R. H. *The English Church and Nation.* 1952.
MOORMAN, J. R. H. *History of the Church in England.* 1943.
NEALE, J. E. *Elizabeth I and her Parliaments.* 1953.
NEILL, S. *Anglicanism.* (Pelican) 1958.
NEWMAN, J. H. *Apologia pro Vita Sua.* 1864.
OLLARD and CROSSE. *Dictionary of English Church History.* 1912.

PECK. A. L. *Anglicanism and Episcopacy.* 1958.
PROCTOR and FRERE. *A New History of the Book of Common Prayer.* 1900.
RAMSEY, A. M. *From Gore to Temple.* 1960.
SPINKS, G. S. *Religion in Britain since 1900.* 1952.
STEPHENS, W. R. W., and HUNT, W. (editors). *History of the English Church.* 9 vols. 1899-1910.
SYKES, N. *The English Religious Tradition.* 1953.
SYKES, N. *From Sheldon to Secker.* 1959.
SYKES, N. *Old Priest and New Presbyter.* 1956.
TOWNSEND, WORKMAN, EYRES. *A New History of Methodism.* 2 vols. 1909.
WAKEMAN, H. O. *History of the Church of England.* 1896.
WAND, J. W. C. *High Church Schism.* 1951.
WAND, J. W. C. *The Second Reform.* 1953.
WAND, J. W. C. *Anglicanism in History and Today.* 1961.
WEBB, C. C. J. *Religious Thought in the Oxford Movement.* 1928.

SCOTLAND AND AMERICA

BACON, L. W. *History of American Christianity.* 1899.
BRYCE, J. *American Commonwealth.* 1888 (chs. 102, 3, 4).
BUCHAN and SMITH. *The Kirk in Scotland 1560-1929.* 1930.
BURLEIGH, J. H. S. *Church History of Scotland.* 1960.
CAMPBELL, A. J. *Two Centuries of the Church of Scotland 1707-1927.* 1930.
COLEMAN, L. *History of the American Church.* 1906.
DAWLEY, P. M. *Episcopal Church and its Work.* 1955.
FOSTER, W. R. *Bishop and Presbytery.* 1958.
GEWEHR, W. M. *The Great Awakening in Virginia.* 1930.
GOLDI, F. *Short History of Episcopal Church in Scotland.* 1951.
HIGHET, J. *The Scottish Churches.* 1960.
MCCONNELL, S. D. *History of the American Episcopal Church.* 1890.
MACLEAN, D. *Aspects of Scottish Church History.* 1927.
MITCHELL, A. *Short History of the Church in Scotland.* 1907.
MUIR, E. *John Knox.* 1929.
REID, J. M. *Kirk and Nation.* 1960.
RITCHIE, J. *Reflections on Scottish Church History.* 1927.
SNOW, W. G. S. *Time, Life and Thought of Patrick Forbes.* 1952.
SPERRY, W. L. *Religion in America.* 1945.

SELECT BOOK LIST

STEPHENS, W. *History of the Scottish Church.* 2 vols. 1893-6.

EUROPE

BAIRD, H. M. *The Rise of the Huguenots.* 2 vols. 1880.
BARRETT, E. B. *The Jesuit Enigma.* 1928.
BREMOND, H. *Literary History of Religious Thought in France from the Wars of Religion.* 1928. (Vols. I and II.)
BURY, J. B. *The Papacy 1864-1878.* 1930.
BUTLER, C. *The Vatican Council.* 2 vols. 1930.
CHADWICK, O. *The Reformation.* (Pelican) 1960 ff.
CLARK, G. N. *The Seventeenth Century.* 1929.
CRAGG, G. R. *The Church and the Age of Reason.* (Pelican) 1960 ff.
CUTHBERT, FR. *The Capuchins.* 2 vols. 1928.
HAGENBACH, K. R. *History of the Reformation in Germany and Switzerland.* 2 vols. 1878.
HAGENBACH, K. R. *German Rationalism.* 1864.
JERVIS, W. H. *History of the Church of France from 1516.* 3 vols. 1872-82.
MOLLARD, E. *Christendom.* 1959.
MOORE, E. C. *Outline of History of Religious Thought Since Kant.* 1912.
NIELSEN, F. H. *History of the Papacy in the Nineteenth Century.* 2 vols. 1906.
OGG, D. *Europe in the Seventeenth Century.* 1925.
RANKE, L. VON. *History of the Popes* (convenient edition 1907).
RAWLINSON, G. C. *Recent French Tendencies.* 1917.
SANDERS, E. K. S. *François de Sales.* 1928.
SIMPSON, W. J. S. *French Catholics in the Nineteenth Century.* 1918.
SOLTAU, R. H. *Pascal, the Man and His Message.* 1927.
VIDLER, A. R. *The Church and the Age of Revolution.* (Pelican) 1960 ff.
WAKEMAN, H. O. *The Ascendancy of France.* 1923.
WHALE, J. S. *The Protestant Tradition.* 1955.

EASTERN CHURCHES

ADENEY, W. F. *The Greek and Eastern Churches.* 1908.
BIRKBECK, W. J. *Russia and the English Church.* 1895.

HISTORY OF THE MODERN CHURCH

FEDOTOFF, G. P. *The Russian Church Since the Revolution.* 1928.
FORTESCUE, A. *The Orthodox Russian Church.* 1916.
FRERE, W. H. *Links in the Chain of Russian History.* 1918.
HEADLAM, A. C. *The Teaching of the Russian Church.* 1897.
KIDD, B. J. *The Churches of Eastern Christendom.* 1927.
NEALE, J. M. *A History of the Holy Eastern Church.* 1850.
ZERNOV, N. *Eastern Christendom.* 1961.

VARIOUS

BELL, G. K. A. *Documents on Christian Unity.* Three Series 1924–48.
BOUNIOL, J. *The White Fathers and Their Missions.* 1929.
GARBETT, CYRIL. *Claims of the Church of England.* 1947.
GARBETT, CYRIL. *Church and State in England.* 1950.
GEORGE, E. A. *Seventeenth Century Men of Latitude.* 1908.
GILES, R. A. *Constitutional History of the Australian Church.* 1929.
GOODALL, N. *The Ecumenical Movement.* 1961.
INGE, W. R. *Studies in English Mystics.* 1907.
JENKS, D. *A Study of World Evangelisation.* 1926.
MAYHEW, A. *Christianity and the Government of India.* 1929.
NEILL, S. *Twentieth Century Christianity.* 1961.
POLLARD, A. F. *Wolsey.* 1953.
ROBINSON, C. H. *History of Christian Missions.* 1915.
ROUSE and NEILL. *History of the Ecumenical Movement.* 1954.
ROWLEY, O. R. *The Anglican Episcopate of Canada and Newfoundland.* 1928.
SIMPSON, P. C. *The Church and the State.* 1929.
SLOSSER, G. J. *Christian Unity.* 1929.
SMYTH, N. *A Story of Church Unity.* 1923.
UNDERHILL, E. *Mysticism,* 1911.
WAND, J. W. C. *The Anglican Communion.* 1948.
WARNECK, G. *Outline of a History of Protestant Missions.* 1906.

RECENT BIOGRAPHY

BELL, G, K, A, *Randall Davidson.* (2 vols.). 1935.
BENNET, G. V. *White Kennett,* 1957.
CALDER, I. M. *Activities of Puritan Faction.* 1957.

SELECT BOOK LIST

CARPENTER, E. *Protestant Bishop.* (Henry Compton.) 1956.
CARPENTER, J. *Gore.* 1960.
DAVIES, G. C. B. *Henry Philpotts.* 1954.
DAVIES, G. C. B. *Early Cornish Evangelicals.* 1951.
EVERY, G. *High Church Party.* 1956.
GILL, J. C. *Ten Hours Parson.* (G. S. Bull.) 1959.
TINDAL HART, A. *William Lloyd.* 1952.
HENNELL and POLLARD. *Charles Simeon.* 1959.
HUGHES, H. T. *Piety of Jeremy Taylor.* 1960.
KEMP, E. W. *K. E. Kirk.* 1959.
KIRK-SMITH, H. *William Thomson.* 1958.
MAYCOCK, A. L. *Chronicles of Little Gidding.* 1954.
PRICE, H. A. L. *Thomas Ken.* 1958.
RIDLEY, J. *Thomas Cranmer.* 1962.
SMYTH, C. *C. F. Garbett.* 1959.
STRANKS, C. J. *Life and Writings of Jeremy Taylor.* 1952.
TREVOR, MERIOL. *Newman.* (Vol. I.) 1962.
WEBSTER, A. B. *Joshua Watson.* 1954.
WELSBY, P. A. *Lancelot Andrewes.* 1958.
THOMPSON, H. P. *Thomas Bray.* 1954.

PRINCIPAL EVENTS, 1509–1929

England	Germany	France and Italy	The Rest
1509 Accession of Henry VIII			
	1517 The 95 Theses 1521 Edict of Worms	1515 Francis I	1517 Death of Ximenes 1521 Conversion of Ignatius Loyola
		1523 Oratory of Divine Love	
	1524 Peasants' Revolt 1525 Battle of Pavia		1526 Battle of Mohacs Pizarro conquers Peru 1527 Westeras Recess
		1527 Sack of Rome 1529 Treaty of Cambrai	1529 Lutheranism in Sweden
1529 Divorce Trial begins 1530 Death of Wolsey 1531 Premunire revived 1533 Cranmer Archbishop 1534 Authority of Pope ended	1529 Marburg Conference 1530 Diet of Augsburg		1531 Zwingli slain
	1534 Anabaptist excesses	1534 Jesuits founded	
1535 Act of Supremacy 1536 Pilgrimage of Grace 1539 Six Articles 1540 Fall of Cromwell			1536 Calvin's *Institutes*
	1541 Diet of Ratisbon		1541 Calvin dictator at Geneva
	1545 Council of Trent 1546 Death of Luther	1542 Inquisition in Rome 1545 Francis exterminates Vaudois	

1549 First Prayer Book	1547 Battle of Mühlberg	1547 Death of Francis	1547 Ivan takes title of Tsar
1552 Execution of Somerset	1552 Treaty of Passau		1552 Death of Xavier
Second Prayer Book			1553 Burning of Servetus
1553 Accession of Mary			1557 Lords of Congregation in Scotland
1555 Martyrdom of Latimer, etc.			
1558 Accession of Elizabeth		1559 *Confessio Gallicana*	1560 *First Book of Discipline*
1559 Third Prayer Book		1560 Amboise	
		1562 French wars of religion begin	
1563 Heidelberg Catechism		1563 Trent ends	1564 Death of Calvin
1568 Catholic reaction			1572 Socinus in Poland
1577 Formula of Concord		1572 S. Bartholomew	1584 Death of Ivan the Terrible
		1584 Death of Borromeo	1589 Moscow Patriarchate
1564 Vestiarian Controversy			
1570 Elizabeth excommunicated by Pius V			
1587 Mary executed		1593 Henry IV adopts Catholic religion	
1588 Armada		1598 Edict of Nantes	
1592 Presbyterianism established in Scotland			
1604 Hampton Court Conference			
1605 Gunpowder Plot			
1607 Occupation of Donauwörth			

PRINCIPAL EVENTS, 1500–1929—continued

Great Britain	Germany	France and Italy	The Rest
1618 Five Articles of Perth	1618 Thirty Years War	1610 Henry IV murdered. Jesuits in Paraguay	1611 Gustavus Adolphus
1628 Petition of Right		1622 Congregation *de Propaganda Fide*	1613 Michael Romanov
	1630 Arrival of Gustavus Adolphus	1629 Peace of Alais	1618 Synod of Dort
		1635 Jansen's *Augustinus*	1620 Puritans land in America
1639 Scots abolish episcopacy			
1643 Solemn League and Covenant			1645 Death of Grotius
1645 Directory replaces Prayer Book	1648 Treaty of Westphalia		
1649 Charles I executed		1656 Pascal's Provincial Letters	
1661 Savoy Conference			1672 Synod of Jerusalem
1672 Declaration of Indulgence			
1673 Test Act	1675 Spener's *Pia Desideria*	1682 Gallican Articles	
1685 Accession of James II		1685 Revocation of Edict of Nantes	
		1687 Innocent XI condemns Molinos	

1688 Trial of Bishops William and Mary		
1689 Toleration Act		1689 Peter the Great
1690 Non-Jurors		
1701 S.P.G.		1700 Moscow Patriarchate suppressed
1710 Trial of Sacheverell	1703 Revolt of Camisards	
	1710 Destruction of Port Royal	
1714 Schism Act	1713 Bull *Unigenitus* against Quesnel	
1717 Convocation closed		
1729 Methodist Society at Oxford	1727 Moravians	
	1751 First volume of Encyclopedia	
	1756 Frederick the Great begins Seven Years War	
	1759 Jesuits expelled from Portugal and	
	1767 from Spain and France	
		1775 American Independence
	1776 Joseph II establishes religious liberty	
1780 Gordon No-Popery Riots	1789 Fall of Bastille	
1799 C.M.S.		
	1806 Francis II gives up title of Holy Roman Emperor	
1807 Slave-trade abolished	1809 States of Church added to French Empire	
	1815 Congress of Vienna	1814 Ferdinand VII restores Spanish Inquisition
		1817 Educational reforms by Alexander of Russia

PRINCIPAL EVENTS, 1509–1929—continued

Great Britain	Germany	France and Italy	The Rest
			1821 Murder of Patriarch of Constantinople
1828 Repeal of Test Act 1833 Oxford Movement Slavery abolished			
	1841 Jerusalem bishopric		
1843 Free Church of Scotland 1845 Newman becomes Roman Catholic 1850 Gorham Judgment 1852 Canterbury Convocation		1852 Treaty between France and Turkey about holy places	
1860 'Essays and Reviews'			1858 Alexander II liberates serfs 1861 Formation of Rumania Civil War in America
1867 First Lambeth Conference 1869 Irish Church disestablished	1870 Old Catholics	1870 Vatican Council declares Infallibility Papal states annexed to Kingdom of Italy	

1871 Religious tests abolished at Oxford and Cambridge	1872 Act against Jesuits		
1874 Public Worship Regulation Act	1893 Anti-Jesuit Act repealed	1880 Expulsion of religious Orders from France	1894 Armenian massacres
		1907 Encyclical against Modernism	
1908 Pan-Anglican Congress	1914 Great War		1917 Abdication of Tsar of Russia
1919 National Assembly created			
1920 Welsh Church disestablished	1922 Evangelical Church Federation		
1928 Prayer Book controversy		1929 Concordat between Papacy and Italy	
1929 Presbyterian Reunion in Scotland			
1930 Lambeth Conference	1933 Hitler Chancellor		
1936 Edward VIII abdicated	1939 Second World War		1941 U.S.A. joins war
1944 Education Act			1947 Church Union in S. India
1948 Lambeth Conference			1948 World Council of Churches
		1950 Dogma of Bodily Assumption of B.V.M.	

LIST OF POPES AND ARCHBISHOPS OF CANTERBURY

Popes		*Archbishops*	
1492.	Alexander VI.	1486.	Morton.
1503.	Pius III.	1502.	Dean.
1503.	Julius II.	1503.	Warham.
1513.	Leo X.		
1522.	Adrian VI.		
1523.	Clement VII.		
1534.	Paul III.	1533.	Cranmer.
1550.	Julius III.		
1555.	Marcellus II.	1555.	Pole.
1555.	Paul IV.		
1559.	Pius IV.	1559.	Parker.
1566.	Pius V.		
1572.	Gregory XIII.	1576.	Grindal.
1585.	Sixtus V.	1583.	Whitgift.
1590.	Urban VII.		
1590.	Gregory XIV.		
1591.	Innocent IX.		
1592.	Clement VIII.		
1605.	Leo XI.	1604.	Bancroft.
1605.	Paul V.	1610.	Abbot.
1621.	Gregory XV.		
1623.	Urban VIII.		
1644.	Innocent X.	1633.	Laud (executed 1645)
1655.	Alexander VII.		
1667.	Clement IX.	1660.	Juxon.
1670.	Clement X.	1663.	Sheldon.
1676.	Innocent XI.	1677.	Sancroft.
1689.	Alexander VIII.		
1691.	Innocent XII.	1691.	Tillotson.
		1694.	Tenison.
1700.	Clement XI.		
1720.	Innocent XIII.	1715.	Wake.

LIST OF POPES AND ARCHBISHOPS

Popes		*Archbishops*	
1724.	Benedict XIII.		
1730.	Clement XII.	1736.	Potter.
1740.	Benedict XIV.	1747.	Herring.
1758.	Clement XIII.	1757.	Hutton.
1769.	Clement XIV.	1758.	Secker.
1775.	Pius VI.	1768.	Cornwallis.
1800.	Pius VII.	1783.	Moore.
		1805.	Sutton.
1823.	Leo XII.		
1829.	Pius VIII.	1828.	Howley.
1831.	Gregory XVI.		
1846.	Pius IX.	1848.	Sumner.
		1863.	Longley.
1878.	Leo. XIII.	1868.	Tait.
		1883.	Benson.
		1896.	Temple.
1903.	Pius X.	1903.	Davidson.
1914.	Benedict XV.		
1922.	Pius XI.	1928.	Lang.
1939.	Pius XII.	1942.	Temple (Wm.).
1958.	John XXIII.	1945.	Fisher.
1963.	Paul VI	1961.	Ramsey.

INDEX

Abbot, Archbishop, 124 f.
Abdul Hamid II, 243
Abjuration, Act of, 168
Adderley, Father, 220
Additional Curates Society, 206
Address to the Christian Nobility, 17
Adiaphoristic Controversy, 39
Admonitions, 83, 86
Adrian VI, 23, 28
Adventists, 254
Advertisements, 83
Aequiprobabilism, 196
Age of Faith, 2, 10
Aids to Reflection, 207
Alais, Peace of, 109
Albert of Brandenburg, 15, 98
Alciphron, 176
Alexander IV (Pope), 13
Alexander VI (Pope), 3, 8, 14
Alexander I (Russia), 233 f.
Alexander II (Russia), 235
Alexander III (Russia), 236
Alexis, 134 f.
Allegiance, Oath of (England), 122, 125, 165
Allegiance, Oath of (French Republic), 200
Allen, Dr., 84
Alva, Duke of, 71, 95 f.
Amboise, Peace of, 77
Anabaptists (cf. Baptists), 22, 30, 34, 58, 94 f.
Analogy of Religion, 176, 186
Ancient Mariner, 207
Andrewes, Lancelot, 124, 257
Angélique, Mère, 114
Anglican and Eastern Churches Association, 262
Annates Act, 44, 80, 169

Anne Boleyn, 42 f., 82
Anne of Clèves, 49
Anne, Queen, 167 f., 186, 247
Apologia pro Ecclesia Anglicana, 88
Apostolic Succession, 212 f.
Apostolicæ Curæ, 259
Aquinas, 171, 202
Armada, Spanish, 85, 162
Arminianism, 95 f., 125, 190 f.
Arnauld, 114 f.
Arndt, 182
Arnold, Matthew, 210
Arnold, Thomas, 208 f., 269
Arsenius, Archbishop, 260
Articles, Forty-two, 57
Articles, Thirty-nine, 80 f., 121, 126, 215 f., 228, 257
Articles, Lambeth, 86
Ascent of Mount Carmel, 75
Aske, Robert, 47
Askew, Anne, 50
Association of Friends of the Church, 213
Astruc, 222
Atomic Energy, 294
Augsburg, Confession of, 33, 57, 93 f., 185, 216
Augsburg, Diet at, 31
Augsburg, Interim of, 39, 70
Augsburg, Peace of, 39, 105 f.
Augustine, S., 6, 13 f., 82, 114 f., 158
Azariah, Bishop, 275

Babington, 85
Babylonish Captivity, 17
Bacon, Lord, 171 f.
Bagot, Bishop, 215
Bakunin, 235

814 HISTORY OF THE MODERN CHURCH

Bancroft, Archbishop, 123 f.
Bangorian Controversy, 173
Baptists (cf. Anabaptists), 269, 273
Barcelona, Peace of, 26
Barlow, Bishop, 82
Barnabites, 64
Barth, Karl, 295
Bartholomew's Day Massacre (1572), 77, 85
Barton, Elizabeth, 46
Basle, Council of, 68
Baur, F. C., 221
Baxter, 182
Bayly, 182
Baynes, A. H., 224
Beaton, Cardinal, 100 f.
Beecher, Lyman, 250
Beissel, Conrad, 185
Belgic Confession, 95
Bell, Dr., 227
Bellarmin, Cardinal, 125
Benedict XIV, 140, 194 f.
Benson, Archbishop, 218
Benson, R. M., 220
Berkeley, George, 175 f.
Beza, 76, 84, 136
Bible, translations of, 21, 35, 49 f., 121 f., 138, 224, 235, 273, 277
Biondo, Flavio, 1
Bismarck, 203
Black Acts of Edinburgh, 103
Black Letter Days, 82
Black rubric, 57, 81, 101, 131
Bockholt, John, 34
Boehme, Jacob, 177
Bohemian Brethren, 98 f.
Bohler, Peter, 188
Bologna, Concordat of, 9, 35
Bolshevists, 156, 237 f.
Bonner, Bishop, 58 f.
Book of Common Order, 102 f.
Book of Common Prayer, 50, 54 f., 81 f., 121, 127 f., 165 f., 205, 209 f., 247, 267, 274, 286 f.
Book of Sports, 123, 127
Books of Discipline, 76, 84, 102 f.
Booth, Bishop Charles, 166
Borromean League, 74

Borromeo, Charles, 73
Bossuet, 122, 118 f., 132
Brahe, Tycho, 172
Bramante, 2
Bray, Dr., 143, 168
Breda, Declaration of, 130, 133
Bressani, 138
Brethren of the Common Life, 3
Briçonnet, Bishop, 35
Briggs, C. A., 255
British and Foreign Bible Society, 273
British and Foreign School Society, 227
British Empire, 289
British Magazine, 206
Britto, John de, 140
Browne, Sir Thomas, 176
Bucer, Martin, 33 f., 55 f., 136
Buchanan, 103
Buckingham, Duke of, 109
Bugenhagen, 94
Bull, Bishop, 132
Bunyan, John, 130, 182
Burnet, Bishop, 165
Butler, Bishop, 176, 186, 189
Bye Plot, 121

Cæsar Borgia, 3, 8
Cajetan, Cardinal, 16
Calvin and Calvinism, 35 f., 49, 55, 75 f., 83 f., 92 f., 115, 136 f., 147, 159 f., 165, 170, 180 f., 205, 211 f., 248, 267
Cambrai, League of, 9
Cambrai, Peace of, 26
Cambridge Platonists, 176 f.
Camden Society, 217, 229
Camisards, 114
Campeggio, Cardinal, 23, 42
Campion, 84 f.
Canon law, 82
Cappel, Wars of, 30, 33
Capuchins, 64, 74, 140, 146
Caraffa, 63 f., 71
Carey, Wm., 274
Carlowitz, Treaty of, 147
Carlstadt, 17, 22, 24, 30
Carlyle, 13
Carmelites, 74 f., 197 f.
Carranza, Archbishop, 67

INDEX

Cartwright, Thomas, 83, 86 f.
Casaubon, 267
Case of Reason, 177
Catechism of John Hamilton, 110
Catherine II, 232
Catherine de Medici, 76
Catholic Emancipation Act, 193
Catholic Institute of Paris, 225
Cavalier, 114
Centum Gravamina, 23
Challoner, Richard, 192 f.
Chalmers, James, 281
Chalmers, Thomas, 264
Champlain, 138
Chancellor, Richard, 151
Chantal, Mme. de, 110
Chantries Act, 56
Charlemagne, 6
Charles I (England), 125 f., 147, 260
Charles II (England), 130 f., 162, 257, 268
Charles III, 194 f.
Charles V, 6, 19 f., 25 f., 31 f., 42, 61, 70 f., 94
Charles IX, 76 f.
Chateaubriand, 201
Chayla, 114
Chichele, 45
Chillingworth, 127
China Inland Mission, 279
Christ and Time, 294
Christian II, 91 f.
Christian III, 94
Christian IV, 107
Christian Civic League, 30
Christian Perfection, 177
"Christian Union," 30
Christian Year, 207 f.
Christianity as Old as Creation, 177
Christianity not Mysterious, 176
Church Association, 218
Church Building Society, 206
Church Commissioners, 295
"Church Congress," 266
Church Missionary Society, 273 f
Church, R. W., 217
Church of South India, 293
Civil Constitution of the Clergy, 198 f.

Clarendon Code, 133
Clarke, Samuel, 174
Clarorum Virorum Epistolæ, 3
Clement VII, 23, 26, 42, 93
Clement VIII, 88
Clement XI, 115
Clement XIV, 161, 195
Cobham, Lord, 121
Coblentz, Articles of, 161
Codex Alexandrinus, 147
Cognac, League of, 25
Coke, Dr., 190
Colbert, 143
Colenso, Bishop, 223, 278
Coleridge, 206 f.
Colet, John, 4 f.
Coligny, 76 f.
College of the Propaganda, 142
Collegia Philobiblica, 183
Collegia Pietatis, 182 f.
Columbus, 8, 136
Comenius, 105
Commission of Triers, 129
Communism, 290 f.
Community of the Resurrection, 220
Complutensian Polyglot, 65
Compton, Bishop, 260
Concerning Christian Liberty, 18
Condé, 77
Confessio Belgica, 95
Congregation of Jesus and Mary, 111
Congregation of Missions, 111
Congregationalists, 246 f., 265
Consilium de Emendenda Ecclesia, 65
Constance, Council of, 17, 68
Constitution of the Christian Church, 173
Constitution of Church and State, 207
Consultatio (Hermann), 54 f.
Contarini, Cardinal, 34, 63 f.
Conventicle Act, 133
Cooper, Bishop, 87
Cop, Nicholas, 36
"Copec," 231
Copenhagen Decree, 94
Copernicus, 172
Copleston, 208

Cordier, 36
Corporation Act, 133, 193
Corporation of Sons of the Clergy, 169
Cortez, 137
Council of the Hundred Chapters, 151
Courtenay, 61
Coverdale, 49 f., 82
Cowley Fathers, 220
Cowper-Temple Clause, 228
Cranmer, 43 f., 53 f., 99
Crimean War, 234
Critique of Pure Reason, 178
Cromwell, Oliver, 128 f., 138, 263
Cromwell, Richard, 130
Cromwell, Thomas, 46 f., 86
Crowther, Samuel, 276
Cujus regio, ejus religio, 25 f., 40, 98, 160, 245
Cullmann, 295
Cummins, Bishop, 251

Darwin, 223, 280 f.
Davenport, C., 257
Davidson, Archbishop, 287
Day, Bishop, 58
De Antiquitate Britannicæ Ecclesiæ, 82
De Imitatione, 187
De Jure Belli ac Pacis, 96
De Legitima Ordinatione, 56
De Libero Arbitrio, 24
De Propaganda Fide, 142
De Servo Arbitrio, 24
De Statu Ecclesiæ, 160
Declaration of Sports, 123 f.
Defenestration of Prague, 106
Deism, 172 f., 186, 197 f.
Descartes, 116, 172 f.
Diamper, Synod of, 140
Diaz, Bartholomew, 7
Dimitri, 152
Dionysius, 153
Directory of Worship, 128, 131
Discourse concerning Baptismal and Spiritual Regeneration, 168
Dispensations, 45
Dodd, 295
Dogma of Bodily Assumption of B.V.M., 291

Döllinger, 202
Dominicans, 3, 20, 138 f.
Dominus ac Redemptor Noster, 195
Donaldson, Bishop, 284
Donation of Constantine, 8
Donatism, 215
Dorner, 222
Dort, Synod of, 96 f., 125, 165, 182, 267
Doukhobors, 234, 237
Dover, Secret Treaty of, 133
Driver, S. R., 224
Duchesne, Louis, 225
Ductor Dubitantium, 133
Duff, Alexander, 274
Dupin, 258

Ecclesiastical Commission, 163, 295
Ecclesiastical Polity, 88
Ecclesiastical Sonnets, 207
Eck, 16 f., 33
Edict of January (1562), 76
Edinburgh, Synods of, 100
Education Acts of 1944, 1945, 295
Edward VI, 53 f., 80, 86, 99, 129, 151
Edwards, Jonathan, 246
Eichorn, 222
Eikon Basilike, 128
Eliot, John, 138
Eliot, T. S., 296
Elizabeth, 44, 61, 79 f., 101, 124, 146
English Church Union, 218
Enlightenment, the, 172 f., 221, 289
Ensor, George, 279
Epistle to the Terrible Priests, 87
Epistolæ Obscurorum Virorum, 3
Erasmus, 4 f., 24, 28, 35, 41, 49, 99, 171
Erastus and Erastianism, 97 f, 125, 173
Eremites (Augustinian), 13, 20
Eric XIV, 92
Erskine, 264
Eschatology, 295

INDEX 317

Essay Concerning Human Understanding, 174
Essay on the Development of Doctrine, 217
Essays Catholic and Critical, 225, 288
Essays and Reviews, 223
Etcetera Oath, 127
Eudes, Père, and Eudists, 111
Eutyches, 215
L'Evangile et L'Eglise, 225
Ewald, 222
Exposition of the Creed, 132

Faber, F. W., 217
Falk Laws, 203
Farel, 35 f.
Farrar, F. W., 223
Febronius and Febronianism, 160 f.
Fénelon, 118 f.
Feodor I, 152
Feodor II, 156
Ferdinand, Emperor, 25, 33, 71 f.
Ferdinand, King of Bohemia, 106
Fernandez, Juan, 142
Ferrar, Nicholas, 132
Fichte, 180
Firmian, Archbishop, 159
Fisher, Bishop, 46
Five Mile Act, 133
Fletcher of Madely, 191
Fogazzaro, 226
Foundations, 288
Fox, George, 131
Foxe, John, 82
Francis I, 6, 9, 19, 25, 35, 38, 42, 75
Francis II, 200
Francis de Sales, 110
Franciscans, 20, 64, 137 f.
Francke, Hermann, 183 f.
Franklin, Benjamin, 190
Fraser, A. G., 276
Frederick I, Duke of Schleswig-Holstein, 93
Frederick, Elector Palatinate, 106
Frederick, Elector of Saxony, 14 f.

Frederick the Great, 160 f., 178
Frederick William III, 180
Free Church National Council, 266
French, Bishop, 282
Frelinghuysen, 246 f.
Friars Observant, 46
Froude, R. H., 210 f.
"Fundamentalism," 255

Gairdner, W. H. T., 282
Galileo, 172
Gallican Declaration, 112, 197 f.
Gama, Vasco da, 7, 139
Gandhi, 275
Garibaldi, 201
Garden of the Soul, 193
Gardiner, Stephen, 43, 54, 58 f.
Gauden, John, 128
General Council of Church of India, Burma, Ceylon, 293
"German Evangelical Church Federation," 264
George I, 172, 177, 192
George III, 193
Giberto, 63
Gillespie, 264
Gladstone, W. E., 214, 219
Gobat, John, 261
Godounov, Boris, 152
Goethe, 179
Gordon Riots, 193
Gore, Bishop, 220, 225, 231
Gorham Case, the, 218 f.
Graf, K. H., 222
Grand Remonstrance, 127 f.
Gray, Bishop, 223, 278
"Great Awakening," the, 246 f.
Greater Catechism, 26
Grebel, 30
Gregory XIII, 92
Gregory XV, 142
Grey, Lady Jane, 58, 61
Grey, Lord, 209
Grindal, 84 f.
Groot, Gerhard, 3
Grotius, 96, 136
Guardian, The, 217
Guise, Henry, Duke of, 78
Gunpowder Plot, 122, 162

Gustavus Adolphus, 107 f., 153, 263
Gustavus Vasa, 91 f.
Guyon, Mme., 118

Halifax, Lord, 258 f.
Hallam, 89
Hamilton, Alexander, 250
Hamilton, Patrick, 100
Hampden, R. D., 214 f.
Hampton Court Conference, 121
Hannington, Bishop, 277
Harmonia Apostolica, 132
Hawkins, 208 f.
Heath, Bishop, 58
Hegel, 180, 221, 235
Heidelberg Catechism, 264
Heiler, Dr., 288
Henry, Duke of Guise, 78
Henry II (France), 39, 71, 76
Henry III (France), 78
Henry of Navarre = Henry IV (France), 77 f., 103, 108 f.
Henry V, 45 f.
Henry VII, 4
Henry VIII, 18, 34, 38, 41 f., 56 f., 80, 122, 150, 266
Henry the Navigator, 136
Herbert, George, 132
Hermann, 54 f.
Hickes, Bishop, 173
High Commission Court, 80, 86 f., 122 f., 163
Hinduism, 139 f.
History of the Expansion of Christianity, 296
Hoadley, Bishop, 173 f.
Hobbes, 175
Hodgkin, Bishop, 82
Holy Catholic Church of China, 278
Holy Catholic Church of Japan, 280
Holy Dying, 133
Holy League, the, 9
Holy Living, 133
Homilies, Books of, 54, 81
Hooker, Richard, 84, 88 f., 125, 205, 208
Hooper, Bishop, 58, 62
Hort, F. J., 224

Howley, Archbishop, 213
Hubmaier, 30
Hughes, Marion R., 219
Humble Petition and Advice, 129
Hundred Grievances, 23
Hundred Years War, 6
Hunt, Robert, 139
Huntingdon, Lady (Connexion of), 191
Hupfeld, 222
Huss, 17, 98, 105, 184 f.

Ideal of a Christian Church, 216
Ilminski, 158
Immaculate Conception (Dogma of), 201
In Memoriam, 223
Independence, American War of, 245 f.
Index (of prohibited books), 67, 72, 96 f., 117, 160, 226
Indulgence, Declarations of, 130, 133, 164
Injunctions, Elizabethan, 80 f.
Innocent X, 115
Innocent XI, 112, 163
Innocent XII, 118
Inquisition, The, 38, 65 f., 72, 76, 86, 94, 118, 139, 161, 193 f.
Institutes, 36, 170
Institution of a Christian Man, 51
Instructions, 26
Instrument of Government, 129
Introduction to the Devout Life, 110
Irenæus, 212
Irénikon, 259
Irish Church, Disestablishment of, 219
Isabella, Queen, 137
Ivan III, 149
Ivan the Terrible, 150 f.

Jacobi, 179
James I (England) = James VI (Scotland), 103 f., 120 f., 260
James II, 139, 162 f., 258, 268

INDEX 319

Jansen and Jansenism, 114 f., 197, 202
Jebb, John, 206
Jefferson, President (U.S.A.), 245
Jeffreys, Judge, 163
Jerusalem, Council of (1672), 147, 154, 257
Jesuits, 65 f., 73 f., 84, 95, 109, 112 f., 137 f., 160 f., 194 f., 201 f., 232
Jewel, Bishop, 87 f., 125
John III, 92
John of the Cross, 75
John Frederick, Elector of Saxony, 38 f.
John à Lasco, 99
John the Steadfast, 25 f.
Johnson, Dr., 176, 205
Joseph II, 161
Joseph, King of Portugal, 194
Jowett, Benjamin, 223
Julius II, 2, 8 f., 14, 42
Julius III, 39, 42, 70
Juxon, Archbishop, 130 f.

Kant, 178 f.
Karlsburg, Synod of, 148
Katherine of Aragon, 42 f, 59
Keble, John, 206 f.
Kepler, Johann, 172
Keith-Falconer, Ian, 282
Kelly, Father, 220
Kelpius, John, 185
Kempis, Thomas à, 187
Ken, Bishop, 167
King, Bishop, 218
Kingdom of Christ, The, 230
Kingsley, Charles, 231
Knox, Alexander, 206, 214
Knox, John, 62, 87, 101 f.
Kraus, Franz, 226

Lainez, 66, 76
Lambert, De la Motte, 142
Lambeth Articles, 86
Lambeth Conference, 267, 269, 292, 293

Lamenais, 201
Lancaster, J., 227
Lang, Archbishop, 287
Laporte, 114
Las Casas, 137
Lateran Council, Fifth General, 9, 63
Latimer, Hugh, 60, 62
Latourette, 296
Laud, William, 126 f., 139, 257, 260
Lausanne, Conference at, 271
Law, William, 177, 187
League of Nations, 288
Lefèvre d'Etaples, 35
Leibniz, 119, 174, 178
Leith, Convention at, 103
Le Maistre, 114, 201
Lenin, 237
Leo X, 5, 9, 15 f., 23, 63, 91
Leo XIII, 202, 225
Lepanto, Battle of, 7
Lessing, 179
Lewis, C. S., 296
Liberty of Prophesying, 133
Liddon, H. P., 225
Lightfoot, Bishop, 224
Liguori, S. Alphonsus, 195 f., 201
Lincoln, Abraham, 253
Litany (English), 51
Livingstone, David, 273 f.
Locke, 174
Loci Communes, 21
Loi de la Séparation, 203
Loisy, Alfred, 225 f.
London Missionary Society, 273, 277 f.
Louis II, King of Hungary, 25
Louis XI, 6
Louis XII, 9
Louis XIII, 109 f., 258
Louis XIV, 112 f., 133, 141, 146
Louis XV, 194, 197
Louis XVI, 197
Lowder, Charles, 218
Loyola, Ignatius, 36, 65 f.
Lubeck, Peace of, 107
Lucar, Cyril, 147, 154, 235, 260
Lull, Raymund, 282
Lupfen, Countess von, 24

320 HISTORY OF THE MODERN CHURCH

Luther and Lutheranism, 12 f., 28 f., 49, 55, 65, 69, 74, 92 f., 136 f., 146, 157 f., 171, 179 f., 263 f., 275, 288
Lux Mundi, 225

Machiavelli, 3, 46, 118
Mackonochie, A. H., 218
Madrid, Treaty of, 25
Main Plot, the, 121
Maintenon, Mme. de, 113, 118, 232
Manning, Cardinal, 219
Mansel, Dean, 230
Mantua, Council at, 65
Manz, 30
Margaret, Queen of Navarre, 35
Margaret of Valois, 77
Maronites, 146, 244
Marquette, Père, 138
Marsden, Samuel, 280
Martin Marprelate Tracts, 87
Martyn, Henry, 274, 282
Mary I, 58 f., 80 f., 99 f.
Mary Stuart, 53, 79, 85, 101
Mathew, Bishop, 268
Matthias, Emperor, 106
Maurice, 38 f., 171
Maurice, F. D., 230
Maximes des Saintes, 118
Maximilian I, 19
Maximilian, Duke of Bavaria, 106 f.
Mazarin, 112, 143
Meditations, 193
Melanchthon, 21 f., 33 f., 53, 65, 94, 136, 146, 260, 236
Melbourne, Lord, 215
Melville, Andrew, 103 f.
Mercier, Cardinal, 259
Methodism, 187 f., 205, 227, 265
Michael Romanov, 153
Michelangelo, 2
Middleton, Bishop, 274
Millenary Petition, 120
Miller, William, 254
Milman, H. H., 222
Miltitz, Charles von, 16
Milton, 129
Missionary Council, 283
Moffat, Robert, 277

Mogila, Peter, 154
Mohacs, Battle of, 7, 25, 149
Mohammed II, 145
Mohammedans, 135 f., 145 f., 151, 158, 235, 257, 276, 282 f.
Molinos, Miguel de, 117 f., 182
Monasteries, Suppression of, 48
Monmouth, 163
Monsieur, Peace of, 77
Monstrous Regiment of Women, 101
Montague, Bishop, 257
Montague, Richard, 125 f.
Montespan, Mme. de, 119
Moral Reflections on the N.T., 202
Moravians, 184 f., 267, 272 f.
More, Hannah, 22
More, Henry, 176
More, Sir Thomas, 4, 44, 46
Mormons, 253
Morrison, Robert, 278
Mozley, J. B., 217
Mühlberg, Battle of, 39
Munzer, Thomas, 22, 30
Murdites, 146
Murray, John, 248
Mylne, Walter, 101
Mystical Element in Religion, 226

Nag's Head Tavern, 82
Nantes, Edict of, 78, 108, 113, 164
Napoleon Bonaparte, 199 f., 233
Nathan the Wise, 179
National Assembly (C. of E.), 285
National Society, 206, 227
Neale, J. M., 217 f.
Neander, 222
Necessary Doctrine and Erudition, 51
New England Company, 143
New Testament, Translations of, 5, 21, 49, 224, 274
Newman, J. H., 74, 206 f.
Newton, Isaac, 164, 172
Nicholas I, 233
Nicholas II, 236 f.
Nicolai, Archbishop, 158
Nikon, 154 f.

INDEX 821

Nippon Sei Kokwai, 280
Nitschmann, 186
Noailles, Cardinal de, 258
Nobili, Robert de, 140
Noetics, 208 f., 223
Non-Jurors, 165 f., 261
Nördlingen, Battle of, 108
Northumberland, Duke of, 57 f.
Nürnberg, Diet of, 23, 66
Nürnberg, Peace of, 33

Oates, Titus, 134
Occasional Conformity Act, 170
Ochino, Bernadino, 64
Odense, Diet of, 93
Oecumenical Movement, 289 f.
Olaf Petersson, 92
Old Believers, 155 f., 232 f.
Old Catholics, 202, 262, 268
Olier, M., 111
Oratorians, 74
Oratory of the Divine Love, 63 f.
Orchard, Dr., 288
Order of Communion, 54
Order of the Theatines, 64
Order of the Visitation, 110
Ordonnances Ecclesiastiques, 37
Origin of Species, 223
Ornaments Rubric, 81
Orthodox Confession, 154
Osiander, 43
Oxford Movement, the, 213 f., 230, 251, 258, 261, 269, 288

Pallu, François, 143
Palmer, William, 261
Panzani, 257
Papal Infallibility, Doctrine of, 202 f.
Pappenheim, 107 f.
Parker, Matthew, 82 f., 122
Parma, Duke of, 95
Parsons, 84 f.
Pascal, Blaise, 114 f., 172
Pascendi, 226
Passau, Convention of, 39
Passau, Treaty of, 57
Paton, J. G., 281
Patteson, Bishop, 281
Paul III, 34, 39 f., 65 f.
Paul IV, 71

Pearson, Bishop, 132
Peasants' War, 23 f.
Penn, William, 131
Penry, 87
Peter of Alcantara, 75
Peter the Great, 156 f., 232, 238
Peter Magnusson, 92
Peter Martyr, 56 f., 64, 76
Petite Église, La, 200
Philaret, 153, 234
Philip V, 193
Philip of Hesse, 23, 31, 34, 38
Philip of Spain, 61, 71, 85, 94 f.
Philip Neri, 74
Philpotts, Bishop, 218
Pia Desideria, 183
Pietism, 172, 182 f.
Pilgrim Fathers, 123, 138
Pilgrimage of Grace, 47
Pilgrim's Progress, 130, 182
Pitt, 193, 227
Pius IV, 72 f.
Pius V, 84
Pius VI, 162, 199
Pius VII, 200 f.
Pius IX, 219
Pius X, 203, 225, 254
Pius XII, 291
Platon, 234
Pobiedonostseff, 236 f.
Pocoke, Dr., 129
Poissy, Colloquy at, 76
Pole, Reginald, 59 f.
Pombal, 194
Portal, Abbé, 258 f.
Practice of Piety, 182
Pragmatic Sanction of Bourges, 8 f., 35
Prague, Peace of, 108
Praise of Folly, 5
Prayer Book (*see* Book of Common Prayer)
Premunire, Act of, 44
Presbyterians, 170, 246 f., 264 f., 288
Preservative against the Principles and Practices of the Non-Jurors, 173
Prierias, 16
Priest to the Temple, 132

Privy Council, 86
Probabilism, 196
Programme of Modernism, 226
Prohibition, 250
Providentissimus Deus, 225
"Provincial Letters," 116
Provoost, Bishop (U.S.A.), 247
Public Worship Regulation Act, 218
Pusey, E. B., 211 f.
Pym, 128

Quakers, 131, 209, 230, 245, 269
Queen Anne's Bounty, 169, 295
Quesnel, Père, 115, 202
Quietism, 74 f., 117 f.

Racovian Confession, 99
Raikes, Robert, 227
Rakoczy I, George, 148
Raleigh, Sir Walter, 121, 138
Raphael, 2
Rasputin, 237
Ratisbon, Colloquy of, 34, 65
Ratisbon, League of, 23 f.
Reasonableness of Christianity, 174
Redemptorists, 196
Reformatio Legum Ecclesiasticarum, 82
Reimarus, 179, 222
Religio Medici, 176
Religion of Protestants, The, 127
Religious Tract Society, 273
Remonstrants, 96 f.
Renaissance, 2 f., 35, 46, 63 f., 79
Renan, E., 222
Repeal, Act of, 60
Restraint of Appeals Act, 44
Reuchlin, 3, 49
Reuss, E., 222
Rhodes, Alexandre de, 141
Ricci, Bishop of Pistoia, 197
Ricci (Jesuit), 141
Richelieu, 108 f.
Ridley, Nicholas, 60 f.
Ritschl, 180
Robertson, F. W., 223
Rogation-tide Processions, 81
Roger (of St. Paul's), 62

Romanov Dynasty, 153 f.
Romantic Movement, 179 f., 201
Rose, Bishop, 167
Rose, H. J., 206, 211 f.
Rousseau, 175
Royal Supremacy, 43 f., 53, 60, 80 f., 121 f., 134, 163
Russell, Lord John, 218
Rye House Plot, 134

Sacheverell, Dr., 170
Sadoleto, Cardinal, 37
Saints' Everlasting Rest, 182
Sancroft, Archbishop, 163, 166
Sandys, George, 260
Saravia, 267
Satolli, Mgr., 254
Savonarola, 3
Savoy Conference, 130, 268
Scell, Hermann, 226
Schelling, 180
Schism Act, 170
Schleiermacher, 180, 186
Schmalkaldic League, 33, 38
Schmalkaldic War, 70
Schmidt, George, 277
Schwabach, Articles of, 31
Schwartz, Christian, 275
Schweitzer, A., 222, 295
Scipio, 88
Scory, Bishop, 82
Scott, Sir Walter, 206 f.
Scripture Doctrine of the Trinity, 174
Seabury, Bishop, 247
Secker, Archbishop, 176
Second World War, 288 f.
Seguier, 114
Selwyn, Bishop, 280
Semler, 179
Serious Call, A, 177
Servetus, 37 f.
Seven Years War, 160
Sheldon, Bishop, 131 f.
Sherlock, Bishop, 175, 247
Short Catechism, 26
Sigismund I, 98
Sigismund II, 98 f.
Sigismund III, 93
Simon, 222

INDEX   323

Sisters of Charity, 111
Sisters of Mercy, 219 f.
Six Articles, 50
Sixty-seven Articles, 29
Slavery, Abolition of, 227
Smith, Bishop George, 278
Smith, John, 176
Smith, Joseph, 253
Smith, Robertson, 224
S.C.M., 255
S.D.C., 220
S.P.C.K., 143, 168, 273
S.P.G., 143, 168, 187
S.S.J.E., 220
S.S.M., 220
Sobieski, John, 147
Société des Missions Etrangères, 142
Society for Promotion of Temperance, 250
Society for the Propagation of the Faith, 273
Society for Reformation of Manners, 168
Society of Friends, 131
Socinus and Socinianism, 96 f., 99, 174
Sokoli, 149
Solemn League and Covenant, 128, 131
Solyman the Magnificent, 7, 25, 31
Somerset, Protector, 53 f.
Sophia (Russia), 156
Soubise, 109
South India United Church, 265
Southey, 219
Speier, Diet of, 25
Spener, Philip, 183 f.
Spirit of Love, The, 178
Spirit of Prayer, The, 178
Spiritual Exercises, 66 f.
Spiritual Guide, 117, 182
Stanley, A. P., 223
Staupitz, 14
Stern, Dr., 130
Stevenson, R. L., 281
Stillingfleet, Bishop, 165
Stockholm Conference, 231
Strafford, 127
Strauss, D. F., 221

Stundists, 236
Sublapsarians, 95
"Submission of the Clergy," 44
Succession Act, 46
Sulpice, S., 111
Supralapsarians, 95
Sweden, 268
Syllabus of Errors, 201

Talleyrand, 197 f.
Tauler, 14
Tausen, 93
Taylor, Jeremy, 132 f.
Teelink, 183
Telemachus, 118
Temple, Archbishop, 223, 289
Ten Articles, 50 f.
Tenison, Archbishop, 165, 247
Tennyson, 223
Teresa, Maria, 148, 161
Teresa, S., 74 f., 117
Test Acts, 134, 163, 169, 193
Tetrapolitana, 33
Tetzel, John, 15 f.
Theologia Germanica, 14
Theological Colleges, 229, 249
Theophilanthropy, 198
Thirty Years War, 105 f.,159,184
Thomas, S. (Canterbury), 49
Thornton, D., 282
Tikhon, 238 f.
Tillotson, Archbishop, 165
Tilly, 107
Tindal, Matthew, 177
Toland, John, 176
Tolentino, Peace of, 199
Toleration Acts, 165, 170
Toleration Edict (1781), 162
Tolstoy, Leo, 237
Toplady, 191
Torgau, League of, 25
Torquemada, 11
Tortus, 125
Tracts for the Times, 213
Travers, Walter, 84, 88
Treasons Act, 46, 54
Trent, Council of, 38 f., 68 f., 79, 88, 94 f., 106 f., 216, 288
Trotsky, 237
True Christianity, 182

Truth of the Christian Religion, 96
Tryal of the Witnesses of the Resurrection, 175
Tunstall, Bishop, 58 f.
Turenne, 119
Tutiorism, 196
Tyndale, 5, 49 f.
Tyrrell, George, 226

Udall, 87
Ultramontanism, 201, 258
U.M.C.A., 273, 276
Uniformity, Acts of, 54, 57, 81, 131
Unigenitus, 115
Unitarians, 64, 230, 247 f., 269
United Nations, 288
Universalists, 248
Ursulines, 64, 138
Utraquism, 105
Utrecht, Union of, 95

Valdes, Juan de, 64
Valla, Lorenzo, 8
Vassili, 150
Vater, 222
Vatican City, 290
Vatican Council, 202, 258
Vaughan, Cardinal, 258
Venn of Huddersfield, 191
Verbal Treasons Act, 46, 54
Via Media, 214 f.
Victor Immanuel, 201
Vincent de Paul, 110
Vincentian Canon, 206
Voet, Gisbert, 182
Voltaire, 160, 178, 191
Von Hügel, Baron, 226

Wake, Archbishop, 173, 258, 261, 267 f.
Walker of Truro, 191
Wallenstein, 107 f.
Walpole, 173
Walton, Isaac, 167
Ward, W. G., 216 f.
Warham, Archbishop, 4 f., 43
Wars of the Roses, 6
Warwick, Duke of Northumberland, 57 f.
Waterland, Daniel, 174

Watson, William, 121
Welfare State, 289
Welsh Church (Disestablishment of), 285
Wesley, Charles, 186 f.
Wesley, John, 186 f., 195, 206
Wesley, Samuel, 189
Westcott, B. F., 224, 231
Westeras, Diet of, 91 f.
Westeras, Recess of, 92
Westfield College, Hampstead, 289
Westminster Confession of Faith, 128, 167
Weston, Bishop, 269
Westphalia, Peace of, 108, 159
Whately, 208 f.
Whichcote, Benjamin, 176
White, Bishop (U.S.A.), 247
White, Blanco, 208, 214
Whitefield, George, 187 f., 246
Whitgift, John, 83 f.
Whole Duty of Man, The, 129
Wilberforce, 227
William and Mary, 163 f., 193
William of Nassau (The Silent), 95
Williams, Charles, 294
Williams, George, 262
Williams, Isaac, 215 f.
Winchester, Elhanan, 248
Wiseman, 215
Wishart, George, 100 f.
Wolff, C., 178
Wolsey, 8, 42 f., 60
Woodruff, Wilfrid, 253
Woolston, 175
Wordsworth, John, Bishop, 268
Wordsworth, William, 206
"World Call, The," 283
World Conference on Church, Community and State, 290
World Council of Churches, 290
World Meeting of International Missionary Society, 290
Worms, Diet of, 20
Worms, Edict of, 20 f.
Wren, Sir Christopher, 139, 169
Wyatt's Revolt, 61
Wycliffe, 17, 49
Wyttenbach, 28

Xavier, Francis, 66 f., 139 f.
Ximenes, 11, 65

Y.M.C.A., 255
Young, Brigham, 253

Zelo Domus Dei, 108
Znzendorf, Nicolaus von, 184 f.
Zwickau Prophets, 22
Zwilling, 22
Zwingli, 28 f., 49, 56 f., 97 f., 136

For Product Safety Concerns and Information please contact our EU
representative GPSR@taylorandfrancis.com
Taylor & Francis Verlag GmbH, Kaufingerstraße 24, 80331 München, Germany

www.ingramcontent.com/pod-product-compliance
Lightning Source LLC
Chambersburg PA
CBHW052145300426
44115CB00011B/1528